TEN REMARKABLE AUSTRALIANS

*they made their mark
on the world
but were forgotten*

IAN MACFARLANE

Foreword by Geoffrey Blainey

Published in 2019 by Connor Court Publishing Pty Ltd

Copyright © Ian Macfarlane 2019

All rights reserved. No part of this book may be reproduced or transmitted in any form or by any means, electronic or mechanical, including photocopying, recording or by any information storage and retrieval system, without prior permission in writing from the publisher.

ISBN 9781925826524

Connor Court Publishing Pty Ltd
PO Box 7257
Redland Bay QLD 4165
sales@connorcourt.com
www.connorcourtpublishing.com.au

Printed in Australia

Front Cover Design: Ian James

CONTENTS

	Foreword by Geoffrey Blainey	5
	Introduction	7
1	Harry George Hawker: Aviator and Aeroplane Designer	15
2	George Finch: Mountaineer and Scientist	39
3	George Ernest Morrison: Adventurer, Doctor, Journalist and Political Adviser	69
4	George Hubert Wilkins: War Photographer and Explorer	97
5	Ethel Florence Lindesay Richardson: Novelist and Musician	125
6	Lyndhurst Falkiner Giblin: Prospector, Sportsman, Politician, Soldier and Scholar	147
7	John Peter Russell: Artist and Engineer	173
8	George Gilbert Aime Murray: Scholar and worker for Peace	197
9	Reginald Leslie Baker: Sportsman and Showman	223
10	Frederick Septimus Kelly: Concert Pianist, Composer and Oarsman	251
	Bibliography	275
	Index	281

FOREWORD

GEOFFREY BLAINEY

It is rare for someone to reach the top of his profession and then, after retiring, venture into a part-time calling that is completely different. Ian Macfarlane, once the Governor of the Reserve Bank, decided to be a biographer. He began to investigate and write about not one, but ten Australian lives. All were born in Australia, in roughly the same era, but won their fame overseas.

Today, even well-informed readers have probably not heard of most of these names. As a life-long historian I must confess that I had not heard of one life vividly narrated in this book: George Finch's. We learn that "he excelled at two completely unrelated activities – mountaineering and science – when most of us cannot achieve even one". His fame has been eclipsed by a member of the next generation of Finchs, Peter Finch the actor.

I found the book engaging as well as revealing. It is partly the colloquial or under-played style. It is partly the author's own surprise as he uncovers the details of the ten lives. His own views of human nature he drops into the narrative, but not too frequently. Of Professor Gilbert Murray, perhaps the most widely known scholar in Britain in the 1920s, we are told "The worst that could be said of him is that he tended to make the mistake of thinking everyone was as reasonable as he was". Of Ethel Richardson, the Melbourne piano student who later shone as a novelist in London, we learn that "The last two words you would ever use to describe her are lighthearted or frivolous".

The research that underwrites the book is extensive. Running my finger down the list of books he has consulted, I count almost 90. A wide cross-section of people could read these lives, not only with gain but also with quiet pleasure. The book makes me think that, in an era when Australian history implants boredom in many senior students, biography may be one way of recapturing their interest.

INTRODUCTION

When I first approached a publisher with plans for this book, he assumed it would be about economics because he knew me by my former occupation. I said I was sorry to disappoint him, but I had a more interesting book in mind and, in fact, it was already half-written.

It was a collection of short biographies of ten remarkable Australians who deserved to be better known. In fact most were well known, even famous at one stage in twentieth-century history, but have since been largely forgotten. As I sought to learn more about these people and their achievements, I wanted to give modern readers an opportunity to discover them too.

How did I come across these people in the first place? Mainly by accident, I must admit. On a number of occasions I found myself reading a book by an English, American or Canadian writer that had nothing to do with Australia, but at some stage in the story an unusual Australian whom I had never heard of popped up. This aroused my curiosity and I made a mental note to find out more about them when I had the time. As I learned more about them, I realised their stories would make a very interesting read. That is the origin of this book.

Let me give you some examples. When reading a biography of Rupert Brooke by an English author, I came across an Australian who was both a concert pianist, classical music composer, and a world champion oarsman who won the Diamond Sculls at Henley three times as well as an Olympic gold medal. On another occasion when I was reading a book by a Canadian author about attempts to climb Mount Everest in the 1920s, I came across an Australian who was probably the most accomplished mountaineer in the world and who had climbed higher than anyone else to that date. In a biography of the Norwegian explorer Roald Amundsen, I discovered an Australian photographer who was twice decorated for bravery in the First World War, then become a polar explorer and the first person to fly across the Arctic Sea from America to Europe. In Bertrand Russell's autobiography, I came across an Australian professor at Oxford who was the world's foremost authority on Ancient Greek and a major force behind the League of Nations. And in a secondhand book catalogue, I stumbled across a young Australian who was a daring aviator and perhaps the most important aeroplane designer during the First World War. There was also an extraordinary man who was a doctor and a journalist, who managed to get himself speared in New Guinea and shot during the Boxer Rebellion in China, but went on to become the political adviser to the President of China.

I could go through all ten people whom I have chosen, but I will leave it to the reader to discover them in later chapters. All ten led separate lives and, to the best of my knowledge, never met each other. But they had a lot in common. All were born in the second half of the nineteenth century in colonial Australia before Federation. They reached their peak in the period around the First World War, an event that figures prominently in most of their lives. As well as being gifted, energetic and ambitious, they were all outward-looking.

INTRODUCTION

Their achievements mainly took place overseas and that is where they made a name for themselves. They were the first wave of Australian expatriates. Some of their lives were extremely adventurous, others were notable for artistic, intellectual or sporting achievements. The ten consist of an explorer, an artist, an aviator, a sportsman, an economist, a journalist, a novelist, a scholar, a composer and a mountaineer. But to characterise them by one activity understates their achievements. All were versatile in that they excelled in more than one field. Today, intense competition means that nearly everyone has become a specialist, but that was not the case more than a hundred years ago. I have tried to indicate the range of activities each person excelled at in the title of each chapter, and sometimes I had to list not just two, but three or four.

It would have been easy to write about famous Australians from this era, but that was not my aim: I wanted to revive the forgotten, not celebrate the famous. A Melba, Monash, Mawson or Kingsford-Smith would not make my list because they are still famous and have been honoured with knighthoods and their portraits on banknotes. Thirteen people born in Australia have been commemorated on banknotes, but none are in this book. This gives me comfort that I am not simply duplicating what is already well known. I have shown my list to friends and they have had trouble identifying even one or two of these people, so readers should not feel inadequate if they have not heard of them. Although they have been forgotten by the general public, it is possible to find out quite a lot about them. Most were subjects of biographies and feature in other books written during their lifetime, although many of these publications are now out of print. As well, there are some small groups of enthusiasts who try to keep their memories alive.

When these people were born, Australia was just a collection of British colonies dependent on the production of wool and gold. We picture our country at that time as being small, isolated and inward-looking with most people living in the bush. The population in 1900 was 3.8 million, so we were certainly small, but we weren't mainly from the bush. We had some big cities and were one of the most urbanised countries on earth, as we still are. We were also quite wealthy by world standards; measures of national income per head place Australia near the top of world rankings in 1880. This wealth comes through clearly in some of the biographies. But we were certainly disadvantaged by what Geoffrey Blainey called the "tyranny of distance". A trip to Europe took several months, was expensive and beyond the means of most people. Besides, there were plenty of challenges at home to occupy us as the land was explored and developed, self-government introduced into the colonies and finally, Federation achieved as a sovereign country.

However, it is wrong to think that Australians were inward-looking. It is true that the governments of the day restricted the import of people and goods through their immigration and tariff policies. But the Australian people, particularly those of talent, were outward-looking. In fact, smallness makes people outward-looking. In large countries, there is a tendency for people to think that everything important is made at home, or at least is available at home. That was not the case here; if anything there was a tendency at this time to think that everything of value came from abroad, especially from Britain. This is not surprising as most of my subjects' parents were born in Britain and Australians looked to it as the mother country. All the people in this book spent time in Britain, but the United States, Canada, France, Switzerland, China and Germany also feature in their stories. An ambitious young Australian was far more likely to look abroad for inspiration than someone from Britain, America or France. This tradition has continued, but I found it surprising that it started so soon in our history.

I think there is a tendency for each generation to think that their predecessors were inward-looking, and that openness arrived only recently. This is particularly so for those with a short span of reference. As recently as last year, film director Jeremy Sims is quoted in *The Australian* as saying, "We were an inward-looking nation until the 1980s – then there was everything from Greg Norman to Paul Keating, INXS to Kylie Minogue and Wayne Gardner." I hope these essays will act as an antidote to this type of myopia.

The accounts I give of these ten lives are quite short – they are biographical essays rather than formal biographies as would be written by an academic or historian. I have had to be selective and leave out unnecessary details, and I have avoided footnotes. But I have tried to give an account that is logically ordered and easy to follow. I frequently include dates and, more importantly, my subject's age when key events happened. In each essay there are interesting questions to be answered, conflicts to be resolved and issues to be raised. Not all aspects of these people are totally praiseworthy, and I have not been afraid to be critical at times. Similarly, not everything that has been previously published on their lives is entirely accurate, so on several occasions I have tried to set the record straight. I have mainly used written material about my subject, their contemporaries and their times, although in five cases I consulted original diaries and letters where they were available in Australian public libraries.

A lot has changed in the 100 years or so since the events covered in this book, including placenames, units of measurement and monetary values. I have chosen to use the modern version of placenames, although most of my sources use the original and often more colourful version. So, for example, I have used Istanbul rather than Constantinople, Yangon rather than Rangoon, and Ethiopia rather than Abyssinia. Sometimes I have included both, such as Beijing and Peking. Although my sources gave distances in miles, I have converted them into kilometres for the convenience of readers, but retained feet and inches for people's heights. In updating monetary values, I have avoided the practice of scaling up the original sums by the subsequent rise in the consumer price index because this always results in an underestimate (for reasons I won't go into). Instead, I have chosen to present monetary values in their original pounds, and give some yardsticks for comparison. The reason for this is that for nearly all the period under discussion, inflation was very low; indeed there were some years of deflation. At that time, you could buy your grandfather's house for the same price he paid for it. The comparison points I have chosen are: for a postmaster's income, 80 pounds per year plus board; for a university lecturer's starting salary, 120 pounds per year; for a surgeon, 450 pounds per year. In 1907, the basic wage in Australia for a man supporting a wife and three children was set at little over 100 pounds per year.

I have always been attracted to the format of a collection of small biographical essays rather than a single large one. I believe it is a better way of getting the reading public to become aware of these interesting people. A reader is unlikely to pick up a 300-page biography of someone they have never heard of, but is more likely to read a collection of stories about ten different people, even if most of the subjects are people whom they have not heard of. At least, I hope that is the case. There are some celebrated earlier examples of this approach, such as

INTRODUCTION

Aubrey's *Brief Lives* and Strachey's *Eminent Victorians*. An Australian example is John Hetherington's *Australians: Nine Profiles,* and a more recent one is Ross McMullin's *Farewell Dear People*.

Finally, I would like to acknowledge the helpful discussions I have had with, among others, Michael Ackland, William Coleman, Ann Galbally, Greg Growden, Angus Houston, Carol Jones, Chris Latham, Jeff Maynard, Wayne Tunnicliffe, and especially Geoffrey Blainey for his encouragement. The staff at the State Library of New South Wales, the National Library of Australia and the Reserve Bank Archives also gave generously of their time. I would like to acknowledge the great help I received from my editor, Sally Asnicar in polishing the final draft.

Harry Hawker in front of a French monoplane before the First World War.

1

HARRY GEORGE HAWKER

Aviator and Aeroplane Designer

You don't have to be an aviation enthusiast to have heard of aeroplanes built by the Hawker company. Hawker was probably the best-known name in British military aviation in the twentieth century. The Hawker Hurricane fighter, the workhorse of the Royal Air Force in the Battle of Britain, was built by Hawker, as was the first vertical take-off plane 30 years later – the Hawker Harrier Jump Jet, and many others. Company names such as Hawker Siddeley and Hawker de Havilland are also well known. So, it was somewhat of a surprise to me to discover that the name comes from an Australian of humble origins who had a brief but spectacular career in the British aviation industry. I was curious to know who Harry Hawker was, and how he came to have this famous company bear his name.

In 1919, King George V was so concerned about the welfare of Harry Hawker that he sent two telegrams to Hawker's wife: the first a message of condolence, and the second, two days later, of congratulations. What had Hawker done to deserve the attention of the monarch who at the time headed the mighty British Empire? And why did Banjo Paterson write a poem in Hawker's honour? Clearly,

Harry Hawker must have had an eventful life.

Harry Hawker was born in January 1889 in Moorabbin (some record it as South Brighton), an outer suburb of Melbourne. The son of a blacksmith, he left school at fourteen years of age, as most students did at the time, and so had little formal education and none at all in engineering or higher mathematics. Nevertheless, he was extremely interested in all things mechanical and spent a lot of time in his father's workshop. Although his father was trained as a blacksmith and wheelwright, he was also a versatile, self-taught engineer. He had built a two-cylinder steam engine and boiler to power his workshop, and later he constructed a steam-powered car. The youthful Harry Hawker learned to experiment like his father and in a short time was able to emulate him by building his own machines.

Harry's first job was with a firm making bicycles and invalid chairs – not a promising start to a career in aviation – but he soon moved on to better things. He became a chauffeur-cum-mechanic to several wealthy rural car owners in Victoria. One of these, a Mr De Little, was a generous employer for whom he worked for three years. Mr De Little had two cars: an Argyle and a Rolls Royce Silver Ghost. Both were relatively new and required little maintenance. Hawker was provided with his own workshop and had plenty of time to spare, which he put to good use.

Like his father, Harry first built an engine to power his workshop, but his was an internal combustion engine, not a steam engine like his father's. Then he built his first motorbike, but instead of buying an engine to power it, he built his own engine from scratch. This did not satisfy him, so he built a second and much more powerful machine. Again he built his own engine, which he modelled on the English J.A.P. engine (the biggest motorbike engine so far built), but incorporated some of his own improvements.

It is difficult now to understand that in those days, if you had a limited income and you wanted to own a motorbike, the best solution was to build one, or at least assemble one from the parts you could find or buy. Hawker was not the only one to follow this path; his two best friends also built their own motorbikes, and the three friends raced them against each other. At first they raced in a banked wooden circuit designed for normal bicycles, but were soon barred from that, so they raced on country roads.

A very formative event in Hawker's life occurred in 1910, when he was twenty-one. He and his friends went to Diggers Rest near Melbourne to see the first manned flight in Australia. When they arrived there were two planes, each with its own pilot, sitting in a paddock waiting to take off when weather conditions became suitable. After a long delay, one of the planes – a French Voisin biplane – succeeded in becoming airborne. Its pilot was Ehrich Weiss, better known as Houdini, the famous illusionist and escapologist. It was hardly a spectacular display; the plane looked like a large box kite with a propeller, and the longest flight lasted a little over three minutes with the plane reaching a height of 30 metres.

Nevertheless, for someone who had never seen a manned flight before, it would have been a revelation. Hawker was immediately smitten with the desire to fly himself. This was the turning point in his life. Motorbikes and cars no longer satisfied his mechanical curiosity; mentally he had moved onto aeroplanes. It wasn't just the mechanical side of aeroplanes that fascinated him, it was the act of flying them that became his goal. There was little or no chance of him achieving his ambition in Australia as it had no aviation industry, so in 1911 he and two like-minded friends sailed for England.

It was a huge gamble on Hawker's part. He was a small man who looked a lot younger than he was, and he had a quiet, reserved manner. He was entirely self-taught with no formal qualifications in engineering and no references, and yet he hoped to pursue a career in an industry that was at the cutting edge of the technology of that era. He wanted to fly; getting work as a mechanic in the aviation industry might be a useful stepping stone, but flying was his ultimate aim. His prospects did not look good, yet we know that in the next ten years he achieved so much that his name became synonymous with the industry, even though the man behind the name was hardly known at all.

After arriving in London, Hawker found temporary work as a mechanic at several car companies. But his big break came in June 1912 when he was hired as a mechanic by the Sopwith Aviation Company. This company had been established only a few years earlier by Tommy Sopwith, a well-to-do gentleman sportsman interested in aviation, yachting and motor racing, and who had both entrepreneurial flair and sound business sense. Tommy Sopwith was a remarkable man; he was a stalwart of the British aviation industry in two world wars, at one point held the world water speed record, challenged for the America's Cup in yachting twice and lived to be one hundred and one years of age. Tommy Sopwith (later Sir Thomas Sopwith) became the most important influence in Harry Hawker's life; as well as being his employer, he was his patron, colleague and friend.

When Hawker joined Sopwiths he was twenty-three years old and his progress with the firm was rapid. He quickly gained a reputation as an outstanding mechanic, and his future in that capacity was now secure. But he wanted to be a pilot, and this turned out to be easier than he expected as Sopwiths also ran a flying school. Hawker enrolled, but was worried that he might damage the planes. Tommy

Sopwith recorded that in answer to the question "What happens if you break the aeroplane?" Hawker took 50 pounds from inside his sock – perhaps his entire life savings – and asked if that would do. It turned out that he was a naturally gifted pilot and qualified for his aviator's certificate within a month. Tommy Sopwith recognised Hawker's exceptional talent and immediately appointed him as chief test pilot for the firm. By October 1912, he was representing the Sopwith Company in flying competitions.

There were many sponsored competitions for aeroplanes at this time; some for speed, some for altitude and some for duration aloft. One such competition was the British Empire Michelin Cup, sponsored by the Michelin Tyre Company. It was awarded to the pilot who could stay airborne for the longest time. The planes flew circuits of the Brooklands motor racing track, and to conserve fuel they flew as slowly as possible. They also flew close to the ground; Hawker stayed at about 100 metres, while his main competitor – Fred Raynham – flew even lower, sometimes as low as five metres. At one stage during the race Tommy Sopwith jumped into another of his planes and flew alongside Hawker, waving encouragement.

It was hardly an exciting spectacle and not surprisingly it was not a big crowd puller, particularly as the small crowd had to wait for eight hours and 23 minutes for Hawker to finish in darkness as the winner. In the process he not only won the cup and earned 500 pounds for Sopwiths, he also broke the British flight duration record. The thing that is surprising from a contemporary viewpoint is that he achieved this victory within a few months of obtaining his pilot's licence. In the infancy of an industry unusual things are possible, and this was certainly one. Tommy Sopwith, an accomplished pilot himself and not much older than Hawker, must have had enormous faith in Hawker's ability for him to entrust the company's fortunes to one so young and new to the game.

Throughout 1913 Hawker continued his work at Sopwiths, combining the roles of test pilot, engineer and competitor in aeroplane racing events. Although his main job was test pilot, this was not simply a matter of taking up new planes and seeing how well they flew. Aeronautical engineers can only do part of their job on the ground; a lot of the fine tuning of the plane is done by the test pilot in the air. In fact, not only can a good test pilot point out weaknesses in the current design, but he can also put forward new design suggestions to correct them, which Hawker did. He also conducted experiments on new flying techniques, particularly how to get out of difficulties. These experiments were quite dangerous, but he made important contributions to developing the range of skills needed to be a professional pilot. His most important discovery was to find a way of getting out of a spin, which until then was regarded as fatal because the pilot could not use the control surfaces (ailerons) on the wings to recover the aircraft.

Hawker also continued to enter competitions. In May 1913, the Royal Aero Club held a competition where pilots attempted to break the British Altitude Record. Hawker was the winner in a plane known as the Sopwith Tractor, reaching an altitude of 3,470 metres. A more important competition was the one organised by Lord Northcliffe, proprietor of the *Daily Mail*. Contestants were required to fly their seaplanes in an anti-clockwise, circular course of 2470 kilometres around the United Kingdom within 72 hours. The course started at Southampton and contestants had to touch down at Ramsgate, Yarmouth, Scarborough, Aberdeen, Oban, Dublin and Falmouth before returning to the finish line at Southampton. Four teams entered, with the winner to receive a prize of 5000 pounds.

In the event, Hawker, in a Sopwith seaplane, and co-pilot Harry Kauper, one of the friends who accompanied him on his initial move to England, were the only team to start. They were going well until an engine problem forced them to come down in the sea 25 kilometres short of Dublin. The ditching was not successful as it damaged the plane and broke Kauper's arm. They were unable to continue but had covered 1670 kilometres in two-and-a-half days, which was regarded as a creditable effort. The *Daily Mail* awarded Hawker 1000 pounds for his brave attempt.

In early 1914, Hawker returned to Australia for a visit in which he would give flying demonstrations. He came by ship accompanied by his plane – a Sopwith Tabloid – in crates, which was quickly re-assembled upon arrival in Melbourne. Hawker's exploits in England had received a reasonable amount of newspaper coverage in Australia, and so he was a minor celebrity who many people were keen to meet. His Sopwith Tabloid was much more sophisticated than any plane previously seen in Australia, so pilot and plane attracted a lot of attention wherever they went. Hawker's purpose in coming to Australia was to promote Sopwith planes for commercial and military use, and he met with the minister for defence, the postmaster general and many other potential customers. He was received in the highest quarters and even took the governor-general for a flight. But he also had to attract as much publicity for the company as he could and this was done by exhibition flights, aerobatics and paid joy flights.

An immediate challenge was where to take off and land, as at that time there were no airports. In Melbourne, the first flight took off from a public road – New Street, North Brighton – but it was soon found that the fairways at the Elsternwick Public Golf Course were a better option. The first exhibition flights took place from here and could be viewed from most points between Elsternwick and the city.

In these, Hawker flew to 1500 metres and executed various turns, banked to over 45 degrees and dived sharply at times. The flight took about 20 minutes before he glided to a smooth landing at the golf course. It was a spectacular display, far surpassing anything previously seen in Australia.

A bigger event took place at the Caulfield Race Course, where a crowd of between 20,000–30,000 came to see the exhibition. Later, in Sydney, a similar sized crowd turned out at Randwick Race Course to watch Hawker fly. Exhibition flights also took place at Albury, Bendigo and Ballarat. Commenting on the various flight displays in Australia, *The Australian Motorist* magazine wrote in March 1914:

> The young aviator, he is only 22 years of age [actually he was 25], scored a great triumph. His predecessors, Houdini, Hammond, MacDonald and Hart, had given aerial demonstrations that had been recorded as successful, but none of them had attempted the daring feats that Hawker accomplished. His manoeuvres were of a totally different standard. It was the difference between an amateur and a professional. Hawker impressed everyone with the fact that he possessed complete mastery of his machine.

The Tabloid was a two-seater, and passengers were taken up one at a time for joy rides. The price per joy ride was 20 pounds for about ten minutes, and the money raised helped to defray the cost of Hawker's Australian visit. Towards the end of his stay in Australia, Hawker was forced to land in a paddock well short of his intended landing place in Albury. The plane ended up with its nose in the ground and its fuselage pointing vertically upward. It was extensively damaged, but Hawker was unhurt. This was not the first time Hawker had crashed a plane, nor was it the last. On one occasion in England he had even landed in a tree, but climbed down unharmed.

Although there were fatalities at times, it is surprising how often these early planes crashed without killing or seriously injuring the pilots. There are a number of reasons for this. For a start they did not fly very fast, usually less than 150 kilometres per hour. The biplanes had a large wing area and could glide easily if the engine failed and land at low speed. They didn't need to find an airport as they could land on a road or a grassed surface. The planes were light – made mainly of a wooden frame and stretched fabric – so they crumpled easily, cushioning the impact of the crash. In later years, when planes became bigger and faster, they became more reliable and so had fewer crashes, but when crashes occurred they were often fatal.

The Australian visit had been a great success even though it had failed to attract any new orders for Sopwiths. The lack of orders for new planes was not a problem because Sopwiths was already having trouble meeting demand for military aircraft from the British Armed Forces, with the Royal Flying Corps established in 1912.

Hawker returned to England in June 1914, two months before the start of the First World War, and for the next four years his work was dominated by the testing, design and manufacturing of fighter planes. His skill as a test pilot and aeroplane designer meant there was no question of risking him as a combat pilot, whose life spans were notoriously short. Instead, he concentrated on designing and producing fighter planes for the British and French armed forces. He also added a third string to his bow as production manager, but it was as a designer that he was most valuable.

The first of the fighter planes that Sopwiths designed was the Strutter. It was a great success and 5400 were produced. Of these only 246 were manufactured by Sopwiths, with some of the rest being built in other British factories, and 4000 being built in France. This emphasises the fact that Sopwiths was principally a design shop, although it did a lot of manufacturing too, and at its peak during the war it had a workforce of 5000 employees. Hawker worked tirelessly throughout the war, improving designs and co-ordinating production from the various manufacturing plants. He made frequent visits to France to sort out production problems.

The Sopwith Strutter was soon followed by the Sopwith Pup, which was smaller, more agile and better suited to aerial combat. Again, most of the planes were produced in factories not owned by Sopwiths. The Pup was a stepping stone to the Sopwith Camel, the best-known of the fighters used in the war and the one that downed the most enemy aircraft. It was a Sopwith Camel that the Canadian pilot Roy Brown was flying when he was credited with downing the legendary German ace Manfred von Richthofen – the 'Red Baron'. (An equally likely explanation for von Richthofen's demise was ground fire from Australian soldiers.)

The Camel was also the plane flown by the fictional character Squadron Leader James Bigglesworth, better known as Biggles. In fact, the first collection of *Biggles* stories put together by Captain W.E. Johns was called *The Camels are Coming*. Incidentally, the rank of captain was self-awarded: Johns' actual rank in the Royal Flying Corps was flying officer, equivalent to lieutenant in the army.

Of the 5600 Camels that were built, Sopwiths built 503. The Camel's main improvement was that it had increased fire power in the form of two Vickers machine guns, rather than just one on the Pup. This would have increased the weight of the plane, but many other design improvements more than offset this. As a result, the Camel could climb much faster than the Pup; it took 8.5 minutes to reach 3000 metres, compared with 12.5 for the Pup. Like the Pup, the machine guns fired through the propeller using the Sopwith–Kauper gun interrupter gear to make sure the bullets went through the gaps between the whirring propeller blades. This device had been invented by Harry Kauper, Hawker's Australian friend and co-pilot in their earlier Round Britain flight.

Camel is a curious name for an aeroplane, but there is a reason for it. The plane had a hump between the propeller and the pilot, and the hump had a purpose. A common problem encountered by First World War fighter planes was when they reached a high altitude, parts of the machine gun and ammunition feeding belts froze. The hump on the Camel was a metal cowling that permitted the heat from the engine to flow over the machine guns, thus preventing freezing. Other Sopwith planes followed the Camel later in the war, but none achieved its fame or its production levels.

No one could doubt Hawker's value as a test pilot, but at first I found it hard to believe that someone so young and lacking in technical education could really be an important engineer and designer. However, all references in the British aviation literature refer to him as an aircraft designer as well as a pilot. Some cite him as having a very major role in the design of the Sopwith Tabloid, Pup and Camel, but other designers are also recognised. It is very difficult to assign precise responsibility because design was essentially a co-operative activity. But the person best able to judge was Tommy Sopwith himself. In the foreword to Lou Blackmore's biography of Hawker, a very old Sir Thomas Sopwith reflected on the Hawker years and in 1987 he wrote:

> Not only was he a natural pilot, he also had a very good eye for the design of aeroplanes, and I give him most of the credit for the success of the aeroplanes we went on to make.

While it's possible that Sir Thomas was overly generous in giving so much of the credit for the designs to Hawker, it seems unlikely as other sources have confirmed Hawker's importance as a designer. Three quotes from the authorised biography of Sir Thomas Sopwith by Alan Bramson support this:

> The importance of Hawker to the Tommy Sopwith story cannot be over-estimated. (page 41)

> Hawker's contribution to Sopwith Aviation was not confined to demonstrations, tests and competition flying. He was also an 'ideas' man with sufficient grasp of engineering principles to convert thoughts into hardware. (page 56)

> Tommy Sopwith regarded his prodigy [Hawker] as a genius and many of the outstanding qualities of Sopwith aircraft have rightly been attributed to him. (page 96)

On the basis of these testimonies, it is reasonable to conclude that the most important aeronautical designer in the British aviation industry during the First World War was a self-taught Australian in his twenties with only half a dozen years' of design experience.

While Hawker was extremely busy during the war, it cannot have occupied all his time. He often went shooting at Tommy Sopwith's estate. He was an excellent shot – like his father, who had represented Australia at rifle shooting – and on one occasion Harry bagged two stags.

More importantly, in 1915 he met his future wife and married her in 1917 when he was twenty-eight. Their first meeting was a case of a 'damsel in distress'. Eighteen-year-old Muriel Peaty was driving in the countryside with a friend when her car ground to a halt. Hawker, who happened to be driving by, came to their rescue. He quickly got Muriel's car started again and the romance developed from there. The wedding took place in London, and Harry's older brother, Captain Bert Hawker of the AIF (Australian Imperial Force), obtained leave from France to attend as best man.

Soon after the war ended, Lord Northcliffe renewed his pre-war offer of 10,000 pounds to any aviator who flew non-stop across the Atlantic Ocean. The Royal Aero Club was to conduct the competition, and Sopwiths immediately announced they would enter. Hawker was the obvious choice as pilot, and he chose wartime colleague and friend Lt Commander Kenneth Mackenzie-Grieve as his navigator. Several other aviation companies – Vickers, Handley Page and Martinsyde – also announced their intention to enter the competition.

It was an extremely dangerous undertaking. No one had ever flown anywhere near as far across water before. Hawker had done a number of daring things in his life, but this represented an altogether higher level of danger than anything he had previously undertaken. It took great courage on the part of the pilots to attempt such a crossing; if anything went wrong with the plane, the most likely outcome would be a fatal crash into the sea. Although steps were taken to reduce the risks, it remained an extremely dangerous flight given the state of aeroplane technology at the time.

The first step to increase the likelihood of success was to choose the shortest route. This was between the easternmost part of the Dominion of Newfoundland (not part of Canada until 1949) and the westernmost point in Ireland, a distance of 3008 kilometres, all over water.

The next step was to choose a plane that had the capacity to fly over such a long route. Hawker chose a modified Sopwith B1, the largest plane that Sopwiths made. It had a water-cooled V12 Rolls Royce engine of 360 horsepower, much larger and more powerful than wartime Sopwith planes. Nevertheless, it was still an open-cockpit, single-engine biplane. He christened it *The Atlantic* and incorporated several unusual, if not unique, features into it.

The air resistance caused by the wheels sticking out of the bottom of a plane reduces its speed and increases its fuel consumption. Modern planes overcome this by having a hydraulic mechanism that retracts the landing gear into the wings or fuselage so they maintain a smooth, aerodynamic shape. Hawker's solution to this problem was simpler; after becoming airborne in *The Atlantic*, he would pull a release trigger and the whole undercarriage would fall off the plane into the sea. This meant that when he reached his destination, he would have to make a crash landing – not a very triumphant conclusion to a heroic journey.

A second modification was to construct the part of the fuselage behind the cockpit out of plywood in the shape of a boat. If things turned out badly and they were forced to ditch the plane into the sea – hopefully without it breaking up or seriously injuring them – they would detach this boat and get into it while awaiting rescue. A final precaution was to equip themselves with insulated rubber suits incorporating airbags front and back. These would keep them warm and provide flotation if they ended up in the water.

Thus equipped, the team took a ship to Newfoundland with *The Atlantic* crated up in the hold. They found the best field they could to use as a runway, re-assembled the plane and waited for suitable weather. In the same area, Raynham and Morgan of the Martinsyde team, old rivals but friends of Hawker, also waited for their opportunity.

At 5:42 p.m. local time on 18 May 1919, Hawker took off and flew east in the first ever attempt to fly across the Atlantic. Things went well at first, but the weather worsened and there was little visibility. This did not deter them, but then the engine began to overheat and was losing water. After exhausting all attempts to overcome this problem, by which time they were halfway across the Atlantic, Hawker realised they could not make it and so would have to ditch the plane. But fortunately, they had a Plan B. This was to fly to the shipping lanes and look for a ship – not a very likely outcome with limited visibility in the middle of the Atlantic.

However, fortune favoured the brave, and after an hour and a half's frantic searching, they spotted the Danish ship the *Mary*. After firing their emergency flares they ditched two kilometres in front of the ship, fired more flares, climbed into their plywood boat and waited for rescue, which duly came after an hour due to high seas.

They had covered 1680 kilometres, and the elapsed time between departure and being picked up was 14 hours 30 minutes. They still had enough fuel in *The Atlantic* to have made it to Ireland had not mechanical problems intervened. At least they had done better than Raynham and Morgan, who crashed on take-off but survived.

While they were recovering on the *Mary* as it sailed towards England, their failure to arrive was causing great unease at home. The *Mary* did not have a wireless and so the wider world did not know of the rescue. Days went by and nearly everyone assumed Hawker and MacKenzie-Grieve had been lost at sea. They were given up for dead and there was much outpouring of public grief. On 24 May, six days after they left Newfoundland, King George sent a delicately worded letter of condolence to Muriel Hawker (no doubt drafted by one of his personal staff). It read:

> The King, fearing the worst must now be realised regarding the fate of your husband, wishes to express his deep sympathy, and that of the Queen, in your sudden and tragic sorrow. His Majesty feels the Nation lost one of its most able and daring pilots who sacrificed his life for the fame and honour of British flying.

Word had also reached Australia about Hawker's disappearance over the Atlantic. On 24 May, the same day as the King's message, Banjo Paterson burst into print with a requiem for the dead Hawker in *Smith's Weekly*. Its final verse reads:

> Though Hawker perished, he overcame
> The risks of the storm and the sea,
> And his name will be written in stars of flame
> On the topmost walls of the temple of fame
> For the rest of the world to see.

Interestingly, Muriel Hawker was the one person who hadn't given up hope. On 26 May, eight days after *The Atlantic* had taken off from Newfoundland, the *Mary* reached Scotland and was finally able to report that Hawker and MacKenzie-Grieve had been saved. There was now much public rejoicing; it was as though they had come back from the dead. The King was quick to respond, sending a telegram saying:

> The King rejoices with you, and the Nation, on the happy rescue of your gallant husband and he trusts that he may be long spared to you.

Hawker and MacKenzie-Grieve came ashore and made a triumphal return to London, where they went by motorcade to Buckingham Palace with crowds lining the streets to salute their achievement. At Buckingham Palace, the King invested them with the Air Force Cross. Hawker became the first civilian to receive this honour. They had become national heroes. Even though they had not succeeded in obtaining their objective, Lord Northcliffe awarded the pair 5000 pounds.

Ironically, within two weeks of their arrival in England, Alcock and Brown in their twin-engined Vickers, succeeded in flying across the Atlantic, also from Newfoundland to Ireland. They thus won the prize, were also feted for their effort and were both knighted by the King, but their public reception was not as great as for Hawker. Could this have been because the British public celebrate noble failure more than success – such as the case of Scott and the South Pole, or Mallory and Everest – or was it because of 'the coming back from the dead'

Hawker's joyous reception in London after his Atlantic flight.

aspect of Hawker's adventure? Probably the latter.

Despite the exploits of Hawker and MacKenzie-Grieve and more so, of Alcock and Brown, most people associate the first crossing of the Atlantic with Charles Lindberg. He was the first to do it solo and he flew a much longer route from New York to Paris. However, he did it in 1927, by which time planes had become much more powerful and reliable. But history records that the first attempt to fly across the Atlantic was by Hawker and MacKenzie-Grieve, and the first successful crossing was by Alcock and Brown. Both events occurred in 1919, eight years before Lindberg.

After the transatlantic adventure, Hawker spent a well-earned motoring holiday with his wife. He was by now a father, as Muriel had given birth to a daughter, Pamela, before the transatlantic adventure. A second daughter was born a year after; she was named Mary after the ship that had rescued her father.

Hawker then turned his attention to car racing. He purchased a Sunbeam racing car that had been built for the Indianapolis 500 and he won several races at Brooklands with it. His other achievement was to be the first person to break 100 miles (160 kilometres) per hour in a light car, where light is defined as being powered by an engine of less than 1500 cc. Hawker achieved this by acquiring an AC car, then stripping it and fitting a very aerodynamic aluminium body of his own design to it. He then raced a more powerful version of the Sunbeam, but without much success. He managed to have two crashes with this car, but fortunately was not seriously injured. However, these crashes, coming on top of the earlier aeroplane crashes, were taking their toll on his body and he was experiencing chronic back problems. Whether the back problems were caused by the crashes or whether there was something more deep-seated was not known at the time.

But this didn't deter him from further racing activity – this time in powerboats. There seemed to be no form of motorised racing that Hawker did not try; from racing motorbikes in Australia, to aeroplanes, to racing cars, and now powerboats. He must have had a love of speed, and of course he had Sopwith's support in a lot of this. The assumption must have been that if you are good at one of these forms of motorised racing, you will probably be good at the others. In recent years we have seen examples of sportsmen who achieved success racing both cars and motorbikes, but attempting it in four different forms of racing is probably unique. In any event, his foray into powerboat racing was not a great success. His boat was enormously powerful, using four, 12-cylinder Sunbeam engines delivering total power of 1600 bhp. It was the fastest boat in England, but despite its power it was beaten by two American boats into third place in the British International Trophy.

While all this racing activity was taking place, a far more important and disturbing development was occurring – the Sopwith Aviation Company was getting into financial difficulties. When the First World War ended, all orders for military aircraft were cancelled, so Sopwiths had to close their production lines and dismiss their large workforce as there was almost no work for them to do. To make matters worse, there was an overhang of military surplus planes dumped onto the market. As Sopwiths struggled with these problems by trying to diversify into car body and motorbike manufacturing, they were hit with a third blow: the government introduced a punitive Excess War Profits Duty on suppliers of military equipment. The Sopwith Aviation Company now had no future; it repaid its creditors and what it could to the Treasury, and closed its doors.

In late 1920, the H.G. Hawker Engineering Company Ltd. was

formed by the four most senior executives from the now defunct Sopwith Aviation Company, one of whom was Harry Hawker. Each of them contributed a quarter of the 20,000 pounds of initial capital. By now Hawker, at thirty-one years of age, was a respected designer/manager and reasonably well-off; it was no surprise that the company was named after him and that he was appointed chairman. Tommy Sopwith joined slightly later in order to distance himself from the transition. Legally it was independent from Sopwiths, but in practice it had many characteristics that linked it to Sopwiths. Not only were all the senior staff ex-Sopwiths, but it had also bought all the patent rights held by Sopwiths for aircraft, motor cars, motorbikes and engines. It managed to pull itself together by manufacturing motorbikes and reconditioning aeroplanes, and so returned to profitability. Some observers said that it was sad that the company carried Hawker's name rather than Sopwith's, given his company's great contribution during the war. With typical generosity of spirit, Tommy Sopwith said, "I didn't mind. He [Hawker] was very largely responsible for its growth during the war too."

But just when things were returning to normal, tragedy struck. In July 1921, Hawker, at thirty-two years of age, was killed in a practice flight. Having survived countless dangerous situations over the previous decade, he died in a routine practice session that involved neither great speed nor endurance. He had entered the Aerial Derby and was trying out his new plane – a Nieuport Goshawk built in England from a French design. Onlookers said they saw it dive, then pull out of the dive too late, and crash into the ground.

What could have caused this tragic event? There are two competing explanations. The initial Coroner's Report said that Hawker was suffering from deep-seated and extensive tubercular disease of the spine (hence the chronic back problems) and that this haemorrhaged, causing him to lose control of the plane. There is no doubt that he had this condition and if it is any consolation, it provided his family and friends with some comfort knowing that the disease would have restricted him to only a short life even if he hadn't crashed. But did it cause the crash?

A more thorough assessment was carried out by the Accident Investigation Branch of the Air Ministry in August 1921, which for some reason was marked "Secret. Not to be Released for 50 Years". When it was eventually released in 1972, a different conclusion emerged. It agreed that Hawker was suffering from a tubercular disease of the spine, that a haemorrhage had occurred before the crash and that it might have disabled his legs. But it also found, as witnesses had reported, that flames were coming out of the underside of the engine well before it crashed. This was because petrol was escaping through the unscrewed cover of one of the three carburettors. Further evidence for this was that, even though Hawker was thrown out of the plane on impact, and so was well clear of the burning wreckage, his shoes and ankles were severely burned. This could only have happened while he was still in the air attempting to control the plane. The clear conclusion was that fire was the main cause of the crash. Surprisingly, the official history of the Hawker Aviation Company still sticks to the earlier explanation.

Hawker's death was a huge loss to British aviation and he was widely mourned in England and Australia. The King was quick to send his condolences, as was British Prime Minister David Lloyd George.

Hawker's main legacy is the company that bore his name. Tommy Sopwith took over as chairman of H.G. Hawker Engineering upon

Hawker's death and under his leadership it thrived and Sopwith became an extremely wealthy man, as did the senior executives. In 1933 it changed its name to Hawker Aircraft Ltd., and in 1935, when it took over Armstrong Siddeley, it became the Hawker Siddeley Aircraft Company with capital of five million pounds. It built many different types of military aeroplanes, but the most successful was the Hawker Hurricane fighter used in the Second World War, of which 15,000 were built. The most famous of the group's post-war planes was the Hawker Harrier Jump Jet, which could take off vertically.

The aviation industry has been a very unstable one, with firms coming and going regularly and takeovers and mergers common. Hawker Siddeley survived this turmoil until 1977, when the British government decided to nationalise the British aviation industry to form British Aerospace. The name Hawker thus disappeared from the English aviation industry, but the non-aviation parts of the business survived.

Interestingly, the only aviation part that survived under the Hawker name was in Australia, where it operated as Hawker De Havilland until 2009 when it was taken over by Boeing. There are still two remnants of the original company using the Hawker name that I could find. Hawker Pacific, headquartered in Sydney, sells other companies' planes and helicopters but does not design or build. It recognises its heritage and features a photo of Harry Hawker on its website. The other is Hawker Pacific Aerospace, which specialises in maintenance and is now owned by Lufthansa and headquartered in Burbank, California. I wonder how many of its employees know where the name Hawker came from.

The fact that Hawker's name lived on in a company that he only had a brief association with is mirrored in another industry in which he participated – motor racing, where Bruce McLaren, the New

Zealand racing driver, established his own company, McLaren Racing Ltd. in 1963. Like Hawker, he died at age thirty-two while practising for a race in 1970. McLaren's company outlived him and thrived under later management, going on to win eight Formula One world constructers championships and it is still a major producer of luxury, high-performance sports cars.

Looking back over the life of Harry Hawker MBE AFC, the thing that still surprises me is that someone could have achieved so much in just one decade. He arrived in England in 1911 having never set foot in an aeroplane, yet a decade later he was acknowledged as one of the most important aeronautical designers in the world, a multiple prize-winning pilot, daring sportsman, national hero and successful businessman. It was only possible because his greatest interest in life and his hobby – what we would now call his passion – coincided exactly with his job. And, more importantly, he was gifted from an early age with exceptional, intuitive ability in this field. Few people are ever so fortunate to have these three things line up so exactly. He also had a well-deserved reputation as a tireless worker, but did he regard it as work? Was there anything else that he would rather have been doing? I doubt it.

There are other Australian names in the history of aviation that are better remembered than Hawker's: Charles Kingsford-Smith, Bert Hinckler, and Keith and Ross Smith, for example. But Hawker is not completely forgotten. In 1978, a stamp was issued to commemorate him and in 1989, Moorabbin Airport changed its name to Moorabbin (Harry Hawker) Airport.

I hope this biographical essay will help people to recognise Harry Hawker's remarkable achievements. It certainly helped me to appreciate what he achieved in such a short time.

George Finch in alpine hut 1911.

2

GEORGE FINCH

Mountaineer and Scientist

I first became aware of George Finch when I was reading Canadian writer Wade Davis's superb book, *Into the Silence: The Great War, Mallory and the Ascent of Everest*. This book explored British attempts to climb Mount Everest in the 1920s. Even though the main figure in the book was English mountaineer George Mallory, an Australian mountaineer named George Finch was a major player and something of an unsung hero of Mount Everest. This man from the world's flattest continent succeeded in climbing higher than anyone in the world had done to that date.

When I looked into Finch, more fascinating stories unfolded, particularly his conflict with the British mountaineering establishment, his turbulent private life and his career as a successful scientist. But no account of him would be complete without exploring his relationship with another Finch who was Australia's outstanding actor in the twentieth century.

To understand the story of George Finch, you have to go back a couple of generations. Charles Wray Finch, George's grandfather, the son of a poor clergyman, was a soldier who came to Australia from England in 1830. He switched careers to become a magistrate, and then a squatter, and a successful one at that. He was well-enough connected to acquire a very large piece of land in the fertile Wellington Valley near Orange in New South Wales. It eventually carried 20,000 sheep and 800 cattle, and required 25 farmhands to run it. It made him a rich man and showed that the allocation of land was often the key to wealth in a settler society like Australia in the nineteenth century. If you missed out, you usually struggled. Charles Finch moved to Sydney in 1855, built a large house on Greenwich Point, was elected to New South Wales parliament and became a pillar of society. His transformation in one generation from humble beginnings to wealthy landowner and member of the establishment would have been impossible in England. George Finch's grandfather was the source of the wealth that kept the Finches in good stead for the next two generations.

His son, Charles Edward Finch – George's father – was born in 1843, educated at the Kings School, Parramatta, and commenced his career as a surveyor. Like his father, he realised that land division was a good business to be in. He married in 1870, but his wife died shortly after and he remained a bachelor for 16 years. He inherited the properties at Wellington Valley and Greenwich Point on his father's death in 1873, and then returned to the Wellington Valley in 1885, by which time he had become Chairman of the Land Board. In 1887, aged forty-four years, he married Laura Isobel Black, aged nineteen years. She was a teacher in Orange, a great beauty and quite well educated, but from a poor family. She later claimed she had married Charles in order to discharge a debt owed by her father.

The couple soon had three children: George, the future mountaineer, who was born in 1888, his younger brother Max and a sister, Dorothy. George's upbringing in Australia was reasonably conventional for a well-off country boy. He went to school locally, and spent a lot of time riding, hunting and helping around the farm. He loved the outdoor life and grew strong and athletic.

At first Laura Finch enjoyed her life as the wife of one of the richest and most important men in the district, as well as being the mother of three small children. But things soon began to change. She turned her attention increasingly towards Sydney and away from Orange, she started to view herself as more refined than the locals, and she took up singing and gave concerts in Sydney. But what she really longed for was Europe. In the end it was her conversion to the cause of the Theosophical Society that changed the course of the Finch family's life.

I will not attempt to explain the principles of theosophy, other than to say it attempts to blend science and a generalised concept of religion, particularly Eastern religion, into a way of life. Its principles are not easy to summarise as it has frequently changed and splintered into smaller sects, some of which emphasise spiritualism and the occult. It was hearing a speech by its leading advocate, Annie Besant, in Sydney in 1894 that turned Laura Finch into a lifelong devotee of the movement, even though she retained some characteristics, including a degree of snobbishness, which seemed to conflict with its principles.

George, when he was old enough to understand, had no time for his mother's philosophical or artistic views, which he regarded as muddle-headed. But she had a lot of willpower and her much older husband was no match for her. She eventually prevailed and Charles

Finch took time off work to take his family to Europe for a year in 1902. George was fourteen years old when he left Australia for what was intended to be a year abroad.

The Finch family initially settled in England near Cambridge, where the Finchs had originally come from. Both Charles and Laura were pleased to find they had some connection with noble English ancestors, who now went by the double-barrelled name of Ingle-Finch. They changed their name to Ingle-Finch, but this seems only to have caused confusion. Although that was now the family's official name, most people continued to call them Finch, and George is rarely referred to as anything other than George Finch. That is the name I will use in this account of his life.

The Finch family's stay in England was short-lived as Laura longed for Paris, which was the centre of the theosophy movement. They soon moved there and Laura felt immediately at home as she already spoke good French and immersed herself in artistic circles and the theosophy movement. Charles, unable to speak French and now sixty, did not fit in at all. This was a watershed in the family's life, and it was resolved in a way that seems sad and difficult to understand.

In the end, Charles returned to Australia; his wife and children stayed in Paris, and he continued to support them financially so that they could lead comfortable and interesting lives. Apart from his daughter Dorothy, he never saw his wife or children again. What is even more remarkable is that the children liked and respected their father, but had reservations about their mother's erratic behaviour and enthusiasm for strange causes. Nevertheless they stayed with her in Paris, but continued to correspond affectionately with him. What would have been the outcome if there had not been a steady flow of money from Charles in Australia to support their lifestyle in Paris?

Why did he not cut it off and ask them to return? No one knows.

To add insult to injury, Laura took up with a French painter named Konstant and gave birth to a son in 1904. Konstant was probably the father, but the child was christened Antoine Konstant Finch. Charles Finch had been gone from Paris by the time the baby was conceived, but he was willing to let his name be used to lend a veneer of legitimacy to the birth. As we will see, this would not be the last time such an event occurred.

Despite this family scandal and other sources of conflict, the children stayed with Laura and settled into French life. She was not a neglectful mother and took her duties seriously; in fact, she was quite demanding about their health and education and placed strict limits on their adventurous activities.

George's time in Paris was notable for two achievements. First, with the help of private tutors, he became a good enough student to gain entry into the medical faculty of the University of Paris. However, medicine did not suit him and after two years he left to study chemistry in Zurich. Second, he and his brother Max became enthusiastic mountain climbers. George's interest in climbing had been aroused in England when he read the book *Scrambling among the Alps* by Edward Whymper, the first man to climb the Matterhorn. In late Victorian times, mountain climbing was becoming a popular pastime for the English and was regarded as a gentleman's sport. It was not for the masses as it involved considerable expense on equipment, travel, accommodation and the hiring of guides. The Alpine Club of London had been founded in 1857 and became, in a sense, the governing body of English mountain climbing. It was run like a London gentlemen's club in that members had to be nominated and seconded by existing members.

George and Max Finch became very active mountaineers. They had the advantage of being closer to the Alps than English climbers, and they spoke fluent French and German. From the moment they arrived in Paris they commenced a series of climbs, starting with the lower mountains (at Laura's insistence) and working up to the higher peaks and more difficult climbs. They could pay for the best guides, whose methods they studied closely. In time they knew everything the guides could teach them and so were able to climb without their assistance.

George moved to Zurich in 1907 and enrolled at the Federal Institute of Technology, where he proved to be an excellent student. This was a very high-class university, which counted Albert Einstein as an ex-student and later as a professor. It was during these years in Zurich that George developed into an accomplished leader of climbing teams and president of the very active university mountaineering club. The Italian climber Count Aldo Bonacossa, writing about the Zurich mountaineers, said:

> The recognised number one mountaineer and the most outstanding personality among them by far was George Finch. He was tall and wore his hair long and untamed, quite unlike other men in Switzerland ... this gave him an exotic look. Moreover he came from the Antipodes and as a result was nicknamed 'the Australian'.

George climbed most of the well-known peaks in the Alps – the Wetterhorn, the Jungfrau, the Bifertenstock, Monte Rosa, the Matterhorn and Mont Blanc. But it was not just a matter of ticking off the peaks one by one, eventually leading to the highest one. Climbing the most difficult face of a medium-sized mountain counted for a lot more than reaching the peak of a higher one by an easier route. Being the *first* to reach a peak by a previously unclimbed route (unclimbed presumably because it was regarded as too difficult) counted most of all. George did this on at least six occasions in the Alps. This was the most difficult form of mountaineering and required great ingenuity, agility, endurance and courage. Climbing in winter counted for more than climbing in summer. George specialised in climbing in winter when snow and ice presented the most serious obstacles and it was necessary to cut steps into the ice with an axe. His reputation as a climber, particularly in snow and ice, grew among the elite climbing fraternity in Europe and began to filter back to London.

George graduated in early 1911, winning the gold medal for the top student in chemical technology. After 18 months working in Zurich and then at the German chemical company BASF, he moved to England in October 1912. His first job was at the Royal Arsenal, then in 1913 he was appointed to an academic position at Imperial College London, a first-rate university specialising in engineering and science. George joined the newly established School of Chemical Technology, which was to remain his base during his long academic career.

He was now twenty-five and in a very comfortable position because he had a secure academic job with flexible enough working arrangements to allow him time to pursue his mountaineering, where his exploits were attracting increasing attention. The salary was modest, but when augmented by his allowance from Australia, he could live well. Unfortunately, this idyllic existence did not last long because within a year, the First World War broke out.

Britain declared war on 4 August 1914, George's twenty-sixth birthday. He volunteered for the British Army in September 1914, and after training was commissioned a second lieutenant in the Royal Field Artillery. Most of his first year in the army was spent in England, training and training others. He expected to be sent to France, but instead was sent to the Balkans in November 1915 to fight German and Austrian troops who were attacking Greece and Albania. By now he was in the Ordnance Division, where his main job was to restore damaged artillery shells. This was dangerous work, but with his scientific background he excelled at it. He returned to England for a time in early 1917, but was back in the Balkans for a second stint until he contracted malaria and was sent back to England shortly before the war ended.

The First World War was a gruelling experience, but George came through it in better shape than most. He was not sent to the bloodbaths of Gallipoli or the Western Front, and apart from malaria, he finished in good enough shape to be able to continue his mountain climbing. He finished the war as a captain and was awarded an MBE.

It is relatively easy to summarise George's military experience during the war, but much more difficult to describe his turbulent personal life. While an officer still serving in England, he met the glamorous and flirtatious Betty Fisher in early 1915 and married her in June 1915. Their time together was brief as he was sent to the Balkans on 28 November of that year. When he returned to England in January 1917, he found that Betty had given birth to a son on 28 September 1916, ten months after he had left England. Betty had not been able to remain faithful even for a month. The real father was identified as a Scottish officer called Jock Campbell. George chased him to France, beat him to unconsciousness and was nearly court-martialled for his efforts.

Like his father before him, he allowed the baby boy to take his surname and so avoid the stigma of illegitimacy. The boy's full name was Frederick George Peter Ingle-Finch, but he was better known as

Peter Finch. We will hear more of him as the story unfolds.

As marriage to Betty was moving to an inevitable end, another relationship was beginning in the Balkans. As George was recuperating from malaria in hospital in Salonika, he met Gladys May, a quiet, practical nurse – the absolute opposite of Betty. She helped him to recover, their friendship grew and they became lovers when they returned to England in 1918. His aim then became to obtain a divorce from Betty, get custody of Peter and marry Gladys.

After a lot of effort he traced Betty across England, found evidence of continuing adultery, took possession of Peter and then filed for divorce on the grounds of adultery (she was pregnant again to Campbell by this time). The case was uncontested and so George obtained what he sought. It is no surprise that he obtained the divorce and that Campbell had to pay the legal costs, but it may seem surprising that George obtained custody of Peter. However, the fact that George was not the biological father of Peter Finch was a closely-kept secret. George, Betty and Campbell knew, but each of them had good reasons to keep it secret. As far as we can tell, no one else knew. Laura Finch, George's mother, who was given the task of raising Peter, believed that he was the biological father, so did Charles Finch back in Australia, and so did Peter himself until the truth was revealed to him in his mid-forties. Almost certainly the court assumed, or was told, that George was the biological father, and so had no trouble in awarding him custody. A greater puzzle is why he wanted custody at all, since we know he farmed Peter off to his mother and other members of the Finch family for his upbringing and never saw him again until late in life. Presumably he felt that Betty was unfit to be the boy's mother, even though she had looked after him for the first two years of his life.

But just as the first marriage was being put to rest, the proposed second marriage took a new direction. By this time Gladys was pregnant and looking forward to marriage, but George changed his mind and decided he did not want to spend the rest of his life with her. He went through with the marriage in November 1920 so that the child (a son) would be legitimate, but three weeks after the wedding he moved out of the house, never to return. He had treated Gladys appallingly, and his offer to pay maintenance for the child's upkeep was little compensation. Preparations for a divorce commenced, but as was the practice in those times, an adultery event had to be contrived – this time with George as the guilty partner. It took the best part of a year to finalise.

Another event that had a big effect on George's life occurred a few years earlier – the Russian Revolution in 1917. It turned out that the endowment established by Charles Finch to support his family in Europe had been invested heavily in Russian railway bonds, which paid high interest. But when the new Bolshevik government came to power, it refused to honour the debts of the previous Czarist regime and the bonds became worthless. The endowment shrank, as did the income it produced. It is not clear how far George's Australian-sourced income fell – his biographer Wainwright implies it fell to zero – but, on the evidence of his later spending patterns, I think there must still have been some money coming to him above his academic salary. But he definitely suffered a reduction in his income.

Shortly after leaving Gladys, George met Agnes Johnson, who was to become his third wife in six years. She was a graduate of Edinburgh University, had worked in the Foreign Office and was applying for a position at Imperial College when he met her. Agnes hated her first name and was usually known by her nickname – Bubbles – which suited her cheerful personality. This was a case of 'third time lucky' for George as they were ideally suited to each other. They married after the divorce from Gladys came through, remained together for the rest of their lives and raised three daughters.

I can now leave George's complicated marital story behind and concentrate on what he is best known for – his mountaineering exploits and the attempts to conquer Everest, which took place in three stages. First, there was a reconnaissance expedition in 1921 to map out the territory and explore possible routes. Second, there was the first attempt to climb Everest in 1922. When this failed, there was a second attempt in 1924. Further attempts were made in later years, but they need not concern us in this essay. Everest was not finally climbed until 1953 in the tenth British attempt.

Everest is in an extremely remote location bordered by Tibet, Nepal and India. The mountain was named after Sir George Everest, the former Surveyor General of India, even though he didn't discover it, nor did he survey it, and it is doubtful whether he even saw it. Furthermore, he objected to it being named after him because he would have preferred a local name. But there were too many different local names, so his was chosen. Incidentally, he pronounced his name 'Eve Rest', the first syllable pronounced the same as in Adam and Eve.

Permission to enter Tibet was needed, and this was granted by the Dalai Lama in 1920. It may seem surprising that he would be so generous to an expedition partly sponsored by Sir Francis Younghusband, who had led a British Army force into Tibet in 1904 during which 500 Tibetans had been massacred. The reason was that in the meantime, much more brutal Chinese aggression in Tibet had made the British seem the lesser of two evils. In fact, by 1920

Tibet looked upon Britain as a protector against Chinese designs. In understanding subsequent events we have to bear in mind that the British, through their imperial control over India and Nepal and their new relationship with Tibet, had a monopoly on Everest exploration. That is why they could exclude other countries or non-British climbers from participating.

In January 1921, the Alpine Club and the Royal Geographical Society announced a joint expedition to Everest and appointed an Everest Committee to organise it and, most importantly, choose the members of the party. As soon as the expedition was announced, Percy Farrer, the president of the Alpine Club, said the climbing party should be headed by George and Max Finch and Marcel Kurz. Max was unavailable and Kurz was ruled out because he was Swiss. So of Farrer's preferred trio, only George would be eligible.

The Everest Committee had eight members, four from each organisation, but it was dominated by the aforementioned Sir Francis Younghusband, the President of the Royal Geographical Society, and its Secretary, Arthur Hinks. Both disliked George from the outset and opposed his membership of the expedition. Hinks was the main problem; a man who had never climbed higher than a staircase, and was so conservative that he even disapproved of the telephone. He went to great lengths to lobby against George's inclusion. I will take up the subject of why these people objected to him later in the story.

Despite their opposition, George was selected alongside Mallory as the main climbers in the four-man climbing party. The other climbers were Harold Raeburn, aged fifty-six, and Alexander Kellas, aged fifty-three. Their ages were a great disadvantage, but they were chosen because they had previous Himalayan experience.

The choice of George Mallory was not a surprise. Few doubted his ability as a climber or his courage, and he also had an aura of glamour about him. A Cambridge man and very good-looking like his friend and contemporary Rupert Brooke, he moved easily in refined and artistic circles. He was widely admired and lusted after by the likes of Lytton Strachey, who in a letter to Virginia Woolf described him as "six-foot high, with the body of an athlete by Praxiteles, and a face – oh incredible – the mystery of a Botticelli ... the youth and piquancy of an English boy".

George moved in different circles and was a much more down-to-earth character – Australian by birth and European by education – but both men were accomplished climbers. In Robert Wainwright's biography of George, he quotes the respected English mountaineer Geoffrey Winthrop Young who wrote in his book *Mountain Craft* that Finch was the pre-eminent snow-and-ice man of his generation and the perfect foil for Mallory, whose strength was climbing on rock.

Two weeks before the party was due to depart, Hinks insisted on a final medical check by two Harley Street doctors. This was expected to be routine, but to everyone's surprise, George was found unfit. How a man who had recently been scaling high peaks could be found unfit is a mystery. Was it part of a conspiracy or an error? There is no evidence for the former so we have to conclude it was the latter. A replacement for George was found.

Even though he was disappointed, George continued to help the team by using his scientific knowledge. He devised a new type of Primus stove that would work at heights of over 7000 metres. To test it he operated it in a special pressure chamber at Oxford University, which recreated such high-altitude conditions. He also underwent tests on his endurance at these altitudes and achieved the best results of any of the thousand volunteers who had taken the tests. His supporters were quick to relay this information to Hinks, but it was too late now that a replacement had been announced.

As the expedition was proceeding in India, George returned to the Alps to look for new challenges. His main achievement that year was to climb the south face of Mont Blanc. One of his main supporters, Percy Farrer, wrote to Hinks stating, "Our invalid Finch took part in the biggest climb done in the Alps this summer."

As George was climbing in the Alps, the Everest expedition was on the hazardous march towards Mount Everest. They left England in April 1921 and started their 300-mile trek towards Everest from Darjeeling in India in May. Although the purpose of the expedition was officially for reconnaissance, Hinks let them know that if they had an opportunity to climb Everest they should, or at least get as far up as possible.

The party comprised nine Englishmen, 40 coolies, 100 mules, four cooks and two translators. Progress was painfully slow and there were many health problems, particularly dysentery. On 7 June, Kellas, who was an experienced climber but fifty-three years old, died. The party moved on and eventually made it to the foot of Everest. Mallory and Bullock (Finch's replacement) were able to climb to the base of the North Col to a height of 7200 metres. This was achieved nearly three months after they left Darjeeling. It was the highest point reached, but was still 1650 metres below the summit of 8848 metres. This is a long way short of success. Because the air gets thinner the higher you go, each hundred metres is harder to climb than the previous one. The party then headed back to India and were able to return to England by November.

The publicity surrounding the reconnaissance expedition had been superbly managed by Hinks, and the media regarded it a success.

Expedition members were in great demand and Mallory alone gave 30 well-attended public lectures. The public was impatient to see the obvious next step – the climbing of Everest – and in response, the committee brought forward the second expedition so that it started in March 1922, less than six months after the first had returned to England. This time George was among the six designated climbers chosen in an expedition team of 13, and the press statement made it clear that he and Mallory were the two to make the final assault on the mountain. Despite their reservations about George, the committee could not overlook his climbing ability. Colonel Strutt, the deputy leader of the expedition, said of George in a reply to Hinks, "He is the one man that I would back to reach the summit, and we should always remember that." So in December 1921, at age thirty-three, George married Bubbles and then took off in March 1922 for five months or so in the Himalayas.

This time he passed his fitness test, as did the expedition leader, Brigadier- General Charles Bruce, who was fifty-six years old and suffered from high blood pressure and various war wounds: so much for the objectivity of the medical examination process. George embraced his new opportunity enthusiastically and once again used his scientific knowledge to advantage. In their biography of Mallory, Peter and Leni Gillman report that:

> Finch and fellow climbing team member – Sommervell, subjected themselves to further tests in the Oxford pressure chamber – Finch again performed superbly, while Sommervell passed out.

George strongly believed that to succeed at the altitudes encountered on Everest it was necessary to carry supplies of oxygen, and he spent a lot of time learning how to operate and maintain the equipment. Not everyone agreed; some were totally opposed to its use at all, some reluctantly accepted it but never really learned how to use it properly, while others, like George, felt it was essential to know how to use it. These disagreements led to friction among team members in both the 1922 and 1924 expeditions. As we now know, when Everest was finally climbed thirty years later, it was with the help of oxygen.

George also had strong views about the best clothing to wear in alpine conditions. Until his innovations, mountain climbers wore tweed sports coats, cashmere sweaters and scarves, some even wore pyjamas underneath. They looked like country gents hiking rather than mountain climbers. George had a down-filled jacket and trousers made to his own design. Some fellow climbers ridiculed this outfit, but he remained warmer than they did in the freezing conditions, and again we know that his approach of a down-filled parka is the one used today.

The second Everest expedition left two months earlier in the year than the first in order to give it time to beat the monsoon. It was also bigger, both in number of people and in number of pack animals – 50 mules and 200 yaks. Like the first expedition, it had to make its way through 300 miles of mountains, valleys, jungle, desert, sand dunes and marshes before it reached the base of Everest. When they reached it, their instructions were to make the first attempt without using oxygen. The first attempt led by Mallory was also a four-man team, all of whom were designated climbers. This was contrary to the original intention of having a Mallory–Finch team do the main assault. Eventually the four-man team got as high as 8200 metres before having to turn back.

George was to lead the second attempt, after the first one failed to reach the summit. He was handicapped by not having a designated climber to partner him. Instead, he was to be accompanied by Geoffrey Bruce (the leader's nephew), a strong and brave man, but a novice at

George Finch on right and climbing partner Geoffrey Bruce on left on Everest in 1922. Finch is wearing a down-filled jacket, Bruce is wearing a tweed sports coat and cashmere cardigan.

mountain climbing. They used oxygen and were able to climb at nearly three times the pace of the earlier party, and reached a height of 8325 metres before Bruce could go no further because he had trouble using his oxygen equipment. George was still in good shape and could have gone higher, but had to look after his distressed partner and get him back to safety.

We do not know how much higher he could have gone if he'd had the help of an equally accomplished climbing partner who was equally adept at using oxygen. Could he have reached the top? George never claimed he could publicly, and we don't know his private thoughts. Nevertheless, he had climbed higher than anyone ever had before and he had shown the value, even the necessity, of oxygen.

At the instigation of Mallory, a belated third attempt on the summit was made in which Mallory would use oxygen when he passed 7500 metres. In the event, the climbing party didn't get that far and it proved to be a disaster when it tried to cross unstable snow, leading to the death of seven Sherpas. This reinforced the view of many that Mallory, though brave, was reckless and lacking in judgement. George's reputation, on the other hand, was starting to rise. Before the expedition returned to England, General Bruce proposed him for membership of the Alpine Club, seconded by Colonel Strutt. George, having set the world height record for mountain climbing, was now deemed good enough to be a member of the club.

I am aware that I have skipped lightly over these two gruelling expeditions. For those who would like a blow-by-blow account of the trek, the climbs and the interactions between team members, I recommend the books by Davis and Wainwright that I have already cited.

When the team returned to England, both George and Mallory were received by the public as heroes and embarked on a strenuous round of public lectures. Most of the money so raised went to the Everest Committee, but the lecturers shared in the proceeds. Interestingly, nearly all of the expedition members were either privately wealthy or were supported by the army. The two exceptions were George and Mallory, who needed to maximise the financial gain from their efforts. Mallory was a schoolmaster at Charterhouse and father of three small children, although his teacher's wage was augmented by an allowance from his father-in-law, who also gave Mallory and his wife their family home.

George was mainly dependent on his academic salary and in need of money. But he also had a valuable asset in the photo collection of Everest that he had taken through his own efforts and the expenditure of 200 pounds on equipment. Inevitably a conflict arose between the Everest Committee, which believed it controlled all material emanating from the expedition and George, who believed the photos were his private property to be used as he saw fit after he had finished his lecture tour for the committee. Finally, George threatened to take the matter to court. This was the final straw for the committee – they had never liked him and now they resolved not to have anything further to do with him. He was ruled out of the third Everest expedition scheduled for 1924.

Now is a good time to address two interesting questions. The first is, why did the Everest Committee, the Royal Geographic Society and the Alpine Club have such a hostile attitude to George? Some observers have suggested it was because of his Australian background. For example, Walt Unsworth, in his massive and authoritative book *Everest*, says of George:

Technically he was the best climber on the expedition but his

> Australian unorthodoxy did not go down well with the climbing establishment and he suffered as a result.

I don't think his Australian background was the cause; it was much more complicated than that. Australians have rarely had trouble being accepted in England, particularly if they are highly accomplished in their field. George was an educated professional with a fine military record; he was referred to in Everest Committee documents as Captain Finch MBE. So why did they dislike him so much?

First, he represented a totally different style of mountaineering to them. He had a European approach to climbing, not a British one. He always climbed mountains without guides, he was interested in science, he wore strange clothes unbefitting a gentleman, he had a professional rather than amateur approach and he believed strongly in oxygen. He was not their idea of a gentleman, and the Alpine Club was, as its members pointed out, a club for gentlemen who climb, not a club for mountain climbers. There was also his unusual marital situation; three marriages in six years take a lot of explaining today, let alone 100 years ago.

Second, and I think more importantly, he let the old guard know that he had no respect for them. As long ago as 1913 he had written an article extolling the modern form of mountaineering and virtually ridiculing the old style. He wrote:

> … mountaineering is no longer the monopoly of rich Englishmen. The younger men are taking up the sport and gradually coming to the front … The spirit that saw the Alps a preserve for moneyed and middle-aged Englishmen is dead.

After he had been left out of the first expedition, but was hoping to be included in the second, George was climbing in the Alps when he got into an argument with two senior Alpine Club members. He knew his behaviour was risking his chances, as he confided in a letter to Bubbles: "There will be no Himalayas for me – I was rude to two most important old boys of the Alpine Club who said I should not have come over the Furg Joch [a pass] alone."

Certainly, as a young man he lacked tact, was hot-headed and strongly opinionated. There were also some aspects of his personality that suggest he was insensitive in personal relations. For example, having been inseparable from his younger brother, Max, before the war, they had a falling out and never saw each other again, even though they both lived in England. He also never met again with his father after they parted when George was fifteen, and his treatment of Gladys May was indefensible. He was also very secretive; the existence of his second marriage and son were never revealed to Bubbles and their children.

I am not trying to claim that the rift with the establishment was mainly due to George. The main cause was that Hinks and his colleagues were relentless in their unreasonable opposition to him and the modern approach to mountaineering, but George was not blameless. If the Alpine Club had been a football club, it wouldn't have mattered. Most sporting clubs are meritocracies: they put the best player on the field, even if he annoys them. But the people who move in mountaineering circles are not like the people who move in football circles.

The second interesting question concerns the relative merits of George and Mallory as mountaineers. The conventional view seems to be that they were equally capable, although Mallory was by far the more famous. I started to question this when I read Walt Unsworth's assessment in *Everest*, where he wrote of Mallory:

> How was it that this reluctant young man became a *Boys Own Paper* archetypical hero? The answer is he couldn't help it: he

was cast in heroic mould, both physically and mentally, and he became a child of destiny ... Mallory had greatness thrust upon him. The pity of it was that he had so little actual talent. Mallory was a competent rather than great climber. His record is small, his climbs largely forgotten. Even in his own day they were not particularly hard climbs ... far from being the greatest mountaineer of his day, he was not really in the leading cadre.

I then went back and reassessed the contemporary judgements that I have already quoted. If Mallory was equal to George, why was he not Farrer's first choice when the expedition was announced? More important is the quote by Strutt, who didn't like George personally and was replying to a letter from Hinks that contained derogatory remarks about him. After pointing out that George was the most likely climber to reach the summit, he emphasised to Hinks *"we must always remember that"* (my italics). This was a very emphatic statement of Finch's status by someone not normally on George's side.

In March 1924, the third Everest expedition set off from Darjeeling without George, but with a team of six climbers led by Mallory. It followed the same path as the previous two, but was no more successful. In fact, it ended in tragedy. Two attempts were made to reach the summit without using oxygen; it was only on the third try that it was used. This was carried out by Mallory and his partner, Sandy Ervine, young, strong and brave, but a novice mountaineer. They were last seen heading for the summit and closer to it than any previous attempt, but they never returned. They disappeared somewhere near the top of Everest and the expedition had to return without them. Mallory's last climb had been a do-or-die effort; he was prepared to risk everything rather than be seen to have failed a third time. And he paid the ultimate price. In England there was much public mourning and he became a national hero and martyr.

There was also much speculation about whether the pair had died on the way up or whether they had reached the summit and died on the way down. No one will ever know for sure, but in 1999 Mallory's body was finally found and it provided some clues to help resolve the question. On balance, the verdict seems to be that it was highly unlikely they had reached the top, but not impossible.

Looking back over the three expeditions between 1921 and 1924 poses other questions as well. To me, the big unanswered one is this: what would have been the result if the two top climbers – George and Mallory – had teamed up and been equipped with adequate oxygen support? They never managed to organise it that way, but if they had done so, would the pair have been able to reach the summit? The final assaults were always handicapped by having a novice in the team or a lack of efficient oxygen supply.

Thirty years later, a British expedition enabled a New Zealand beekeeper and a Nepalese guide (hardly the types to be members of the Alpine Club) to conquer Everest, supported by the methodical use of oxygen. Just as Scott perished in the Antarctic partly because of his refusal to use sled dogs, Mallory died on Everest because the teams failed to exploit the advantage of oxygen.

With the three expeditions to Everest behind us, it is now time to find out what happened to the baby boy, Peter Finch. For the first two-and-a-half years of his life he was raised by his mother, Betty, until he was taken by George and put into the care of George's sister, Dorothy Finch, while legal custody was sought. Custody was granted in 1921 and Peter was moved to Laura Finch's care at Vaucresson near Paris. He stayed there with Laura, now in her fifties and becoming increasingly eccentric, for two-and-a-half happy years. When he was nine, Laura decided to move to India, which was now the centre of the theosophy movement and presided over by an ageing Annie Besant. Their stay there was very brief and Laura realised she was no longer able to look after Peter. After consulting senior members of the movement, including Besant, it was decided that Peter and Laura should go their separate ways – Laura to Darjeeling (where she lived until her death) and Peter to Sydney, where members of the movement intended to reunite him with his aunt, Dorothy Finch.

It didn't work out as planned because Dorothy was moving from rural town to town as a nursing sister and could not take care of him. Instead, Peter ended up living in the theosophy movement's Australian headquarters – a grand old mansion in Mosman on Sydney Harbour called The Manor. So, at the age of ten he found himself able to speak English and French, but not able to read or write, and in his fourth country of residence.

Shortly afterwards, Charles Finch, now aged eighty-seven, stepped in to rescue him from the movement he and his son George despised. Charles was too old to be guardian, so he called upon his brother, Edward Finch, now in his seventies, and Edward's spinster daughter, Betty Finch, to take Peter into their home and raise him. Peter lived in this household in Greenwich Point between the ages of ten to fifteen and attended local schools where he made up his educational deficiencies. Although it was a strict and conservative household, Peter put up with it until he got a job as a copy boy at a newspaper, and then 'escaped' to live in Kings Cross. Looking back on his childhood Peter said, "I was passed along the line of Finches like a football through a rugby team."

Despite this unfortunate upbringing, Peter Finch went on to have an extremely successful career as an actor. He was arguably Australia's most successful actor in the twentieth century, and the first

Australian to win an Academy Award for best actor. He started as a radio actor, as most did at this time, and joined the Australian Army as an artilleryman in the Second World War, but soon found himself entertaining troops. In fact, he was allowed time off in 1944 to act in the Australian film, *The Rats of Tobruk*.

After the war he was spotted by Sir Laurence Olivier, who was touring Australia, and at age thirty-two was lured to the London stage. But it was primarily as a movie actor that he excelled. Peter made over 50 films, in most of which he starred, playing alongside such leading ladies as Elizabeth Taylor, Audrey Hepburn, Sophia Loren, Julie Christie, Kim Novak and many more. Most of his films were made in England, but he also starred in Australian classics such as *The Shiralee* and *A Town Like Alice*. He also went on to make some Hollywood films including *Network*, for which he won the Academy Award for best actor. He died of a heart attack in 1977 aged sixty, before the outcome of the award was known, and so became the first actor to win an Oscar posthumously. He had led a colourful, successful and interesting life that became the subject of two full-length biographies.

I felt it was necessary to take this diversion into the life of Peter Finch, both because of its intrinsic interest, but also because the subject of Peter will crop up again later. Returning to George Finch, by 1924 he was reconciled to his new life after Everest. Nothing in future would be as tumultuous as the previous decade, but it would be a long period of accomplishment and satisfaction, followed by a wonderful and deserved finale.

One of George's first acts was to publish a book on his mountaineering experiences. The book is called *The Making of a Mountaineer*, and it became a classic among the mountaineering community. It is not an autobiography, although the first chapter recounts his boyhood experiences in Australia. The main part of the book consists of a series of accounts of mountains climbed and advice on how aspiring mountaineers can learn to master the art of climbing. Lord Hunt, who went on to lead the successful ascent of Everest in 1953, credited this book with being the one that first sparked his interest in mountaineering.

But it was not mountaineering that played the major role in the rest of George's life, but his academic career in chemistry. His speciality was in the chemistry of ignition, combustion and explosions, but he also did valuable work on analysing the surface of metals. His research was widely published, and he worked his way up the academic ladder at Imperial College. He was appointed assistant professor in 1927 and full Professor of Applied Physical Chemistry in 1936. Two years later, he was elected a Fellow of the Royal Society, and was able to put the coveted letters FRS after his name.

George settled into family life in London with Bubbles and they had three daughters in the 1920s – Joyce Anne (nicknamed Bunty) born in 1923, Paolo Jean born in 1924 and Felice born in 1929. The family lived well and had plenty of recreational activity. Mountaineering was not completely forgotten and they spent each Easter climbing in Wales, and in summer a month in the Alps. Bubbles became an enthusiastic and capable climber, as did Bunty, and they all climbed together until 1931 when George had to give up due to health problems. He then switched his main recreational activity to sailing, and in typical George fashion did not do so in half measures. He bought a large yacht – an eight-ton, gaff-rigged cutter with a cabin big enough to accommodate his six-foot two-inch frame and that could sleep the whole family. As well as English coastal sailing, they also sailed to Europe and once rescued a distressed vessel in the

English Channel.

When the Second World War broke out George was fifty-one and too old for active service, but he was able to put his research to good use for the government. He was initially seconded to be scientific adviser to the Ministry of Home Security. In this capacity, his main function was a defensive one of finding ways to *minimise* the fire damage to buildings bombed in the Blitz. Later he joined the Research and Experiments Department and conducted research for the air force. This research played an offensive role in that he was part of a team that developed the J bomb, which when it landed spurted out intense flames horizontally with the aim of *maximising* fire damage to buildings.

When the war ended he resumed academic life, but was to get one more surprise from his past. In 1948 Peter Finch, now an actor in London, traced George and they met again. It was apparently a very strained meeting and Peter was astonished and shocked when George told him, "I am sorry, young man, but I am not your father." When Peter asked who was, George replied, "Ask your mother." Peter then met with his mother, who was non-committal for a long time. Eventually she opened up about her past, then in 1962 when Peter was forty-five, his real father, Jock Campbell, introduced himself. Peter Finch finally knew who his biological father was, but only saw him again once and the relationship did not develop any further.

When George retired from Imperial College in 1952, he was asked by Prime Minister Nehru of India to head up the new Indian National Chemical Laboratory in Poona for five years. George and Bubbles then moved to India and he threw himself enthusiastically into a new challenge. It was fitting that they should be in India in 1953 because this was the year that Everest was finally climbed by

Hillary and Tenzing in an expedition led by Colonel John Hunt (later Lord Hunt). This expedition approached Everest through Nepal and climbed the mountain by the South Face, unlike the expeditions in the 1920s, which had approached through Tibet and attempted to climb the North Face.

After their success, the expedition returned to England through Nepal and India. While passing through Delhi, Hunt met up with George and shortly after wrote:

> It was a particular delight in Delhi to meet again George Finch, veteran of the 1922 expedition and pioneer of the use of oxygen for climbing purposes. His presence among us at the time was the more welcome in that we were so anxious that the tributes with which we were being showered should be shared with those who had shown us the way. As one of the two outstanding climbers of the first expedition to make a definite attempt to reach the summit of the mountain in 1922 – the other was George Mallory – and a strong protagonist for oxygen at a time when there were many who disbelieved in its efficacy, and others who frowned upon its use, no one could have better deserved to represent the past than George Finch. We salute him.

But this was not the only belated recognition for George; an even greater one awaited him when he returned to England after his five years in Poona. In 1959 he was elected the thirty-third president of the Alpine Club of London. The old guard must have been turning in their graves, but the newer generation welcomed him graciously. Among the newer members was his son-in-law, Scott Russell, a respected mountaineer and scientist who had married Bunty.

George could now look back on his career in science and mountaineering with almost complete satisfaction. He and Bubbles retired to the village of Upper Heyford near Oxford and he continued to be involved on a part-time basis in scientific committees and in the affairs of the Alpine Club until his death in 1970 at the age of eighty-two. Bubbles died two years later. In 1989, to commemorate the centenary of his birth, a new edition of *The Making of a Mountaineer* was published with a 100-page introductory memoir of George written by Scott Russell.

Three aspects of George Finch's life interested me and encouraged me to find out more. First, he excelled at two completely unrelated activities – science and mountaineering – when most of us cannot achieve even one. His achievements in science were considerable as Fellow of the Royal Society, winner of numerous awards and foreign honours. Not quite the Nobel Prize, but at least he was appointed to their selection committee. In mountaineering his achievements were even greater. His obituary in *The Times* concluded, "He was one of the two best Alpinists of his time – Mallory was the other." It is interesting that a literature search reveals that there are 16 books written about Mallory, including a novel by Jeffrey Archer, but only one about George (by Wainwright), even though his mountaineering exploits were similar and his lifetime achievement so much greater. I hope this little piece will help to slightly redress the imbalance.

The second reason I was interested in Finch was the rather extraordinary personal relationships early in his life, and the connection with that other larger-than-life character, Peter Finch.

And finally, the third reason was his clashes with the establishment. In his personal life he was particularly good at blocking out events from his thoughts that others would remember and regret. I wonder whether he was equally as good at it in his mountaineering life. Would he have been able to completely block out the possibility that in 1922 he could have been the first to climb Everest if the establishment, with whom he clashed, had given him more support in terms of partners and oxygen supply as they did to others 30 years later?

George Morrison aged nineteen in 1881.

3

GEORGE ERNEST MORRISON

Adventurer, Doctor, Journalist and Political Adviser

George Ernest Morrison was better known as Morrison of Peking, or 'Chinese' Morrison. While his chief claim to international recognition was through his work in China in the second half of his life, his early adventures in Australia, the Pacific and Asia are an even more remarkable story. I found it hard to believe someone could have crammed so much action into so few years, but there can't be any doubt that he did.

Morrison is a good example of someone who excelled in a number of different fields. He was an inveterate traveller who wrote a classic account of his travels that is still in print. He qualified as a surgeon at Edinburgh University and practised medicine for a time. He then turned to journalism and became a famous foreign correspondent for

The Times of London, and ended his career as political adviser to the President of China. Along the way he had numerous extraordinary adventures, some of which nearly cost him his life.

Morrison's father, also called George, migrated to Australia from Scotland in 1858 and married another Scottish immigrant, Rebecca Greenwood, in 1859. Morrison senior founded Geelong College soon after arriving in Australia, became its headmaster and, at one stage, its proprietor. His brother Alexander founded Scotch College Melbourne at about the same time.

George Ernest Morrison was born in February 1862 and educated at Geelong College, where he remained until he was seventeen years old. He was a good student, but more interested in the outdoor life. He was a keen sportsman, representing the school at cricket and athletics. He claims to have faced the great fast bowler Frederick Spofforth, known as the 'Demon Spofforth' in a social cricket match against the visiting Australian team. Unfortunately, he scored only one run. He was also interested in hunting and was a good shot, but his main interest was in walking. In 1878, when sixteen years old, he walked from Geelong to Queenscliff and back within a day, a distance of 67 kilometres. This was a prelude to much greater feats of distance walking in later years. He read widely and his hero was Henry Morton Stanley, the Welsh–American journalist and explorer who found Dr Livingston in Africa and uttered the immortal words "Doctor Livingston, I presume".

In December 1879, when still seventeen years old, in the break between finishing school and starting university, he decided to walk from Geelong to Adelaide via the coastal route. This was a much less populated part of Australia than it is today and was only sketchily mapped. Morrison was mainly reliant on what food he carried in his knapsack and on his small tent for shelter. He completed the journey of over 1000 kilometres in 46 days and arrived in Adelaide a few days after he turned eighteen. He wrote an account of his journey and it was published in *The Leader*, a weekly paper produced by *The Age* newspaper. Thus, he started his career as a journalist at the age of eighteen while still a student.

Morrison entered the Medical Faculty at Melbourne University in March 1880 and completed the first year. While doing so, he prepared for his next adventure by buying a canoe and practising various techniques for paddling, including paddling while standing up. The canoe was named *Stanley* after his hero. In November 1880, aged eighteen, he provisioned the canoe and started the long journey along the winding Murray River from Wodonga to its mouth in South Australia. Again, he had to rely on the food he carried in his canoe plus any game he shot along the way. After a journey of 2480 kilometres, he reached the mouth of the Murray in late January 1881, arranged for the transport of his canoe back to his home and then had to find his own way home. His solution was simple; he walked back to Geelong, this time by the most direct route. His account of his adventure was again published as a series by *The Leader* under the title 'Down the Murray in a Canoe' by G.E.M., Melbourne University.

Morrison then spent the rest of 1881 completing the second year of his medical studies, but in March 1882 he learned that he had failed. It is not clear whether he regarded this as a disaster, or whether it presented him with the opportunity to do something he found more interesting and challenging – probably the latter. In a letter to his mother at this time he wrote about his next foray into journalism:

> I am not taking a hasty step ... In no other way can I see any hope for furthering my wish to become a newspaper correspondent,

and only as a newspaper correspondent can I expect to distinguish myself above the common herd ... In spite of all that is said to the contrary, it is the noblest in my opinion of all the professions and as energy, courage, temperance and truthfulness are necessary to its success, to this fact must be ascribed the high positions occupied by journalists all over the world.

His next venture, agreed to with *The Age*, was to take a boat to the South Pacific Islands to investigate the import of Kanaka labourers to the Queensland cane fields. This dark chapter in Australian history involved bringing workers from the Solomon Islands and Vanuatu (then called the New Hebrides) to work in Australia on three-year contracts. Critics said that deception and force were used to get the men to come, and that they were mistreated and their health neglected once they had been trapped into this form of indentured labour. Defenders of the system said it was necessary, as white men could not perform labouring tasks in the tropics.

In June 1882, only three months after leaving Melbourne University and still aged only twenty, Morrison set off from Mackay in Queensland as a deckhand, on a ship bound for Vanuatu to recruit Kanakas. He observed the system firsthand, then returned to Mackay in September and wrote up his findings, which were published by *The Age* in six weekly instalments. Although he was critical of the neglect of the islanders' health and recorded occasional acts of cruelty, he did not call for the abolition of the system.

But as usual, Morrison was already planning his next adventure, and the one after that. First, he arranged to become a crew member on a boat taking missionaries to New Guinea. This was his first trip to New Guinea and, unlike his later visit, it was relatively uneventful. After a brief spell there, he started his next journey by taking a boat to Normanton on the Gulf of Carpentaria via Thursday Island.

Normanton was to be the starting point for his greatest adventure yet – he planned to walk across Australia from north to south along roughly the same path taken by the ill-fated Burke and Wills expedition 20 years earlier.

In December 1882, still only twenty years old, Morrison started his long journey through this remote part of Australia, much of which was desert. His course, which took him through Queensland and New South Wales to Victoria, was not completely devoid of towns, but there were large stretches between them. From Normanton he went to Cloncurry, Winton, Thargomindah, Hungerford, Wilcannia, Hay, Deniliquin, Echuca, and then through the settled areas of Victoria to Melbourne. Despite the dangers presented by so much desert, his biggest problem was a flood in Queensland in which he was lucky not to drown. He arrived in Melbourne in April 1883, having covered 3260 kilometres in 123 days. Again, his account was published in *The Leader*, but this time other papers throughout Australia also covered the story and it even made it into *The Times* in London. Morrison was starting to become quite well known.

Having returned to Geelong, it didn't take long for him to get back into action. Two weeks after his return he wrote a 2700-word letter to *The Age*, this time taking a much stronger line than in his earlier articles and denouncing the Queensland Kanaka trade. *The Age* endorsed the letter the next day in its editorial and the campaign for the abolition of the Kanaka trade heated up. *The Age*'s rival newspaper in Melbourne, *The Argus*, took a contrary view and attacked *The Age* and Morrison personally. It referred to him as:

> ... this amazing pedestrian ... who has recently acquired some transient notoriety by performing the curious and purposeless feat of walking as a swagman from Carpentaria to Melbourne, and who has previously gratified his love of adventure by taking

some trips to the South Seas in labour vessels.

Morrison shrugged off this criticism and moved onto the next big issue of the time, which concerned Australia's attitude to New Guinea. The Australian colonies had for some time been wary of foreign countries' designs on eastern New Guinea (the Dutch had already annexed the western half). There were fears that the French, Russian, German, even the Chinese government could annex this unclaimed land. Attempts were made by the Australian colonies to get the British government to act, but the British Colonial Office was not interested. In April 1883, the Queensland government unilaterally decided to act. As Cyril Pearl, in his biography of Morrison, describes it:

> The Thursday Island Police Magistrate, Mr Henry Chester was ordered to take formal possession of Eastern New Guinea 'in the name and on behalf of Her Gracious Majesty Queen Victoria, her heirs and successors.' Without Her Gracious Majesty's knowledge or approval, Mr Chester raised the Union Jack at Port Moresby in the presence of the white population of three, and a few bewildered natives, to one of whom he presented a commemorative red felt hat.

With New Guinea now in Australia's grasp, Morrison then saw another opportunity for adventure, this time by making a second trip to that country. Little was known of New Guinea apart from a few coastal settlements; virtually nothing was known about the interior. He approached *The Age* with a proposal, which they accepted. He was given the title 'Special Commissioner of The Melbourne Age' and assigned to lead a small party into the interior of New Guinea and report his findings back to the public via *The Age*. When *The Argus* got wind of this, they financed a rival party to do the same thing.

In June 1883, Morrison, still only twenty-one years old, chartered a boat and led a team of five to Port Moresby, landing three days ahead of *The Argus* team. His team set off into the interior, but found the terrain extremely difficult and the natives less than friendly to the intruders. After 38 days – during which they advanced an uncertain distance through thick jungle – disaster struck: Morrison was speared twice. One spear entered through his stomach just below the chest and the second just below his right eye next to his nose. These were serious wounds. His companions pulled out the spears as best they could, but he lost a lot of blood. Morrison was lucky to be alive, but in serious need of medical attention.

It took 11 days for his team to get him back to Port Moresby and a further 20 to get him back to Cooktown. His weight fell from 70 to 50 kilograms. It was apparent that not all of each spear had been properly removed when, after leaving Cooktown, Morrison blew a piece of wood about two centimetres long out of his nose. When he finally returned home he was operated on by Melbourne's leading surgeon, Sir Thomas Fitzgerald, who removed from his right nostril a splinter of wood about five centimetres long. But there was still part of a spear in his abdomen.

The whole New Guinea expedition had been a failure; it had achieved nothing other than to allow Morrison to write a nine-part series for *The Age*. *The Argus* expedition had done no better, and there was a lot of criticism of these foolhardy ventures. The British Deputy Commissioner for the Western Pacific reported:

> The two so-called exploring expeditions have done no good … It is worthy of notice that the accounts of their doings are very inaccurate … Mr Morrison, a boy of 21 reached a point probably 15, certainly not more than 22 miles from the coast, though he asserts it must have been nearly 100 miles.

I have to confess that, when first reading about these adventures, I couldn't believe that anyone could fit so many activities into such a short time, and when still so young. I decided to go back and construct a timeline, not just in years, but in months, to reassure myself that this sequence of events was possible. There was also the question of authenticity – did all these things occur or were they the product of hindsight and reminiscences? I am now confident that they occurred as I have recounted them. All the original accounts are contemporary; nothing relies on memory. Morrison kept a detailed daily diary from the age of sixteen. He wrote regular letters to his mother during his travels, all of which have survived. And, of course, all his adventures were published in the Melbourne press as they happened.

Fitzgerald, the surgeon, did not feel he had the skill to remove the part of the spear remaining in Morrison's abdomen, which was pressing against his spinal cord and incapacitating his left leg. In his opinion, there was only one surgeon in the world he would trust to do this – Professor Chiene of the Royal Infirmary in Edinburgh. So Morrison and Fitzgerald headed to Edinburgh, where the operation took place. Professor Chiene removed a piece of wood about six centimetres long and one centimetre thick from deep inside Morrison's abdomen. It is preserved in the medical school of Edinburgh University, and an account of the operation was published in their journal. Morrison had to spend 80 days in the infirmary to regain his health, but he made a complete recovery.

After this series of adventures, Morrison's life took a much calmer direction – he entered Edinburgh University to study medicine in January 1885, just before his twenty-third birthday. Although we can't be sure, his parents must have had a hand in his return to medicine. All along they had hoped for this, but had reluctantly indulged his adventures and helped to finance them. Morrison had never had full-time paid employment up to this date, and the little he earned from journalism was not enough to cover his expenses. The final episode in New Guinea, which had achieved nothing and nearly killed him, probably provided the grounds for his parents to reassert their authority.

At this time, Edinburgh had a good claim to being the centre of world medicine. Morrison was fortunate to be accepted as a student, and lucky to have parents who could support him. After two-and-a-half years of intense study, he graduated in 1887 at the age of twenty-five with a medical degree, good references and a career in medicine open to him. But instead, Morrison chose to go travelling again for several months, this time to the United States and the Caribbean.

After returning to Scotland, Morrison found casual work as a doctor, but he struggled to resolve the conflict between his medical career and his desire for further travel. In May 1888, he got his first salaried job when he became medical officer for the Rio Tinto Company at their copper mine in Spain. After a few months his boss resigned, and Morrison became chief medical officer with a staff of 11. The increased responsibilities and salary were not enough to keep him there for long. While he liked Spain, he hated the mine and its polluted environment, and his only consolation was his romance with Pepita, a Spanish woman who fell in love with him and wanted to marry him (her letters survive). After 15 months in the job, he left Rio Tinto and Pepita for about six months' travel in North Africa, Spain and France, and then returned to Australia. In April 1891 he was appointed a resident surgeon at Ballarat and District Base Hospital. This was a good job in a good hospital near his family home, paying 450 pounds per annum. He kept it for two years, but when he resigned it marked the end of his short medical career.

Still restless and dissatisfied, the desire to travel reasserted itself

– this time it was to be Asia. After spending some time in Japan, he went to China and in September 1893, aged thirty-one years, he set off on his most famous journey. This took him from Shanghai to Bhamo in Myanmar, a distance of over 4800 kilometres. He chose to adopt local dress, even adding a false pigtail, because he didn't want to be exploited as foreigners usually were in China. The surviving photo of him in native dress shows that he didn't look remotely Chinese, but this didn't worry him.

The first part of his journey was by boat along the Yangtze, and after that he travelled by foot, pony, mule and, at times, by sedan chair. He was accompanied by three coolies (porters) who carried his luggage. The journey from Shanghai to Bhamo took exactly 100 days. He then went by riverboat to Mandalay, then Yangon, and finally by steamer to Kolkata, where he fell ill with a serious fever. He was nursed back to health by a Eurasian woman called Mary Joplin, who fell in love with him but had the good sense to suggest he marry someone else (her letters to him also survive).

Morrison then returned to Australia, was offered a job back at Ballarat Hospital, but declined it because his interest in pursuing a career in journalism had returned. His attempts to do so in Australia failed, despite trying various newspapers. The editor of *The Argus* rejected him, saying "It is impossible; he cannot write up to our standard." Morrison then took a casual position as surgeon on a ship to London.

Before leaving Australia, Morrison had been working on an account of his Chinese journey, which he now hoped would interest a British publisher. Morrison arrived in London in February 1895 and soon found a publisher. The book was released under the title, *An Australian in China, being the narrative of a quiet journey across China to Burma.*

The book was a success, receiving favourable reviews in a number of newspapers and journals. Although it was out of print for a long time, it has recently been reprinted by a Hong Kong publisher. The success of his book encouraged him to approach a number of British newspapers for a job as a journalist. As in Australia, his approaches were met with rejections, even from downmarket papers that had trouble attracting good journalists. So it was a surprise and a relief to him when he was offered a job by *The Times*, largely on the strength of his book.

The book still makes interesting reading today as Morrison was a skilful and, at times, witty writer, but it is a curious mixture of unresolved and conflicting opinions. He is full of praise for the Chinese because of their hospitality and their law-abiding nature, and we also know that he chose to spend the rest of his life among them. On the other hand, he was a strong believer in the benevolence of the British Empire in China, and at one stage in the book he diverts to make a spirited argument against Chinese immigration into Australia on the grounds that they would out-compete the locals because they work harder and live more cheaply (a common argument at the time). On the subject of Christian missionary activity in China, he was also ambiguous: full of praise for the individual missionaries who helped him on his way, but ridiculing them for their failure to achieve many converts.

Morrison's earlier youthful enthusiasm for journalism when he described it as "the noblest of all the professions" and referred to "the high positions held by journalists around the world" seems strange to modern readers, and was probably not widely applicable even in his own time. But, if there was one institution that could be said to embody those lofty ideals, it was *The Times* of London. Founded in 1785, it was the choice of the British establishment and the upholder of very high standards of reporting. It was the first newspaper to send a war correspondent to a battlefield, which it did during the Crimean War of 1853 to 1856. Its list of resident foreign correspondents was legendary, and together they constituted an alternative diplomatic corps. Morrison reported to the Head of the Foreign Department, Sir Donald Mackenzie Wallace, who was succeeded by Sir Valentine Chirole, who held the post through most of Morrison's time. Both these gentlemen were extremely learned, well-travelled and multilingual. Their decision to offer Morrison a job, however, was a gamble. He had no serious experience as a journalist, no specialist knowledge of international relations, politics or defence matters, nor did he speak mandarin, but they must have felt he had potential. They were also impressed by him as a person. The normally dour official *History of The Times* becomes quite effusive when describing him:

> At thirty-three years of age, Morrison was strikingly handsome, tall and well-built – a magnificent specimen of Australian manhood.

Morrison was offered the post of correspondent in Beijing, then called Peking, but asked instead for the post in Bangkok and backed up his request with good arguments. *The Times* agreed that he could have an assignment in Thailand on probation before taking up his permanent post in Beijing. He wanted to go to Thailand because it was an international trouble spot where tensions between the British and French were flaring up. It was the buffer zone between the French colonies in the East in what is now Laos, Cambodia and Vietnam, and the British colonies in the west, India and Myanmar, and in the south, Malaysia and Singapore. The French were expanding westwards across the Mekong and absorbing parts of Thailand; the British, unusually for them, eschewed their own colonial expansion and preferred to keep Thailand neutral. In the end, a treaty between Britain and France was signed, which ensured that Thailand remained independent.

Morrison arrived in Saigon, now officially renamed Ho Chi Minh City, in December 1895 and then travelled to Bangkok. He wrote a series of articles for *The Times* on the situation in Thailand, but as usual could not resist the desire to travel. He went to Myanmar by bullock cart, on horseback, foot and elephant, and then on to Kunming in China. He then turned westward and traced his way back to northern Thailand and down to Bangkok. His articles were well received in London and so he passed from probationer to full staff member. However, his tendency to travel whenever possible did not escape censure. Chirole sent him a subtle rap across the knuckles when he wrote:

> For our purpose, the incidents and adventures of travel must always be subsidiary to the general information and enlightenment we require for the furtherance of British interests and of an Imperial policy ... Picturesque details should be the garniture, not the foundation of your work.

Note the second part of the first sentence: news was important, but so too was the need to support British interests.

The China that Morrison entered in March 1897, aged thirty-five, had undergone enormous change in the previous 60 years, and was to undergo even more during his time there. It had remained relatively closed until the First Opium War of 1842, when the British captured Shanghai and Zhenjiang on the Grand Canal, thus cutting off Chinese supplies to Beijing. In the ensuing Treaty of Nanjing, Britain gained a colony – Hong Kong – and five coastal trading ports. Trading companies and missionaries flooded in from Britain, followed quickly by French and American ones. In 1858 in the Second Opium War (not primarily about opium this time) British and French troops captured Tianjin and occupied Beijing. In the ensuing Treaty of Tianjin, a further nine trading posts were awarded, including two inland ones, which effectively opened up the Yangtze Valley to trade. Full diplomatic relations with China were established and a number of countries opened diplomatic posts in Beijing.

Although Britain was the most active in opening up the China trade, others soon followed. Russia was more interested in gaining land than trading opportunities and so expanded into Manchuria and established Vladivostok as its base. France moved up from the south and acquired large parts of Indochina in what is today's Vietnam. In 1894 Japan launched a devastating attack, destroying the Chinese Navy and acquiring Korea, Dalian and Taiwan. Under international pressure, they had to relinquish the former two, but retained Taiwan. Two years later, at about the time of Morrison's arrival in Beijing, German forces seized Jiaozhou Bay and most of the province of Shandong, which they proceeded to run as though it was a German colony protected by the German Navy. Further territorial gains were made by Russia into areas that had been relinquished by Japan, and by Britain, which acquired The New Territories north of Kowloon on a 99-year lease.

The period from the First Opium War onwards is referred to by the Chinese as The Century of National Humiliation. Not only was it opened to external influences, it was defeated militarily and parts of it were carved off and dominated by foreign countries competing for ever larger slices. It did not, however, become a colony as India did. Although China received some of the gains from trade, most of the gains went to its foreign trading partners. Those partners, in turn, viewed each other with suspicion; if one country gained a concession from the Chinese, the others would push for their own and even resort to force of arms if necessary.

Morrison and his servants in front of his house in Beijing.

Throughout this period, China was ruled by Manchu emperors of the Qing dynasty. They had ruled since 1644 but had become more and more ineffectual, if not dysfunctional. They had increasing difficulty in ruling their own people and there were frequent domestic uprisings among the various regions, ethnicities and religions that made up the vast country.

China was headed by the Guangxu Emperor when Morrison arrived. He had ascended to the throne at the age of four in 1875, but the real power lay with his aunt, the Dowager Empress Cixi. The central government in Beijing was economically weak, as too much of the revenue it raised was spent on the royal household with its elaborate collection of members of royalty, retainers, attendants, concubines, eunuchs and palaces. The Chinese Army was ill-equipped, badly led and no match for the sophisticated armaments of Britain, France, Germany or Japan. China's bargaining position was extremely weak as seen by all the concessions they had to make in the various treaties, as well as paying reparations for the cost of wars they hadn't started. There was much discontent among the Chinese, which sometimes took the form of sporadic violence against foreign traders and missionaries; there was also a growing opposition against the Qing dynasty.

It was in this time of great power rivalry and domestic instability that Morrison quickly made a name for himself. First, he established a large home with a complement of seven servants. Unlike most foreigners, he chose to live in the Chinese part of Beijing rather than the diplomatic enclave. As usual, his next step was to go travelling. He chose to go north and completed a long loop that took him through Manchuria, Siberia and Mongolia before returning to China. In his travels he saw a lot of Russian soldiers and engineers and concluded they had designs on further incursions into Chinese Manchuria, including by expansion of the Trans-Siberian railway. He raised the alarm against Russian expansionism in his dispatches to *The Times*, although his warnings were disputed by the British Foreign Office.

A year later in March 1898, he became aware that Russia had served a series of demands on China, including that it surrender all sovereign rights over Dalian so that the Russian railway would terminate at that important port. Morrison also knew that China, in response to bribes paid by Russia, had agreed to accept the demands. Again, he explained these developments in *The Times* and again, the Foreign Office disagreed. Once he was proved right, however, questions were asked in parliament and the foreign secretary had to explain why Morrison was better informed than the Foreign Office. As a result, Morrison acquired the reputation as the man you ask if you want to know what is happening in China. From this time onwards, he began to be referred to in England as 'Chinese Morrison' or 'Morrison of Peking'.

He also concluded that war between Russia and Japan was inevitable as they both aimed to expand further into Manchuria. Russia supported the Qing rulers, with whom they did deals, while Japan encouraged the reformers who wanted a constitutional monarchy like Japan, or even a republic. Morrison wrote that a war would be a good thing and was confident that when it came, Japan would win. At this stage he was a strong supporter of Japan and encouraged the British government to conclude a treaty with it.

Meanwhile, a dramatic event was about to take place – the Boxer Rebellion. There had been sporadic acts of violence before, but the Boxer Rebellion of 1900 was of a much greater degree of intensity. It was centred in Shandong province where the flooding of the Yellow River, followed by a severe drought, caused a famine and led many to look for scapegoats. These were soon found in the form of foreign traders, missionaries and Chinese Christian converts. A violent uprising ensued as young men were attracted to a movement known as Spirit Boxers, who not only practised martial arts, but also had a religious belief that they were invulnerable against the weapons of their enemies. The Boxers quickly overran Tianjin and then occupied Beijing. Foreign diplomats, missionaries, Chinese Christians, a small garrison of soldiers and Morrison took refuge in the grounds of the British Legation in Beijing. They were besieged for 55 days, during which they were under constant attack from Boxers and Qing troops – the Dowager Empress having decided to support the Boxers.

Morrison was in his element. Not only was he personally brave, he was a good marksman and a natural leader who raised the morale of the defenders. He also organised parties to strengthen the fortifications and was prepared to take risks under fire. Unfortunately, on one of these sorties the military leader of the garrison was killed and Morrison was shot in the leg, which put him out of action. Morrison's exploits during the siege were widely praised in the accounts written by other defenders. For example, the Head of the British Legation, Sir Claude MacDonald wrote:

> Dr Morrison acted as lieutenant to Captain Strouts [the leader of the garrison] and rendered most valuable assistance. Active, energetic and cool, he volunteered for every service of danger and was a pillar of strength when things were going badly. By his severe wound on 16th July, his valuable services were lost to the defence for the rest of the siege.

During the siege, as the relieving army was approaching from the coast, a correspondent from another paper sent word to London that the legation had been overrun and all those within killed. This led to much public grief around the world, and obituaries of the main defenders published. In Geelong, Morrison's home town, flags were flown at half-mast. When the relieving army finally arrived and freed the captives, Morrison had the rare privilege of reading his own obituaries.

When it was apparent that the uprising had been suppressed, the Qing fled to Xian. They returned after an exile of 18 months and reigned until 1908, when the Guangxu Emperor died (almost certainly poisoned) and the Dowager Empress died a day later. The emperor was succeeded by his three-year-old nephew, Puyi, called the Xuantong Emperor (known to recent generations in the West as the subject of Bertolucci's wonderful film, *The Last Emperor*).

By the early 1900s some of the policies that Morrison had argued for were enacted and some of his predictions had come to pass. In 1902 Britain enacted a treaty with Japan, which strengthened the latter's resolve in dealing with Russia. In 1904, war broke out between Russia and Japan that resulted in a decisive Japanese victory. Morrison's prediction of that war, and his encouragement of it, meant that his name was closely associated with it; in the British press it was sometimes referred to as Morrison's war.

Morrison continued as the China correspondent for *The Times* until 1912. During this period, his reputation continued to grow and he was consulted widely by, among others, the British Foreign Office, other foreign governments and several arms of the Chinese government. An important change in his views occurred in 1908, when he concluded that the main medium-term threat to China was now Japan. He began to be characterised as anti-Japanese, and this brought him into conflict with the British government, which was still pro-Japanese in their Asian foreign policy. Subsequent events showed that Morrison was correct and ahead of his time.

His responsibilities in Beijing did not seem to curb his capacity for travel. He was frequently away from China and his trips could last for many months. On separate trips, he visited Australia, the US, Japan, and was in London for extended stays several times. His views were widely sought outside China and he had discussions with President Theodore Roosevelt and an audience with the Emperor of Japan. His most ambitious trip was overland from Beijing via Turkmenistan to Moscow. This took him six months and furnished him with 12 long articles for *The Times*.

His other great passion, some would say obsession, was book collecting. He specialised in Western language books about China, going back as far as the first edition of Marco Polo published in 1496. Eventually his library amounted to 20,000 books, 4000 pamphlets and 2000 maps, which occupied much of his large house in Beijing and absorbed a considerable amount of his generous income. The other activity that absorbed much of his time was keeping a detailed and extremely frank diary. One of his entries describes a brief liaison with a woman called May Perkins whom he described as "the most thoroughly immoral woman" he had ever met. The Australian sinologist-turned-novelist, Linda Jaivin, used this affair as the basis of her 2009 erotic novel, appropriately titled *A Most Immoral Woman*.

Just as his attitude to Japan had changed, Morrison's attitude to Britain and China was also evolving. While still a firm supporter of the British Empire, he was often frustrated by British officialdom, and found himself disagreeing with aspects of British policy and his employer's views. When abroad, he also found himself as a spokesman for China, where he attempted to counter the extremely negative impression of China's future given by other observers. Within China, he agreed that the Qing dynasty had outlived its usefulness (if it ever had any) and should be replaced by a republic. In 1911, he wrote:

> The Manchu dynasty is in danger. The sympathies of the immense mass of educated Chinese are all with the revolutionaries. Little sympathy is expressed for the corrupt and effete Manchu dynasty with its eunuchs and other barbaric surroundings.

By this time Morrison had become an informal adviser to the supporters of Juan Shikai, who commanded the most effective army in China. When the Qing dynasty abdicated in 1912, Sun Yat-Sen briefly headed a provisional government, but soon Yuan Shikai took over as president. His methods could be brutal and he was more of a dictator than a president, but Morrison and most others felt that he was the one man strong enough to hold the country together after the collapse of the old regime.

The year 1912 was a turning point in Morrison's life. First, he resigned from *The Times* after 17 years' service, 15 of them in Beijing. He did so because he was becoming frustrated with the editors back in London and, more importantly, because he had received an attractive offer from the new Chinese government. He was to be a personal adviser to Juan Shikai, with a salary of 3500 pounds, compared with the already generous 1200 pounds he received from *The Times* (these figures can be contrasted with the 450 pounds he received as a surgeon in Ballarat). Morrison remained an adviser to successive Chinese governments for the rest of his life.

The other big event in 1912 was his marriage. Morrison had never been short of female company who could variously be described as girlfriends or mistresses (or other less flattering terms in his diaries), but he had never contemplated marriage. In fact, the one woman he continued to dote on was his mother back in Australia. Then he met twenty-three-year-old Jennie Robin, who became his secretary. She was a New Zealand-born, British-raised beauty. Despite their age difference – he was fifty – they had a happy marriage that produced three sons.

Morrison's career as a government adviser was a mixed blessing. Although he had direct access to Yuan Shikai until his death in 1916, and to Shikai's successors, he felt they rarely followed his advice. While Yuan Shikai was friendly, he was instinctively secretive and inscrutable. Morrison said he had a better idea of what was going on in China when he was a journalist looking in from the outside than when he was an adviser working on the inside. He advised on a wide variety of issues both of an economic and foreign policy nature, but it is the latter for which he is better known. When the First World War began, Morrison advised China to break off diplomatic relations with Germany, which still held a large part of Shandong province. He later advised China to formally join the allied side. They resisted because they didn't know which side would win the war. Japan, on the other hand, because of its close ties with Britain, joined the allied cause, although it quietly kept its options open with Germany. Eventually in 1917 China joined the allied side, but it was too late to gain any bargaining power in post-war negotiations.

In 1917, aged fifty-five and with the first sign that his health was failing, Morrison began to think of the future security of his wife and three young sons. He decided to sell his library and received offers from America and Japan. He eventually sold it to a Japanese institute for the astonishing sum of 35,000 pounds. What this meant was that in one hit, his hobby had brought him a sum of money equivalent to what he had earned in 20 years of work in China as a journalist and government adviser. The windfall set him and his family up for life.

After the war ended, Morrison accompanied the Chinese

delegation to the peace talks that led to the Versailles Treaty. As he had expected, China's position as a recent addition to the allied cause counted for little, while Japan was treated as a full ally even though its contribution was modest. The final treaty took the German concession in Shandong from them, but awarded it to Japan rather than giving it back to China (a decision later reversed under American pressure).

Morrison, in very poor health by now, was disappointed, but not surprised. He left France and returned to England with his family for medical treatment, but died there from pancreatitis in 1920 at the age of fifty-eight. Sadly, his wife Jennie died three years later, leaving three young sons behind. Fortunately, a combination of Morrison's library windfall and the efforts of Jennie's parents meant that the boys were taken care of. All three were educated in England at Winchester and Cambridge. The oldest boy, Ian, followed his father's footsteps and became a foreign correspondent for *The Times*.

In 1952, a Chinese woman Han Suyin wrote a bestselling autobiographical novel called *A Many Splendoured Thing* about her love affair with a British journalist. It was made into a successful Hollywood film in 1955 called *Love is a Many Splendored Thing*, starring William Holden as the journalist and Jennifer Jones (made up to look oriental) as the heroine. The song of the same name won the Academy Award for best song in 1956, topped the hit parade and became a classic. In real life the journalist was Ian Morrison, George Morrison's oldest son, but he did not live to see any of this as he was killed in Korea in 1950 while covering the war.

It is now time to do a retrospective assessment of Morrison's life. What sort of man was he, what sort of views did he hold, and was he as important as he seemed? The first thing we can say is that he was a man of great energy and daring. He certainly didn't take the safe and well-trodden path that was open to him by virtue of his medical training. He was brave and adventurous – anyone who has been both speared and shot qualifies for that description. Although he spent a lot of time on his own during his travels, he was sociable at other times and had a lot of friends of both sexes. He was intelligent without being scholarly, and was an accomplished and witty writer. One aspect of his life that intrigues me was his passion for collecting – first for books for his library, and second for his thoughts and experiences in his extraordinary diary.

The diary displays his wit as a writer and his tendency to judge others harshly. He regularly describes people as bores, drunks or possessing strange sexual habits. He even passes judgement on the dinners to which he was invited, a common putdown being "it must have been cooked by the gardener". His comments on people could be amusing. He thought the Head of the British Legation in Beijing was a conventional and unimaginative soldier: "the type of military officer rolled out a mile at a time and then lopped off in six-foot lengths". He thought the part-owner of *The Times* Arthur Walter lacked business acumen: "he knows nothing of accounts. He expressed surprise at the remarkable coincidence that the two sides of a balance sheet amounted to exactly equal sums". Even when he approved of someone, there could be a sting in the tail. He describes the then Australian governor-general, Sir Ronald Munro-Ferguson, as a "dapper kindly spoken Scotchman in khaki with a somewhat squeaky voice, suggesting arrested testicular development".

The historical figure that Morrison reminds me of is Samuel Pepys. Both were on the fringes of great events, but not major players, both accumulated celebrated libraries (Pepys donated his 3000 volumes to Magdalene College Cambridge) and, importantly, both kept detailed and extremely frank diaries. Morrison's diaries were edited down to two volumes for publication shortly after his death, but his estate thought it was too soon to publish. By the time this restriction was withdrawn, Morrison had been largely forgotten, so publication never occurred. The full 109 volumes are available in the Mitchell Library in Sydney, and they make fascinating reading. But two volumes of his letters were published, each volume containing over 800 pages. So there is a massive amount of information about him, covering nearly every day of his life.

To a modern reader, Morrison's political views could be dismissed as no more than the standard support for the British Empire, and there is a fair bit of truth in this. Almost all British and Australian citizens at that time held these views. If you came from the prosperous and largely self-governing British colony of Victoria, what was there to object to? In defence of Morrison, it should be recognised that by the time he reached China, the period of British armed aggression had finished 50 years earlier with the end of the Opium Wars. Britain's aims were predominantly mercantile by Morrison's time; the military aggressors were the Germans, the Japanese and the Russians. As well, Morrison had a genuine affection for China; he wanted it to succeed and defended it in international forums, sometimes unwisely. And we know he spent the last part of his career as an employee of the Chinese government.

On the big issues of the day, Morrison's political judgements were generally correct and he saw events unfolding earlier than most others. He was right about Russian ambitions in China, about the need to encourage Japan as a counterweight, and about all aspects of the Russo–Japanese War of 1904. He was also a long way ahead of British opinion in changing his views about Japan. He wasn't always right, of course, and we could say he was a little late in putting his support behind the reform movement for a republic in China. Towards the end of his life he recognised that he had misjudged Sun Yat-Sen and should have supported him earlier. He also had a tendency to downplay the shortcomings of Juan Shikai.

Finally, we come the question: how important a figure was George Morrison? Many would find it hard to see how someone who was no more than a journalist, not even an editor, could be important. But in those days before telephone, radio and television, an authoritative print journalist representing a prestigious paper could become an influential figure. There were no foreign policy experts in academia or think tanks to compete with as there are now. The only expertise on foreign relations was found among diplomats, who had to maintain secrecy, or among reputable foreign correspondents. There was a lot of interest in China; it was the world's largest country and one of the most mysterious, where strange geopolitical events were occurring. Morrison found himself in a unique position; he handled it well and made a name for himself.

While Morrison did not become a household name, he was well known and respected in political, diplomatic and military circles as the person to consult if you wanted to know what was happening in China. Anyone who could meet with the Japanese emperor and the presidents of the US and China must have had high standing. In England he seemed to know everyone, from Rudyard Kipling to Sydney and Beatrice Webb. On his two visits to Australia from China, he spent time with the prime minister, the governor-general and various state premiers and governors. Lord Sydenham, who as Sir George Clarke had been governor of Victoria, said in 1905 that Australia had produced only two people of worldwide reputation:

Morrison and Melba. That may well have been true at the time, but today, although we still remember Melba, the name Morrison does not mean anything to most people.

Hubert Wilkins in arctic gear in the 1920's.

4

GEORGE HUBERT WILKINS

War Photographer and Explorer

Of the people whose lives are recounted in this book, the one who was most widely honoured in his own lifetime was George Hubert Wilkins. As well as being knighted by King George V and King Victor Emmanuel III of Italy, he had the Order of Lenin pinned on him by Joseph Stalin. He was granted a ticker-tape reception in New York after one of his exploits, and received medals from geographical societies around the world as well as military decorations for bravery under fire. He is the subject of seven books, four of which are full-length biographies, and he wrote four books himself. Yet he is hardly known today by the general public, and some of what we think we know about him turns out to be untrue. But by any standards, he was a man of great courage, ingenuity and imagination who must be counted as one of the great explorers of the twentieth century.

George Wilkins' father, Harry Wilkins, was born in 1836 and was possibly the first European person to be born in the fledgling colony of South Australia. After marrying Louisa Smith, he moved 200 kilometres north of Adelaide and established a farm at Mount Bryan East. The couple had 13 children, the last of whom was George, born in October 1888. This was something of a surprise as by then Louise was fifty years of age, Harry fifty-two, and their previous child had been born 12 years earlier.

Farming in this district was always a struggle. We now know the land should be classified as marginal at best because the rainfall is too low and too sporadic. It was a tough upbringing for young George, who had to help on the farm when not at school. He became a very versatile hand, learning all the farm skills as well as becoming a good horseman and hunter.

A severe drought eventually proved too much for the family and they gave up the struggle. They moved to Adelaide in 1905 when George was sixteen, but he always remembered the devastation caused by the drought and the fact that farmers could not prepare for it because its timing was impossible to predict. This was the basis for his lifelong interest in meteorology, and his later hope that if enough weather stations were established around the world, prediction would become possible.

In Adelaide, George studied electrical engineering at the South Australian School of Mines, now part of Adelaide University. Although he did not sit the final exams, he did acquire a good all-round knowledge of engineering and was able to find work in the field, and soon set himself up in business. In 1908, when he was twenty, he moved to Sydney and found work as a projectionist. His involvement in the cinema business deepened and he soon bought his own movie camera, then known as a cinematograph, and started making short films. Sydney at that time had an active film industry making many cheap silent movies, and soon George was in demand as a cameraman, then known as a cinematographer (the word has a broader meaning today). Taking moving pictures of galloping horses, speeding trains, cars and boats was a challenge with the equipment available at the time, but George overcame most obstacles and gained a reputation as an outstanding cinematographer. His reputation spread and he was offered a job in London by Gaumont Pictures, one of the world's leading film companies. He was still only twenty-three, but his life had already been a varied one, going from being a farm boy to an engineer then a projectionist, and now to an established cinematographer. He had stumbled, almost by accident, into an exciting and rapidly growing field with enormous international opportunities.

He arrived in London in early 1912 and his experience as a cinematographer broadened. But before continuing our story, we immediately run into a problem that must be addressed – namely the reliability of the published record of his early exploits. The biographies of Wilkins by Grierson (1960), Thomas (1961), Nasht (2005) and Andrews (2011) give extraordinary accounts of his adventures on the way to England and in the Balkan War (Nasht, at least, did express some reservations about these stories). On the way to England, he is supposed to have stowed away, encountered an Italian spy in Algiers, been captured by slave-traders, taken to an oasis in the desert and then rescued by a beautiful Arabian maiden. In the Balkan War he is supposed to have been put in front of a firing squad three times and somehow ended up in a harem. Reading these four biographies, I found these accounts implausible and inconsistent, or to put it more bluntly – unbelievable. I then discovered I was not alone in my scepticism. Jeff Maynard wrote two particularly good books about Wilkins; one dealt with his experiences in the First World War, *The Unseen Anzac: how an enigmatic polar explorer created Australia's World War 1 photographs*, and the other is *Wings of Ice*, about the air races to the poles. Both books also include a lot of valuable biographical material.

Maynard is an admirer of Wilkins, but he is also realistic about the veracity of some of his stories. He has also done more thorough research than the earlier authors, using Wilkins' letters and records kept in the US. He examined these stories about Wilkins' early years and came to the blunt judgement that "These adventures are fictitious". The explanation is that these accounts came from Wilkins nearly 50 years after the events were supposed to have happened, and by this time he had become immersed in spiritualism and the supernatural and no longer could distinguish between imagination and memory. Wilkins included these stories in his script for a proposed autobiographical radio series to be called *True Adventure Thrills*. The radio series was never broadcast, but the script survived and is the source of these stories. It is a pity that a man who had experienced so many fully authenticated adventures in his lifetime felt the need to embellish the record late in his life, and it surprised me that earlier writers did not question these accounts.

An alternative and more plausible account that Wilkins gave of his trip to London is that he travelled by ship via Sri Lanka, the Middle East, Italy and France and in each place, he recorded interesting events and people with his camera. He quickly settled into his role as a Gaumont cameraman, covering current events in Europe and providing footage for the weekly newsreels that played in cinemas – the forerunner to today's television news programs. He also took an interest in aviation and learned to fly, but did not bother to obtain his pilot's certificate. Soon he was given a more important task – he was to go to the First Balkan War and provide moving pictures for Gaumont and written material for the *Daily Chronicle* in London.

The First Balkan War commenced in October 1912 and was largely completed by an armistice in January 1913, but some fighting continued until May 1913. It was fought between the Balkan League consisting of Bulgaria, Serbia, Montenegro and Greece, all of whom opposed the Ottoman Empire. It was also a war where the Christian Balkan States sought to drive the Muslim Turks out of Europe. In this they were largely successful, and the defeated Ottomans had to give up a large area of Europe and retreat to a small foothold around Istanbul. It was a bloody war, in some ways the first modern war, with heavy use of artillery, machine guns, motor vehicles and even aeroplanes. As such, it was a prelude to the First World War.

Wilkins was part of a group of 27 foreign journalists who followed the war from the Turkish side. They sought to get as close to the front as they were allowed, but mainly they had to retreat with the defeated Turkish soldiers and Muslim refugees from the advancing Bulgarian Army. As in most wars, chaos reigned, supplies were short, transport unavailable, roads clogged, and finally a cholera epidemic ensued.

We know a reasonable amount about Wilkins' experiences in the Balkan War from a contemporary independent source. In the book *Adventures of War with Cross and Crescent*, published in 1913, English journalist Bernard Grant, who travelled closely with Wilkins, speaks highly of him in several places, including the following:

> And here I must pay tribute to Wilkins of the cinematograph, one of the best companions in the world, because of his continued cheerfulness, his knowledge of handicraft, of horses, and all rough work and outdoor life. He is an Australian and has had many adventures in wild places of the world which have taught him valuable lessons, among them being the gift of leadership, instant decisions in moments of peril, and a quick way of righting something that has gone wrong. Personally, I do not know what I would have done without such an experienced fellow by my side, and I am glad to give the praise that was his due.

Wilkins returned to London in early 1913 and was congratulated by his superiors at Gaumont for the movie footage he had taken. They immediately gave him his next assignment in Trinidad, where he made publicity films for Cadbury's chocolates. On his way back he received a telegram from Gaumont offering him a position whereby he would accompany the official Canadian Arctic Expedition of 1913 as cameraman, but still be on the Gaumont payroll.

This became the next big adventure for Wilkins and kept him in the Arctic, away from civilisation, between mid-1913 and mid-1916. The expedition, led by the brave but erratic explorer Vilhjalmur Stefansson, hoped to discover a new land north of Canada and find the fabled 'Blond Eskimos' who were reported to have blond hair, white skin and blue eyes. I will continue to use the word Eskimo, which was the term used during Wilkins' exploration, although the Canadian government now prefers the term Inuit. From the Canadian government's point of view, the main purpose of the expedition was to stake out the western half of Canadian Arctic Territory before it could be claimed by either the United States or Russia.

For Wilkins, the three years he spent in the Arctic consisted mainly of hard work, tough living conditions and danger. The explorers' accommodation consisted of huts, tents and often 'snow houses' (what we would call igloos). Their means of transport were either by boats nudging their way through icefloes, or by dog teams and sleds. Their diet was determined by their hunting success and consisted of seal meat, caribou (reindeer) meat, fish and occasionally even wolf and fox meat. Mostly they were able to cook it, but on occasion they had to eat it raw and frozen.

We know a lot about Wilkins' experiences in the Arctic from the Canadian Stuart Jenness's scholarly book, *The Making of an Explorer:*

George Hubert Wilkins and the Canadian Arctic Expedition 1913–1916. The first thing that stands out from this account is how versatile and hard-working Wilkins was. Although only a cameraman attached to the expedition, he threw himself into all the expedition's work – collecting specimens, building huts and snow houses, surveying and mapping, cooking, hunting and captaining and navigating boats. The second thing that stands out is that he quickly developed qualities of leadership, so much so that Stefansson appointed him as his deputy, even though at that stage he was not actually an official member of the expedition. Twice Wilkins had to lead a rescue by boat to relieve the ice-bound advance party under Stefansson, who later wrote that Wilkins was "easily my best man". Stefansson also spelled out some of Wilkins' qualities thus:

> I have never known anyone who worked harder than Wilkins. He would be cleaning the scraps of meat off the leg bone of a wolf before breakfast and scraping the fat from a bearskin up to bedtime at night. His diaries were filled with information about the specimens he gathered, his fingers were stained with the photographic chemicals used in the development of his innumerable plates and films, his mind was always alert and his response always cheerful when a new task was proposed.

Despite these three years of danger and hard work, the expedition made no great breakthroughs. No new land, apart from a few insignificant islands, was found, and the 'Blond Eskimos' proved to be a myth. Wilkins did, however, meet with and photograph a lot of Eskimos, including some – the 'Copper Eskimos' who were slightly lighter in colour. The Eskimos were very hospitable to the explorers, and some of Wilkins' photos of them in traditional dress became classics. From the Canadian government's perspective, it had not been a waste of time – much of the western Canadian Arctic was mapped and numerous animal, plant and mineral specimens brought back and donated to Canadian museums.

But during the three years that Wilkins was confined in the Arctic, something of much greater significance than exploration was happening – the First World War had begun. It is unclear when Wilkins first heard about this as there were no newspapers, and letters could take months or even up to a year to reach the explorers. But Wilkins must have become aware of it during the second half of his stay in the Arctic and when the expedition was wound up in late 1916, he returned to Australia. When he reached Australia, he volunteered for the recently established air force, where he was appointed flying officer in the 9th reinforcement of the Australian Flying Corps. He then undertook flight training at Point Cook near Melbourne before embarking for England in May 1917. His choice of the air force instead of the army was not accidental; he expected that his proficiency as a pilot would be useful for polar exploration after the war. In fact, when he filled in his recruitment papers, he gave his occupation as explorer, not photographer. But the Australian Armed Forces had a different view on the matter; they felt he would be of more use as a photographer than as a pilot.

C.E.W. Bean, the official Australian war correspondent, and later official historian of Australia's role in the First World War, convinced his superiors that Australia needed two photographers to record the achievements of the 1st AIF. First, Frank Hurley, a member of the Mawson and then the Shackleton expeditions to Antarctica was chosen, and then he in turn recommended his friend Wilkins. So, Australia ended up with two polar explorers as their official photographers in the First World War.

Hurley and Wilkins commenced operations in July 1917, and so they only covered the last 18 months of the war (in fact, Hurley left the Western Front for Palestine before the end of 1917). While they worked well together, the two men were quite different people, and were given very different instructions. Hurley was to take the propaganda photos used to raise civilian morale and encourage recruitment. This suited him as he was essentially a showman with artistic aspirations and was happy to 'create' composite images using multiple overlaid negatives to achieve dramatic effect. Wilkins' job was to record the unvarnished truth about every battle the Australians fought.

For both photographers, their tasks were challenging because the war was fought on a flat landscape with the troops in trenches and out of sight for most of the time. Even when the troops went into combat, they only appeared as small figures against a large, flat background. To get any worthwhile action photographs the photographer had to be in the front line, and so under fire. Both men were prepared to do this, particularly Wilkins, who quickly gained a reputation for bravery and daring.

Both photographers took part in the bloody, but largely inconclusive, Third Battle of Ypres in Belgium, better known as Passchendaele, in the summer of 1917. After that, Wilkins was with the Australian troops during the German offensive of spring 1918, when the German Army broke through and nearly reached the strategically vital city of Amiens. He was also with them during the Battle of Amiens and then during the successful push by the Allies later in 1918, which included the Australian victories at Villers Bretonneux, Hamel, Péronne and the breaking of the Hindenburg Line. Wherever they were fighting, Wilkins was there, either at the front or near it. Bean wrote, "Captain Wilkins has probably been in the fighting more constantly than any other officer in the Corps." Wilkins was frequently under fire and suffered bullet wounds on several occasions. Once near Ypres, an exploding shell knocked him unconscious and he fell into a waterlogged shell crater. Fortunately his chest landed on his bulky wooden camera, which kept his mouth and nose above water level and so saved him from drowning. The still-unconscious Wilkins was rescued by Canadian troops, who took him to a field hospital where he recovered. In late 1917, he was awarded the Military Cross for his bravery during the Third Battle of Ypres.

On another occasion, during the combined Australian–American attack on the Hindenburg Line in 1918, Wilkins found himself in a front-line trench with a group of novice American soldiers. They had lost their officers, were in thick fog, and unsure of where the German counter-attack was coming from. Wilkins, as an officer, took command of the situation, and despite serious casualties he helped the Americans to successfully resist the German counter-attack. For this he was awarded a bar to the Military Cross he had earlier been awarded. I wonder if any of the Americans who recognised his authority as an officer in battle realised that his position in the army was as a photographer.

Despite the danger and the injuries, he produced a complete photographic record of the Australian Army in the Western Front during the last 18 months of the war. He meticulously catalogued it, and it now forms the main visual historical record of the achievements of the Australian Army in the First World War. In his history of the war Bean acknowledged Wilkins, but not Hurley, and Sir John Monash in his book *Australian Victories in France in 1918* also thanked Captain Wilkins MC* for providing all the photographs for the book, which were "taken during the fighting and often under fire". There can be no doubt that Wilkins' photographic work was of the highest standard, as was his bravery under fire. For the former he was promoted to captain, and for the latter he was awarded the Military Cross and bar, making him the only Australian war photographer in any war to be decorated for bravery.

Just as in the First Balkan War and the Canadian Arctic Expedition, in the First World War we have reliable independent records of Wilkins' adventures, achievements and personal bravery. He was clearly the sort of person you wanted to have by your side in any difficult or dangerous situation. He was also noted for his modesty. For example, unlike Hurley he never asked for his First World War photographs to be attributed to him; he was content for them to have an identification number attached. As a result, some of his photographs may have been attributed to others. Today, Hurley is better known than Wilkins as a World War One photographer because of his books and exhibitions, but there is no doubt that Wilkins produced the larger and more important body of work.

After the war ended, Wilkins remained in the army during 1919, photographing with Bean the military remains of Gallipoli, and cataloguing all his war photographs in London. During his time in London he submitted plans to The Royal Meteorological Society asking for their support in establishing weather stations in the Arctic, but was rebuffed. He also met an ambitious explorer called John Lachlan Cope, who was planning a major expedition to Antarctica that he'd named The British Imperial Antarctic Expedition. Wilkins agreed to take part in the expedition after he returned to Australia, but first he had to find a way back. A solution soon presented itself – he would fly back – but this had never been done before.

Australian Prime Minister Billy Hughes' government offered a prize of 10,000 pounds to anyone who could fly from London to Australia. Wilkins was offered a place as navigator in one of the competing teams. They took off from London in November 1919 in a twin-engine Blackburn Kangaroo, and after three stops in France made it to Crete. Their next destination was Cairo, but one of their engines failed and they had to return to Crete, where they made a crash landing in a field. They were lucky to be alive, but their plane was severely damaged and this forced them out of the competition. One of the competing teams, led by Keith and Ross Smith, completed the flight to Australia, won the 10,000 pounds, and achieved lasting fame.

Wilkins eventually sailed back to Australia in 1920, stayed there briefly, then sailed to Uruguay to meet up with Cope and join his expedition to Antarctica. Cope's attempts to find financial backing failed and his grandly-titled expedition consisted of himself, Wilkins and two others. They went by whaling boat to Deception Island just off Antarctica, but failed to reach the Antarctic mainland. They then returned to London; the whole exercise had been a failure, but this did not stop Wilkins in his efforts to reach Antarctica. In 1921 he took part in Sir Ernest Shackleton's fourth Antarctic expedition, in which it was intended that Wilkins would conduct reconnaissance in a small plane. In the event the plane was left behind and the expedition got as far as South Georgia Island, where Shackleton had a heart attack and died. The expedition never reached Antarctica, but Wilkins spent months on the island gathering specimens, which he donated to the British Museum when he returned to London.

It had been a frustrating couple of years for Wilkins' polar ambitions – two failed attempts to get to Antarctica and no support for his planned polar weather stations. But one institution had faith in him: the British Museum was impressed by his record and by the specimens he had provided them. They chose him to lead an expedition into Northern Australia to collect specimens of native animals that they feared were facing extinction as a result of pastoral expansion. It was a major diversion for someone whose heart was still set on polar exploration, but he was now the leader of a well-financed expedition backed by a prestigious institution, which helped establish his reputation as an explorer of substance.

Wilkins spent 1923, 1924 and the first half of 1925 travelling with his three assistants through northern New South Wales, Queensland and the Northern Territory, collecting specimens and observing the land and its people. In total he collected over 400 mammals, 600 birds and 100 reptiles, which were preserved and sent back to the British Museum at its beautiful Victorian Annex in Kensington. The expedition was judged a great success because of its collection and because he completed the whole exercise virtually on budget, a rarity among early explorations. Wilkins was now clearly a man who could be trusted to lead expeditions.

He wrote a book about the expedition, *Undiscovered Australia: being an account of an expedition to tropical Australia to collect specimens of the rarer native fauna for the British Museum, 1923–1925*. Despite its title, it is not about zoology or botany, but consists mainly of an account of his adventures and his views on a range of subjects including Australian farming, Australia's weather, its mistreatment of Aborigines, Aboriginal myths and several accounts of cannibalism. Overall, Wilkins was sympathetic to the plight of the Aborigines and very critical of the settlers and the outback police, but the book had little impact. The London edition was not published until 1928, and the New York edition in 1929. It was, therefore, published after he became famous for his later polar flight, and after he had received his knighthood.

In late 1925, Wilkins finally got his chance to return to his first love – polar exploration. On Stefansson's recommendation, the Detroit Aviation Society chose him to lead an expedition into the Arctic Circle. This was a well-financed venture involving several pilots, two aeroplanes and a large support staff. Wilkins hoped that in the summer of 1926 he would be able to investigate the unexplored territory between Barrow in Alaska (now called Utqiagvik) and the North Pole, and establish once and for all whether there was land beneath the polar icecap. If there was, he hoped to establish a weather station. Finally, he would attempt to fly from Alaska to Spitsbergen, an island off Norway, over the Pole. Flying over the North Pole was third in importance in his list of priorities. He had never been interested in such 'trophy achievements' and besides, all the important ones had already been accomplished: Frederick Cook in 1908 and Robert Peary in 1909 had already claimed to have reached the North Pole by land, and Roald Amundsen had discovered the Northwest Passage between continental Europe and America in 1906 and had also reached the South Pole in 1912.

As Wilkins prepared his equipment and team for their expedition from Barrow in Alaska, two other teams were preparing for polar assaults from the other end. The first was Commander Richard Byrd from the US Navy, who already had a support staff of 50 in Spitsbergen. He was single-mindedly determined to be the first person to fly to the North Pole. The second was a team led by Amundsen, financed by the American Lincoln Ellsworth and piloted by the Italian Umberto Nobile, in a large Italian-built airship. Although Wilkins did not regard himself as being in a race to see who could be the first person to fly to the Pole, the press saw it differently – they rejoiced in the prospect of a three-team race to the Pole and gave it widespread coverage.

Wilkins, now thirty-eight, spent the three years from 1926 to 1928 on his Arctic quest. Success did not come easily and his first year was a big disappointment. All he really achieved was to establish his base at Barrow. Since it was rarely accessible by sea, everything, including fuel, had to be brought in either overland or by air, and this proved difficult due to his two Fokker aeroplanes suffering serious damage and his sled teams and snow tractors not being able to get through because of extreme weather.

Even more galling for him was that the two teams in Spitsbergen were having a much easier time. Byrd was able to bring his aeroplane into Spitsbergen by ship and soon had it ready to fly. The other team's airship made it to Spitsbergen from Rome and was also ready to go. On 9 May 1926, Byrd and his pilot, Floyd Bennett, flew their three-engine Fokker to the Pole and back. The trip covered 2400 kilometres and took over 15 hours. It had achieved nothing of scientific or commercial value, but Byrd was seen to have won the race and he became a national hero. It is difficult to confirm whether he definitely reached the Pole as there are no witnesses and, as they did not land their plane, no signs or flags were left there for others to verify. The South Pole is on land, and so in 1912 when Amundsen reached it, he was able to build a cairn and plant the Norwegian flag, but the North Pole is on an icecap that drifts, so that even if an object had been placed there it would have moved away over time.

On 11 May 1926, two days after Byrd's flight, the Amundsen, Ellsworth, Nobile team left Spitsbergen in their airship with its 16-man crew and reached the Pole the next day. There can be no doubt that they hovered above it on 12 May before moving on to Alaska in a trip that took the best part of four days. All three previous claims – those by Cook, Peary and Byrd – have been disputed, and so the airship was the first to have an undisputed claim to have reached the North Pole.

In the summer of 1927, Wilkins made his second attempt to achieve his Arctic objectives from his base in Barrow. He had a much smaller team this time and lighter planes more suited to Arctic conditions. His immediate objective was the same as in the previous year – to see whether there was land in the unexplored region between Barrow and the Pole. Wilkins and his pilot, Ben Eielson, flew north into this area in March and made the first successful aeroplane landing on the Arctic ice. Wilkins then took depth soundings and discovered that the water under the ice was over five kilometres deep. This put paid to any hope that there might be land under the ice in the unexplored region, and confirmed that the North Pole and its surrounds was one large icecap over the ocean.

After some initial problems the plane took off successfully and headed back to Barrow, but engine failure forced it into another landing. Wilkins and Eielson were stranded on the ice 130 kilometres short of Barrow. For almost anyone other than Wilkins, this would have meant certain death as there was no hope of rescue. But they had brought food and warm clothing with them, and so they set off on the walk over treacherous and shifting icefloes back to Barrow. Wilkins, using the experience of his earlier Arctic expedition, was able to build an igloo for them to sleep in each night. Eventually, after 12 days' walking – and sometimes crawling – through slowly melting ice, they made it to safety. The whole trip was an extraordinary feat of endurance, and it had advanced scientific knowledge of the region and its aviation potential, but it did not represent a 'trophy achievement'.

Two months later, Charles Lindbergh flew from New York to Paris, and in the public's estimation this eclipsed all the efforts of the Arctic

Charles Kingsford-Smith left and Hubert Wilkins right in front of Fokker trimotor "Southern Cross" in 1928.

aviators. The 1920s was the heroic era of aviation, and Lindbergh became its star.

Finally in 1928, things took a turn for the better. Wilkins was able to buy an aeroplane fast and light enough to meet his requirements – a single-engine Lockheed Vega. He partly financed the purchase by selling his old Fokker Trimotor to three Australians in San Francisco who were hoping to fly across the Pacific. The leader of this group was Charles Kingsford-Smith, who reconditioned the plane, fitted more powerful engines, renamed it the Southern Cross and became a national hero by flying it to Australia via Hawaii and Fiji later that year.

In April 1928, Wilkins and Eielson took off from Barrow to fly over another part of the unexplored region and then, they hoped, on to Spitsbergen. They did not fly over the Pole, but chose a slightly longer and more difficult course. It was a major feat of navigation requiring 20 course variations, and took them 20 hours and 30 minutes to fly the 3500 kilometres and reach Spitsbergen, nearly 2000 kilometres of which was over territory that had never before been seen by humans. Everything went smoothly until near the end when they were forced to land on the island of Spitsbergen, but well short of the airport at Green Harbour. Severe weather forced them to stay on the ground in their plane for five days before they could take off and fly the short distance to Green Harbour. Despite this little setback, they had achieved their objective of completing the first intercontinental flight across the Arctic Ocean.

There is little doubt that Wilkins' achievement was a greater feat of exploration and aviation than Byrd's. Wilkins was in the air longer, covered a greater distance, and there can be no question about what he achieved. He left Barrow and arrived in Spitsbergen over 20 hours later. Byrd left Spitsbergen, flew to his turning point and returned to Spitsbergen with his claim that his turning point was the Pole – something that has been disputed ever since. Wilkins' flight was also a greater feat of navigation as he went east–west as well as north–south; Byrd flew only north–south – up a meridian of longitude and back down it. The main danger with these early flights was that the engine would give out and the plane crash, so one had to be brave to take that risk. Byrd had the extra safety margin of three engines, whereas Wilkins had to rely on one.

Wilkins' achievement was quickly transmitted to the world's press and he and Eielson became the latest heroes in the age of aviation. They were feted in Norway, Germany and England, where in June, Wilkins was knighted by King George V and chose to be called Sir Hubert Wilkins rather than Sir George. The two men then travelled to New York where they were greeted by crowds, given the keys to the city and awarded the American Geographical Society's highest honour.

It is interesting that despite Wilkins' earlier protestations to the contrary, they had finally been rewarded for a 'trophy achievement'. At the age of forty, this was the high point of Wilkins' career. He capitalised on his newfound fame by releasing a book, *Flying the Arctic*, as well as an American edition of *Undiscovered Australia*. He became so well known in America that he was used in advertisements for Camel cigarettes, where he is pictured in his fur anorak puffing on a cigarette and proclaiming, "For digestion's sake – smoke Camel".

Despite his achievements and his fame, Wilkins' life had been very precarious and insecure. He had no home country or regular place to live; he had shuttled between Australia, England, Turkey, the Arctic, France, the Antarctic and the US, never spending more than a few weeks in one abode. He also had no secure source of income, and increasingly he had to rely on the patronage of rich people, which effectively meant rich Americans. He appeared to have no private life, which is not surprising as he was so often on the move or in remote corners of the world. But he did not lack female company entirely. Immediately after the First World War he met an English woman to whom he became engaged, but the marriage did not take place. Instead, after he became famous, he met an Australian actress working in New York called Suzanne Bennett. To everyone's surprise, they announced their engagement and were married in August 1929 in the interlude between two of his visits to Antarctica. Not surprisingly, given his peripatetic lifestyle, it was an unusual marriage; they never lived together for more than a few weeks at a time and there were no children. The letters they exchanged suggest that, after an initial period of happiness, the relationship grew more strained.

With his reputation now established, Wilkins' aim was to devote the rest of his life to polar exploration, but he could not do it on his own terms; he was still at the mercy of rich sponsors. Shortly after he returned from the Arctic, he was approached by William Randolph Hearst, the newspaper magnate, who was willing to finance an attempt to fly to the South Pole. Wilkins and Eielson and their trusty Lockheed Vega soon went by whaling boat to Deception Island in Antarctica. In December 1928 they were the first to fly an aeroplane in Antarctica. It was a substantial flight covering over 2000 kilometres out and back and taking 11 hours, but the distances are so huge in Antarctica that it did not get them close to the Pole. They returned to the US and planned another attempt for the next summer.

Meanwhile Byrd, with a party of 80, plus three planes and four ships set off for the Antarctic in October 1928. They had enough food and equipment with them to allow a party of 40 to spend the winter there in buildings erected on Amundsen's old site and prepare for the flight next summer. The contrast between the vast resources available to Byrd and the modest scale of Wilkins' approach could not be starker. But the newspapers, including those owned by Hearst, again covered the events as a race to the Pole between Byrd and Wilkins.

Wilkins was back in Antarctica by early November 1929, but had difficulty finding a suitable site for an airstrip. On 28 November 1929, Byrd's team of four, piloted by the Norwegian Bernt Balchen, flew the three-engine Ford plane to the South Pole and back to their base. Unlike the flight to the North Pole, this flight's achievement has not been disputed.

Back in the US after these two less than successful forays into Antarctica, Wilkins pressed ahead with his next polar adventure. Having flown over the Arctic icecap, he then proposed to traverse it underwater by submarine. His major sponsor was the rich American, Lincoln Ellsworth, who had previously sponsored Amundsen. The venture was called the Wilkins–Ellsworth Trans-Arctic Submarine Expedition, and it was a much more ambitious and expensive project than anything Wilkins had attempted before. Its success was also heavily dependent on the performance of the submarine, and this was its big weakness. The only submarine available was a decommissioned US naval vessel from the First World War, which Wilkins renamed the *Nautilus*. Despite extensive reconditioning and upgrading, it was never likely to be up to the task. For the first time in his life, Wilkins was subject to widespread criticism for undertaking what many people regarded as a reckless adventure that risked the lives of his crew.

In the event, the criticism was largely borne out. The submarine failed to cross the Atlantic successfully and had to be towed to

Ireland for repairs, and then to England for more work. It then made it successfully to Norway, but was again damaged, losing the two rudders that controlled its diving. It never looked like reaching the Pole or traversing the icecap. In fact, its only excursion below the icecap took minutes rather than hours, but at least they did get to see what it was like under there. The whole expedition was a failure; it severely tarnished Wilkins' reputation and left him in debt. Just as the trans-polar flight in 1928 was the high point of his career, the submarine adventure in 1931 was the low point.

In Wilkins' defence, it must be said that his idea was not crazy, but to attempt to do it with the equipment available at the time was hopelessly optimistic. In 1958, 27 years later, two nuclear-powered US submarines successfully crossed under the Arctic icecap, one from east to west and one from west to east. Among the world of submariners, Wilkins is still a hero, his only fault was to be ahead of his time.

But the fallout from the submarine adventure meant that his chances of leading a new expedition in his own name had virtually disappeared. From now on, he would have to play a subsidiary role to others. Lincoln Ellsworth, now even richer after his father's death, still had ambitions to achieve a trophy in the world of exploration. His support of Amundsen and Wilkins had not achieved the results he hoped for, so he set himself a new objective of being the first to fly across the Antarctic landmass from one side to the other. Wilkins was to organise the expedition, but was not allowed to accompany Ellsworth and his pilot on the trans-Antarctic flight.

It took three attempts over three years before the objective was finally achieved. Wilkins spent 1933, 1934 and 1935 either in Antarctica or nearby on Ellsworth's ship, co-ordinating the expedition. Finally, on 23 November 1935, Ellsworth and his pilot,

Herbert Hollick-Kenyon, flew from one side of Antarctica to the other, stopping four times and finally reaching their destination on 5 December. This attempt occupied three years of Wilkins' life, but it was the last time he was associated with a high-profile attempt to achieve a polar breakthrough. He continued to work in polar regions, but on more practical matters.

In August 1937, Russia's greatest aviator, Sigismund Levanesky, piloting a four-engine Tupolev with five crew members, disappeared somewhere in the Arctic on route from Moscow to New York. Wilkins was chosen by the Russian government to lead the search for the airmen and, with pilot Hollick-Kenyon, they flew over 70,000 kilometres, most of it in the Arctic winter. They flew back and forth over the Arctic for seven months, but to no avail; the plane and its crew were never found. But Wilkins' efforts had impressed the Russians and he was invited to Moscow to receive the Order of Lenin, personally pinned on by Joseph Stalin.

During this time, Wilkins became interested in the paranormal, particularly the possibility of extrasensory perception. While in the Arctic, he and a New York-based writer Harold Sherman conducted experiments in transmitting thoughts to one another through space. They became convinced that it was possible, and their experiments formed the basis of a jointly-authored book published in 1942 called *Thoughts Through Space: A Remarkable Adventure in the Realm of the Mind*. Wilkins' interest in the paranormal also led him to the Urantia Movement, a quasi-religion based on revelations that combined Christianity, science, evolution and extra-terrestrial life. Wilkins helped finance their official publication, *The Urantia Book*. This 2000-page volume was his constant companion through the later part of his life. It is also said to have had an influence on L. Ron Hubbard, the founder of Scientology. It is hard not to conclude that as Wilkins' worldly success declined, his interest in the spiritual increased and his grasp of reality gradually declined.

In 1939 Ellsworth made his final foray into Antarctica, again accompanied by Wilkins. It was a strange visit as Ellsworth was attempting to claim land for the US, while Wilkins was doing the same for Australia. Wilkins' aim was to persuade the Australian Government to establish a permanent base there with him in charge of it. The base was established, but Sir Douglas Mawson was chosen to head it.

Soon the Second World War broke out and Wilkins offered his services to the Australian and British governments, but at fifty-one he was too old for active service. He was also too old to continue his career as an explorer. This would only have been possible if he was rich, or if he was valued for fundraising and organisational ability. But Wilkins was not that type of explorer – he was the 'hands-on', physical type who led from the front, and this was difficult to do as he got older. He had to find another form of employment that could use his experience. Fortunately the US Army saw his value and employed him in a civilian capacity, an arrangement that lasted, in one form or another, for the rest of his life. Even though he lived and worked in the US, he retained his Australian citizenship and never acquired a US one. It might have seemed an anticlimax compared with the dangerous and adventurous work that he undertook during the prime of his life, but it suited him. Helping to design equipment and testing it in remote locations was a satisfying job for an ex-explorer.

By this time, his wife had bought a farm in Pennsylvania and lived there with the actor Winston Ross. She named the farm Walhalla after the small goldmining town in Victoria where she originally came from. Wilkins spent time there when he could, but his job, as always, involved an enormous amount of travel. His main position was as a geographer and climatologist with the Quartermaster General Corps, but he also did work for the US Navy's Office of Scientific Research. Initially hired as an Arctic consultant, his job was to improve the standards of clothing and equipment for operations in cold climates. He soon became an expert on all aspects of military equipment, from clothing to sleeping bags, tents and food, and he spent as much time testing equipment in the desert as in the Arctic.

When he became too old for frequent travel to remote places, he was given more sedentary work for the Quartermaster Generals Corps at their headquarters near Boston. He moved there and spent the last five years of his life living in a hotel room in Framingham, Massachusetts. Even though his life was much less exciting than in his exploring days, as best we can judge, he enjoyed the varied work the army required of him and was liked by his colleagues. One of them, Dr Ralph Goldman, recalls:

> I remember Sir Hubert well, mostly for his unusual lifestyle – he lived in a furnished room at a run-down hotel near the Framingham railroad station, drove the pay office wild because he seldom cashed his pay checks and told wild stories about barely escaping with his life from a Sultan's harem ... He was one of the last of his kind.

Note that this reminiscence also alludes to his increasing tendency to tell tall stories about his early years as he got older.

In 1958, after working on his beloved 1939 Chevrolet during the day, he returned to his room, suffered a heart attack and died at the age of seventy. Tributes flowed from those who knew him in many countries, but the most important mark of respect came from the submariners of the US Navy. After his funeral, the submarine

Skate travelled to the North Pole, punctured a hole in the icecap and scattered his ashes at the Pole. Another heartfelt tribute came from his friends in the US Army:

> Quartermasters Corps' most colourful, best known and most beloved employee passed away in his hotel room amidst the mementos of his adventurous life. One of the great and glamorous figures of the first half of the twentieth century, Sir Hubert was born in Australia seventy years ago. Best known for his polar exploits, he spent five 'summers' and portions of twenty six winters in the Arctic and eight 'summers' in the Antarctic. He made the first airplane flights over the Arctic Ocean in 1926, 1927 and 1928 and the Antarctic Ocean and continent in 1928 ... Sir Hubert's immortality is assured ...

Instead, as we now know, Wilkins has largely been forgotten. Why is this so? Certainly not because no one has tried to remind us of his deeds. Four full-length biographies have been published: one by an English author, one by an American and two by Australians, plus a book on his early Arctic exploration by a Canadian, as well as a book on his First World War exploits and another on his polar flights, both written by an Australian. If you have heard of Wilkins and do a bit of research on him, you cannot help but be impressed by his exploits, not just his polar ones. He was truly one of the few great explorers of the twentieth century. But his name does not strike a chord in the popular imagination and he is hardly known, even in his homeland.

In so many fields of human endeavour the public is aware of the few who attain celebrity status, but not of those equally worthy who do not. In exploration, celebrity status is reserved for those who are the first to do something easily measurable. Vasco de Gama was the first to sail from Europe to India, Magellan was the first to sail around the world, and Columbus was the first to reach the Americas (or was he?). In the twentieth century there were few firsts left to achieve, but Amundsen reached the South Pole and Hillary and Tenzing climbed Everest. The development of the aeroplane offered some new opportunities, so aviators such as Bleriot, Lindbergh and Kingsford-Smith achieved the trophies of first across the English Channel, first from New York to Paris and first across the Pacific respectively. Two other aviation firsts that were still available in the 1920s were reaching the North and South Poles. Whether their achievement had any strategic, scientific or commercial value is doubtful. I am not suggesting that detailed exploration and mapping of the polar regions had no value, rather that being the first person to fly over a particular point had little value. However, that is not how the popular press of the day saw it, nor is it how popular history remembers it.

This brings us inevitably to a comparison between Wilkins and Byrd, and the enormous advantage of being a well-connected member of the establishment. Byrd came from an illustrious family, his brother Harry was an influential senator, he had the resources of the US Navy behind him, as well as the wealth of the Rockefellers, Vanderbilts and Fords. His expeditions were ten times the size of the ones Wilkins could put together, and he could concentrate solely on being first to each of the Poles. Wilkins never really had a chance in this contest even if he had concentrated on achieving the trophy. So Byrd is the name that people associate with polar exploration, not Wilkins, even though informed opinion now seems to be that Byrd did not actually reach the North Pole.

The real test of who was the greater explorer is if you consider who would you have preferred to have by your side if you were lost in the Arctic, or who would you have turned to if you needed to search for someone who was lost out there? For me, the answer is definitively Wilkins.

Henry Handel Richardson in Munich in 1896 with ever present cigarette.

5

ETHEL FLORENCE LINDESAY (HENRY HANDEL) RICHARDSON

Novelist and Musician

Ethel Florence Lindesay Richardson was born in Melbourne in 1870. The name is unlikely to bring any nods of recognition, nor is her married name of Ethel Florence Lindesay Robertson. It is under her *nom de plume*, Henry Handel Richardson, that she is best known. She was the author of one of Australian literature's undoubted classics – *The Fortunes of Richard Mahony* – a book that has been referred to by literary scholars as 'the great Australian novel'. She is probably better known today for a smaller and more approachable book, *The Getting of Wisdom*.

But there was more to her than the books she wrote. The first third of her life was devoted to music, and much of it was spent in Germany. She then decided to devote the rest of her life to literature. How she used her early experiences in Australia to provide the inspiration for her Australian novels, written entirely during her long literary career in London, is an interesting story. So is the story of her father, the source of much of her inspiration, so we must start with him.

Walter Lindesay Richardson was of Protestant Irish stock, born in Dublin in 1826 to an aged father and much younger mother. His father died, and he moved with his mother to Scotland where he graduated in medicine from Edinburgh University. Walter migrated to Australia in his twenties, during the Victorian gold rushes, and settled in Ballarat. In 1855 he married Mary Bailey when he was thirty and she eighteen. Mary Bailey had come to Australia from England as a girl of fourteen, following four of her siblings.

After failed attempts at goldmining and shopkeeping, Walter eventually established a successful medical practice in Ballarat, specialising in obstetrics. He became a pillar of colonial society, helped to found Ballarat Hospital, was prominent in the masonic movement and spiritualist circles, was the president of the Victorian Association of Progressive Spiritualists, and was a member of the Senate of the University of Melbourne. He and his wife were also active speculators in goldmining shares. But he was restless and, tiring of colonial society, he and Mary returned to England in 1868. His attempts to establish a medical practice in two English cities failed, so they came back to Australia. By this time, his mining investments had been so successful that he was able to live the life of a prosperous rentier on the dividends. He acquired a substantial house and grounds in the Melbourne seaside suburb of St Kilda, which he filled with books and devoted himself to intellectual pursuits and spiritualism.

After 15 years of marriage, during which Walter and Mary had resigned themselves to being childless, somewhat to their surprise a daughter, Ethel Florence Lindesay, the future novelist, was born in 1870. No one ever called her Ethel, a name that she hated; she was always known as Ettie, so I will follow that practice, as have her numerous biographers. Soon after, a second daughter, Ada Lillian

Lindesay, known as Lil, was born.

Restless again, Walter took his family to Europe for a tour in 1873, but when he returned this time, he found that his fortune had shrunk. He returned to medicine and attempted to establish a practice in the Melbourne suburb of Hawthorn, where he built a large house. This was unsuccessful, so he tried again in Chiltern in north-eastern Victoria with even worse results. By this time, he was showing clear signs of mental illness. He made a final attempt at medicine in Queenscliff on Port Phillip Bay, where he became quarantine health officer. Walter broke down completely here and was committed to what was then known as a lunatic asylum, where he was diagnosed as suffering from General Paralysis of the Insane (GPI). By this time Mary had used her political connections to be appointed postmistress in Koroit in western Victoria at a salary of 80 pounds per year plus board. She managed to have her husband released from the asylum and cared for him in Koroit in the brief period before he died in 1879, when Ettie was nine years old.

It is necessary to go through Walter's life in some detail as I will refer to it when I discuss his daughter's masterpiece – the three volumes that make up *The Fortunes of Richard Mahony*, much of which is based on her father's life. As is apparent from what I have described, Ettie's early life was very unsettled, particularly in the six years when she moved from Hawthorn to Chiltern to Queenscliff and then to Koroit by the time her father died. As well as being physically unsettled, Ettie and her sister were also emotionally affected by the slow and disturbing death of their father.

Things improved somewhat when Mary obtained a better position as postmistress in Maldon, north of Melbourne. It was an old goldmining town that had successfully converted into the prosperous centre of a rich agricultural district. Mary and her two daughters lived in a well-built brick house of six rooms, an enormous improvement on

Koroit. Looking back on it many years later in her last book, a memoir titled *Myself When Young*, Ettie wrote:

> In it I spent the happiest days of my childhood, free at last of unchildish anxieties; and when, of a sleepless night, my thoughts turn homeward, it is usually in these carefree, sunlit surroundings that I find myself.

In 1882 at the age of twelve, Ettie left home to become a boarder at one of Melbourne's finest private schools, the Presbyterian Ladies College (PLC). Her sister followed a year later. Ettie's time at PLC was a successful period for her. Not only did she receive a good education, she later used the experience as the basis for her novel, *The Getting of Wisdom*. The novel is less than flattering about the school. Nevertheless, the experience for her was clearly beneficial. Many years later, in *Myself When Young*, Ettie wrote:

> I cannot remember ever being really happy at school. None the less I should have been sorry to miss a day of the four or five years I spent there. The education provided was a very sound one, and in many ways ahead of its time: this I realised when I came to England and saw what was still considered good enough for the majority of English girls. Our curriculum was based on that of the 'Scotch College' for boys; we learned all that our brothers did, and, like them, were prepared for matriculation and the University. Algebra and Geometry, Latin and Greek, Physics and Biology – none of these subjects were held to be beyond us or outside our sphere. Taken as a whole, and for its day, the training offered us was remarkably thorough and free from prejudice.

Ettie's main interest at school was music, where she both performed and composed, but she also showed interest in literature, history and languages. She matriculated in 1887, won the Senior Pianoforte Scholarship and the school cup in tennis. Although she could have gone to university, she was advised by the school to further her musical studies. After a brief experience working as a morning governess at a school in Toorak, which she hated, Ettie accepted the advice and turned to music.

At this time, if you were really serious about a career in music the best option was to study abroad, especially in Germany. So Mary took her two daughters on a family visit to Europe, travelling first class. The trip was initially conceived as a tour of about a year, supplemented with further musical training. In the event, it became a permanent move for the family to Europe; only Ettie and Lil ever saw Australia again, and that was briefly when they visited for a few months in 1912.

The three Richardsons arrived in London in 1888 and stayed there for a few months before departing to Leipzig in the eastern part Germany in 1889 so that Ettie could enrol in the Leipzig Conservatorium to further her piano studies. This was the start of a long period spent mainly in Germany for the three of them. Ettie lived in Germany for many years and did not leave permanently until 1903, so she mostly read and spoke German. Her mother did not adjust to German life as well as her two daughters, but she stuck it out until her death in 1896.

The years in Leipzig were very happy ones for Ettie. Leipzig was the centre of German music and therefore the centre of the classical music world. Johann Sebastian Bach had composed most of his music there, and Wagner was born in Leipzig. Other names prominent in Leipzig music during the nineteenth century were Schumann, Mendelssohn and Mahler. If you wanted a career in classical music, this was the place to start. Ettie's mother supported her two daughters financially, as well as providing a well-run family home for them. They soon made a circle of friends from the conservatorium and the university, and were never lonely.

Ettie was a good student and had no trouble in completing the three years' study, which qualified her for a director's certificate. But, to her teachers' surprise and disappointment, she did not complete the fourth year, which would have given her a diploma. We do not know why she did not go on with it. Had she lost interest in music, or had she already decided on a career in literature? My guess is that she was realistic enough to know that although she was an excellent pianist, she was not in the elite class that would permit her to succeed as a concert performer. She was still interested in music, but was developing another interest.

While studying in Leipzig, Ettie met George Robertson, a Scotsman who already had a degree in science, but was studying for a PhD in German literature at Leipzig University. He had a passionate interest in literature, particularly German, Scandinavian and Russian. Ettie had always been a voracious reader, but mainly of mainstream English classics. Her reading had no particular purpose behind it, and it always had to take second place behind music in her cultural life. Robertson broadened her literary horizons and introduced her to writers such as Tolstoy, Dostoevsky, Ibsen and various German, Danish and Swedish writers. He realised her potential literary talent and encouraged her to write. So at the same time as Ettie was recognising her limited future as a professional musician, another more promising avenue was opening up. This was the major turning point in her life.

It wasn't just a love of literature that drew the two together; there was a genuine romantic attachment. They spent so much time with each other that Mary thought they should announce their engagement, even though they had no hope of soon marrying. So they became engaged in 1891, but circumstances meant that they lived apart until their marriage in 1895.

After Ettie's studies finished in 1892, Mary and her two daughters returned to live in England for three years, although Mary would have preferred to return to Australia. We know little about this period other than that Ettie, Mary and Lil lived mostly in London, and George remained in Glasgow, with visits to London whenever he could. It was during this period that George encouraged Ettie to translate Jens Peter Jacobson's influential novel, *Niels Lyhne*, into English. Although the novel was written in Danish, she used a German translation as her source, so it went from Danish to German to English. Despite this unorthodox method, the translation was published by Heinemann and received good reviews.

Ettie was strongly influenced by *Niels Lyhne*, as were such writers as Stefan Zweig, Thomas Mann and Rainer Marie Rilke. The book sparked her interest in German romanticism and melancholy Scandinavian themes such as unrequited love, failure to achieve spiritual and artistic fulfilment, and death. Both Jacobson and his fictional hero, Niels Lyhne, suffered early deaths. At this time Ettie also wrote an article in defence of Ibsen, whose sombre outlook on life was under attack from English critics.

Mary and her two daughters returned to Germany in 1895 – this time to Munich. Ettie encouraged George to leave Glasgow and come to Munich so they could marry, but the big obstacle was earning enough money to support themselves. This was overcome by Mary's generosity in providing a wedding present of 300 pounds. In late 1895, they married and settled into life in Munich. But they were only there for nine months when George received an offer of a lectureship in Strasbourg, then part of Germany and called Strassburg. His annual salary was only 120 pounds a year, but with Mary's gift to augment it, they settled into life in Strasbourg. Within the first few months, however, they received news that Mary's health was deteriorating, and she died in Munich in November 1896. This brave and resourceful woman had been Ettie's provider and protector for as long as she could remember. She had always put her daughters' interests ahead of her own and had died in a foreign land, although her heart was always in Australia. Ettie was shaken by her mother's death and felt guilty that she had not shown more appreciation for her while Mary was still alive.

Ettie's next literary effort was a translation of the Norwegian novel *The Fisher Lass* by Bjornstjern Bjornson, published by Heinemann. She refers to herself as Ethel F.L. Robertson as translator of the book. It was in Strasbourg that Ettie decided that her literary future was as a novelist, not as a translator or essayist. She started the long, laborious process of writing her first novel, *Maurice Guest*, soon after they reached Strasbourg in 1896, but it was not finished until 1906 in London, and not published until 1908. This was the main literary achievement of her seven years in Strasbourg.

Meanwhile, George was extremely productive, turning out numerous articles and a major book on the history of German literature. His academic output was rewarded when he was appointed Professor of German Literature at London University in 1903. This was the end of the German phase of their life, and they spent the rest of their days in England.

At first they were disappointed with English intellectual and cultural life, and compared it unfavourably with Germany where they had become thoroughly acculturated. But they eventually settled into English life, first in Hampstead and then for six years in Harrow, where they were living when Ettie's first novel was published.

Like nearly everything she subsequently wrote, *Maurice Guest* is based on her personal experiences – on this occasion, her years in Leipzig as a music student. It traces the doomed passion of a young Scottish music student – Maurice Guest – for a beautiful Australian woman, who is herself in love with another student of much greater musical ability. It ends with Maurice Guest's self-destructive decline and eventual suicide. The book clearly shows the influence of the

Scandinavian outlook on life as epitomised by *Niels Lyhne*. This was the first time Ettie had used the pen name Henry Handel Richardson, which as well as having a musical ring, was the name of one of her departed Richardson relatives. As she had now established herself as an author under this name, I will cease calling her Ettie, and henceforth refer to her as Richardson (I could have called her Henry, as her husband did, but I prefer to use her surname).

It is a big step for a writer to use a pseudonym, especially one that changes their gender. Other female Australian writers from her era, broadly defined, such as Mary Gilmore, Miles Franklin, Katherine Susannah Pritchard, Christina Stead or Henrietta Drake-Brockman each used their own name. So I was surprised that the various biographies of Richardson skip over this issue lightly, and their brief explanations of why she chose this course vary widely. The most plausible explanation to my mind is the one given by Karen McLeod and enlarged upon by Germaine Greer in her introduction to a reprint of *The Getting of Wisdom*. According to Greer, in *Maurice Guest*, "Richardson wished to write the story of a degrading sexual obsession from the point of view of its masculine victim." This would have been seen as unconvincing, and probably unseemly, coming from a female author, so she chose to write under a male name. She was proud of the fact that none of the reviewers guessed the female identity behind the pseudonym.

The book was not a commercial success, though it did go into a second impression. Reviews were mixed, with *The Times* giving it the thumbs down, stating "it is too full of morbid self-analysis and too relentlessly cruel in its *denouement* to be widely popular". But *The Evening News* said it was "one of the most remarkable first novels ever written" and *The Daily News* reviewer said he "could scarcely find its equal for strength of purpose and truthfulness". The book was also favourably reviewed by, among others, John Masefield, Hugh Walpole and H.G. Wells. It gave Richardson the confidence to contemplate an even more ambitious task, which ultimately became *The Fortunes of Richard Mahony*. Before doing so, she produced a much lighter piece of work, *The Getting of Wisdom*, in which she returned to her Australian roots.

Richardson started this short book in 1907 and it was published in 1910, a quick production by her standards. It marked the start of a series of novels that are all inspired by memories of her early years in Australia, but written in the comfort of her family home in London. Like her first novel, it is based closely on her own life, and is almost autobiographical. Set in a private girls' school among a group of boarders, it details the difficulties of a young country girl of modest means adjusting to life among more self-assured older girls. It is therefore similar to Richardson's own experience at PLC and has always been seen in this light, particularly by those who regard it as an unfair criticism of the school. Its main departure from the autobiographical is that the main character – Laura – is depicted as a relative failure academically, whereas Richardson was an excellent student.

Like its predecessor, the book was well received in literary circles but had only modest sales. But it did not fade away. In later years it was reprinted, and for the general reading public it is mainly through this book that they may be aware of Richardson. Its recognition was greatly assisted in the 1970s, when a revival of the Australian film industry led to the production of three films based on novels by female authors whose stories were set in the late 1800s and early 1900s. All three novels have feminine themes, and their authorship is often misattributed. The first film was *Picnic at Hanging Rock* (1975) adapted from a novel by Joan Lindsay, the second was *The Getting of Wisdom* (1977) adapted from Richardson's novel, and the third was *My Brilliant Career* (1979) adapted from the novel by Miles Franklin.

In 1910, at the age of forty, Richardson moved into a large house in Regents Park Road in London and set about writing the three novels that make up *The Fortunes of Richard Mahony*. It was a task she did not complete for nearly 20 years. The first volume, *Australia Felix*, was published in 1917; the second, *The Way Home*, in 1925; and the third, *Ultima Thule*, in 1929. She was a slow, fastidious writer and a careful researcher.

As usual the books are based quite clearly on experiences in her life, but more so on the life of her father, Walter Richardson. All the events are the same, but most of the large cast of characters are fictional, as is the dialogue of course, and the main character differs in a number of respects from Walter Richardson.

Australia Felix tells the story of the main character Mahony's marriage to Mary, the early years of struggle, and the setting up of the medical practice in Ballarat during the gold rushes. *The Way Home* covers their return to England, the lack of success there, the trip back to Australia, the sudden increase in the value of their investments and the brief period of living the good life. The final book, *Ultima Thule*, covers another trip abroad, the loss of wealth, unsuccessful attempts to return to medical practice, the decline into poverty and insanity and finally, the death of Richard Mahony. It is all remarkably similar to the account of Walter Richardson's life I gave at the beginning of this essay.

The books draw heavily on surviving letters between Walter and Mary Richardson, but Richardson felt more research was needed, so in 1912 she, George and Lil journeyed to Australia for several months. They visited Ballarat, Melbourne, Chiltern, Queenscliff and Koroit, and any other site that featured in Walter Richardson's life.

Having completed her research, they returned to London and Richardson settled back into her gracious five-storey Georgian House overlooking Regents Park. She had a very comfortable existence and a disciplined writing routine. All her biographers comment on this, but Michael Ackland, her most recent biographer, summarises it best.

> She had established a strict routine to which she adhered for the rest of her life. Richardson woke to the new day with a cup of tea brought by a servant. She bathed at 7.30, then went back to bed for a leisurely breakfast. During this time her study was cleaned and a tray of light, thin pencils, sharpened by George, was placed on her desk, together with a stack of fresh paper and the typed up pages of what she had written the previous day. At nine she descended to discuss meals and any other issues the housekeeper might want to raise concerning the three maids or the day's tasks. By 9.30 the novelist was in her study, cut off from the outside world by a normal door and an additional sound-proofed one, though still linked by telephone with the housekeeper and kitchen. Outside the stairs were 'heavily padded', servants moved about in felt slippers, so that the very house 'seemed to carry an air of silence'. During the morning Richardson had no contact with family members. George had already been up since five and done a day's work in the study below hers before he breakfasted and set off for the University. From 9.30 to 1.00 pm belonged exclusively to the novelist, who chain smoked as she wrote ('I am a slave to smoking … & can only work with a cigarette between my lips'). 'At about 11.00 am a small cup of mocha coffee with cream and a dish of fruit was taken up to her'. The tray was placed in her study silently, its bearer retreated taking care not to bang either door … A moody, irritable person, she could run through the whole gamut of emotions in her study and move about restlessly between window, fireplace, desk and bookcase when ideas and words came haltingly. The strain of three or four hours of writing was immense.

In the afternoon, she relaxed. Her favourite outlets for relaxation were tennis and walking. Her walking was as disciplined as her writing; she followed the same route each time and walked even on the coldest and wettest days. She still played the piano on most days and read widely. She estimated that she read more than a hundred books a year. Most were serious literature, but she also relaxed with detective stories such as those by Agatha Christie. Like her father, she had a lifelong interest in spiritualism, became a member of the Society for Psychical Research and the London Spiritual Alliance, and attended séances. She also supported the suffragette movement, which was agitating for the right for women to vote in England, attending rallies and donating to the movement. Her sister, Lil, was more active and spent time in jail in 1912 following the destruction of property during a protest. It must have occurred to both sisters that, had they still been in Australia, all this effort would have been unnecessary because Australia had already granted women suffrage in 1902, one year after Federation. England, on the other hand, did not do so until 1928.

When *Australia Felix* was published in 1917, it received a lukewarm critical reception and did not sell well. It was already out of print by the time *The Way Home* was published in 1925, so reviewers had to assess it without the continuity provided by its predecessor. Again, reviews were lukewarm and sales modest. The reception of these two books must have been very disheartening for Richardson. She had worked for 15 years to produce them, and it must have seemed to her that her literary career had been a failure. It required enormous strength of character to return to her writing desk and plough on through to the end of the third volume. She later said, "To go on with volume three after such a failure was the hardest thing I have ever done, and left a mark on me that no success will erase."

Even more bad news was to come. Her publishers, Heinemann, having achieved disappointing sales on the first two volumes and letting them go out of print, rejected *Ultima Thule*. Richardson was not surprised. "I think the stark undiluted tragedy of it has somehow horrified them, and they do not anticipate any great sales. No doubt they are right; the public does not want unpleasant reading, still less the naked truth of things." The ever-supportive George Robertson, however, had faith in his wife's ability and in 1929 he arranged to publish it privately in a print run of 1000 copies.

To Richardson's amazement, it received excellent reviews. The first serious review set the tone. In *The Daily News* the reviewer concluded, "I must record my belief, if our age has produced a masterpiece at all, this is a masterpiece." Other enthusiastic reviews followed, and Heinemann reversed its decision and went ahead and published it. Even more surprising is that in the United States, it was chosen by the Book of the Month Club and over 80,000 copies were sold there.

I must admit I am surprised it was so successful, and I say this for two reasons. First, it was the third book in a fictional biography, where the first two were already out of print. It had to be judged in isolation without the reader knowing the events that led up to its starting point, or how the main characters had developed. Second, it is a story of unremitting decline (as Richardson herself recognised). Unlike its two predecessors, which had periods of decline relieved by other periods of calm or improvement, this novel is a story of unrelieved gloom. This is not surprising from a writer who in her husband's words "upheld the banner of tragic realistic art". *Ultima Thule* records one disaster after another, as Richard Mahony fails in each endeavour, physically and mentally deteriorates, goes mad, and then dies. Viewed as the conclusion of the trilogy, it has a certain logic; viewed in isolation, I am surprised it received the acclaim that its two predecessors were denied.

Nevertheless, it was wonderful news for Richardson, who at the age of sixty had finally received the recognition she deserved. Heinemann subsequently published the trilogy in one volume, and it also sold well. Having achieved success abroad, she was reclaimed by Australia, where *Ultima Thule* was awarded the Australian Literary Society's gold medal.

For the first time also, she received a decent income from her own efforts, although it was hardly a generous reward for 20 years of perseverance.

Richardson's newfound happiness did not last long. In 1933, George died at the age of sixty-six. They had been married for 38 years, and all their friends agreed they had been a very devoted couple. As Ackland puts it, she had lost a "husband, brother, father and best friend in one person". She also had to move out of Regents Park Road, as she could no longer afford it. This did not matter much because it gave her an opportunity to move close to the sea, which she had always wanted.

For more than a decade Richardson had formed a close friendship with Olga Roncoroni, a woman nearly 20 years her junior. Olga often stayed at Regents Park Road and was a family friend, so much so that George, on his death bed asked her to look after his wife. In 1934, Richardson and Olga moved to the small village of Fairlight, near the coastal town of Hastings. Richardson was sixty-four and in declining health when she moved to Fairlight, and she stayed there with Olga until she died in 1946 at the age of seventy-six.

While living in Fairlight, she continued to write and produced a novel, *The Young Cosima*, set in Germany and inspired by the story of Richard and Cosima Wagner. She also completed a book of short stories, *The End of Childhood*, and an autobiographical memoir, *Myself When Young*. None of these later pieces of writing made much impact, and they did nothing to enhance her literary reputation.

Interestingly, shortly before Richardson died the American film company Metro-Goldwyn-Mayer (MGM) bought the film rights to *The Fortunes of Richard Mahony*. They intended to cast Gregory Peck as Richard and Greer Garson as Mary, but the film was never made. In 1954, eight years after she died, MGM did succeed in making a film based loosely on one of her books, *Maurice Guest*. The film was called *Rhapsody*, starring Elizabeth Taylor and Vittorio Gassman. It failed commercially and was described by Bruce Beresford, director of the film *The Getting of Wisdom*, as a "stinker".

Having completed my account of Richardson's life, it is time to address two remaining questions: First, what sort of person was she; and second, what was her place in Australian literary history?

On the first question, the main personal characteristics of Richardson that stand out to me is her seriousness. The last two words you would ever use to describe her are lighthearted or frivolous. She knew what she wanted, and set out methodically to achieve it. She had firm views about what constituted good literature and little tolerance for works of a lower standard. She put a huge amount of time and effort into each book she wrote, her preparation was meticulous and her drafts constantly revised. Richardson was not prepared to compromise, cut corners or seek popularity. A different slant on this is given by another of her biographers, Dorothy Green, who wrote:

> For a writer relieved of the duties of supporting herself, of housekeeping and child rearing, so favoured as to be able to devote her whole time to her work for close to fifty years, the results are meagre in quantity, whatever they may be in quality. As she said herself, she was 'a miserably unproductive writer'.

Richardson's judgement of herself in the last sentence is a bit harsh. Her modest output was not due to inefficiency or laziness, rather it was the result of the type of novel she set out to write. It was not possible to adopt her approach and expect to produce a large output. Of course, an important reason she was able to adopt this uncompromising approach was that she did not have to rely on the sales of her books to support herself. In any event, I don't think a writer needs to apologise for producing only six novels if they are of a high enough quality.

Richardson seems to have been a very private person. There is no element of self-promotion in her make up. In the competitive environment of London literary circles, she tended to stay on the outer. She wrote few reviews, rarely attended book launchings and cultivated almost no influential or career-enhancing friendships among London literary identities. Some describe her as a recluse. This is something of a misstatement because she did have a number of lasting friendships, but few from within her own profession. She was also loyal to her own family, particularly to her sister and nephew.

In her literary and musical tastes, she was very much a highbrow. She identified with serious modern literature, particularly from Europe, her musical tastes were exclusively classical and she loved opera, particularly Wagner. Socially she had been brought up to regard herself as a member of the gentry, and on a higher plane than the common people. This comes across in *The Fortunes of Richard Mahony* and in her memoir *Myself When Young*. Both describe how her mother hated the thought of her children ending up at a state school (which they didn't) and that she would not allow them to play with local children in the various towns in which they lived. Even when times were tough in Australia, the Richardson household could afford to employ at least one servant, usually more. Richardson's experience of a private education in Australia, followed by a grand tour to Europe and further tertiary education there, was an opportunity only available to a tiny minority of better-off Australians.

In *The Fortunes of Richard Mahony*, we are told that the family was reduced to poverty by the father's misfortunes. We must remember this is a work of fiction, and it clearly was not the case in real life. As another biographer Axel Clark makes clear, when Walter Richardson returned from the second London trip he was not ruined; the dividends continued to flow, but at a reduced rate. Nor did he die in poverty, as he left 1850 pounds in his will. This may not sound like much, but it was a lot of money when we compare it to the remuneration of 80 pounds per annum for a postmistress, or the 120 pounds per annum a lecturer at the University of Strasbourg was paid. In addition, the house they owned in Hawthorn was later sold for 4000 pounds. This allowed Mary, a canny manager of money, to provide a private education for her daughters and to support them in Europe for eight years.

Some commentary on Richardson discusses the possibility that she may have been a lesbian, but most biographers dismiss the suggestion. Evidence in support of the view is that she had a crush on another girl while at school, the fact that *Maurice Guest* touches on same-sex attraction and that, after her husband died, she lived with another woman until her death. These are not very convincing arguments. Richardson also had a crush on a young man during her school years, was happily married for 38 years, and was sixty-four and in poor health when she moved in with, and was cared for by, her close friend Olga Roncoroni.

Of course, the subject of her sexual preference should not matter. It is only relevant in Richardson's case for one reason. Everything she wrote was convincing because it was heartfelt and based closely on her own experiences. At the core of her two most important novels are loving heterosexual relationships, and it would be disappointing if we discovered that these were not also heartfelt and based on experience.

We now come to the subject of her place in Australian literature. At the outset, I have to record that I make no claim to any expertise as a literary critic, but even so, I will give my untutored view before moving on to the opinions of others more expert in the field. It is clear that her main claim to literary greatness rests on *The Fortunes of Richard Mahony*, but the trilogy is not an easy read. It is very long and, for the most part, very gloomy, containing three important death scenes. It could more accurately be called the 'misfortunes' of Richard Mahony. I admired many aspects of the work, particularly her skill in handling a multitude of characters, her mastery of dialogue and the subtlety of her observations in drawing the contrast between England and colonial Australia, but it was still hard work to get to the end. At a conference I attended in 2017, one of Richardson's biographers, Professor Michael Ackland, confided that he could not put *The Fortunes of Richard Mahony* on his prescribed reading list for his Australian literature students because they would not get through it.

The majority view among Australian literary scholars is much more positive than mine (and presumably than Professor Ackland's students would be). In fact, Richardson is clearly counted among the literary greats. To get some idea of her place in Australian literary history I consulted *The Oxford Companion to Australian Literature* and *The Cambridge History of Australian Literature*. These two large volumes each contain a collection of essays by leading Australian literary academics covering the full range of Australian authors. The number of times an author is cited gives a reasonable measure of their literary reputation. In my survey, the top five in order were Henry Lawson, Patrick White, Katherine Susannah Pritchard, Henry Handel Richardson and Miles Franklin. Another indication of her place in Australian literary history are the astonishing nine biographies of Richardson: Nettie Palmer (1950), Edna Purdie and Olga Roncoroni (1957), Vincent Buckley (1961), Leonie Kramer (1967), William Elliot (1975), Karen McLeod (1985), Dorothy Green (1986), Axel Clark (1990 and 2001), Catherine Pratt (1999), and Michael Ackland (2004). Ackland's bibliography also cites 77 articles on Richardson or her books in scholarly journals, of which 21 deal specifically with *The Fortunes of Richard Mahony* and seven with *The Getting of Wisdom*.

Richardson's extremely high reputation is not diminished by two very unusual aspects of her major work. First, although it is a work of fiction, it is based heavily on the factual history of one man's life. This has led a number of critics to claim that Richardson was deficient as an imaginative novelist, and too much a chronicler of facts. There is some merit in this argument, but we shouldn't underestimate the purely fictional aspects of the work. For example, Richard Mahoney was portrayed as an introspective outsider, whereas the real Walter Richardson was much more an outgoing public figure and a joiner of clubs and societies. The main character in the book is much more a depiction of the author than of her father.

It is time to reveal that the descent into insanity of Walter Richardson was in fact the result of tertiary syphilis. Even in his own time, it was widely suspected that GPI was the third stage of syphilis, and this was medically proven in 1913. Walter Richardson, with his medical training, would probably have suspected he had tertiary syphilis, and his novelist daughter would have known it when she wrote her major work.

The second unusual aspect of the work is that, although it is set in Australia with Australian characters, it is not in the tradition of Australian literature in any way. Three quotes from different literary critics bear this out.

Robert Dixon wrote:

> *Richard Mahony* is often regarded as 'the great Australian novel' yet as Probyn and Steele [two academic writers] observe 'Richardson herself had little patience with or interest in such an accolade, and … saw her trilogy as a contribution to … a distinctly European genre of novel writing'.

Karen McLeod wrote:

> She has no idea of Australia which she is concerned to uphold,

and when she was writing her books she had read virtually no earlier Australian literature. From an English point of view, she might as well be called a German writer ... Her literary roots were in Europe, and even in *The Fortunes of Richard Mahony*, that is where they continued to be.

While Dorothy Green emphasised the point:

> As far as the philosophic content of Richardson's novels is concerned, it is the Germanic strain in her work which is of primary importance, together with the influence of Jacobson.

I chose to include Richardson in my collection of biographical essays because she was born in colonial Australia, yet went on to become a successful expatriate author in the twentieth century – a sort of forerunner to Christina Stead, Alan Moorehead, Clive James, Germaine Greer, Robert Hughes, or, more recently, Peter Carey. I knew little about her before I started to write, although we have a copy of *Australia Felix* in our bookshelves courtesy of the Victorian Education Department, which made it prescribed reading for English Literature students when my wife sat the Victorian matriculation exam many years ago. My informal enquiries indicate that Richardson is not well known by the general public, although there is a Henry Handel Richardson Society and, as we have seen, she is extensively studied by the Australian academic literary community.

What makes Richardson unusual among Australian literary figures is that her major work, which some have called 'the great Australian novel' was written over a period of 20 years, all of which were spent in England. Even more unusual is that she regarded her writing as being in the European literary tradition, not the Australian. Despite these idiosyncrasies, her writing has endured: *Maurice Guest*, *The Getting of Wisdom* and *The Fortunes of Richard Mahony* – half of her novels – are still in print 70 years after her death. How many authors have achieved this feat?

Portrait of Giblin on his retirement by William Dobell

6
LYNDHURST FALKINER GIBLIN

Sportsman, Prospector, Politician, Soldier and Scholar

Lyndhurst Falkiner Giblin probably takes the prize for having excelled at more activities than anyone else in this book. After schooling in Australia and university in England, he went on to become an international sportsman, a gold prospector, a seaman, a farmer, a politician, a soldier – and several more occupations that defy easy description. He did not find the occupation in which he became Australia's best-known practitioner until his mid-forties. Unlike the others in this book, he did most of his travelling in the first half of his life, before returning home and making his contribution to Australia.

Giblin became an important adviser to the federal government from his base as professor of economics at Melbourne University. He was widely admired by both sides of politics for his sound judgement, even if at first they were puzzled by his eccentric appearance and lifestyle. He also concealed a dark secret that previous writers have hinted at, but I have been compelled to confront.

He came from an old Tasmanian family, his great grandfather having arrived from England in 1827 at a time when Tasmania accounted for a third of Australia's population. Giblin's father, William Robert Giblin, was the first in the family to achieve a measure of fame. Starting from humble beginnings, he became a barrister and later the attorney general, treasurer and then premier of Tasmania in two periods between 1878 and 1884. His political career was dedicated to the moral and social elevation of the underprivileged, and so his political sympathies were closest to those of the English Whigs and non-conformist Christians. He was a tireless worker, and died in 1887 at the age of forty-six.

Lyndhurst Falkiner Giblin was born in Hobart in November 1872, the second son in a family of four boys and three girls. While other members of the family had conventional names, he was given these two unusual, aristocratic-sounding Christian names. Lyndhurst comes from Lord Lyndhurst, who was Lord Chancellor in the Wellington and Peel governments in Britain in the first half of the nineteenth century. Quite why Giblin was named after a Tory Lord Chancellor who left office long before Giblin's birth has not been explained. The only connection I can find between Lord Lyndhurst and Tasmania is that his daughter married Sir Charles du Cane, who was Governor of Tasmania at the time of Giblin's birth. The name Falkiner comes from Giblin's paternal grandmother. I suspect that Giblin didn't much like these names because in his professional career he always referred to himself as L.F. Giblin.

Giblin attended the Hutchins School, a private school for boys that was Tasmania's pre-eminent educational institution, between 1881 and 1889. He was an excellent student and in his final year won a scholarship, which provided him with 200 pounds per year for four years to attend a British university. He enrolled at the University of

London in 1890 at the age of seventeen and studied there for three years. His course covered a wide range of subjects, but concentrated on scientific subjects including physics, mechanics, pure and applied mathematics, zoology and comparative anatomy. He left without taking a degree and it is likely that his London years were preparation for his entry into King's College Cambridge at the age of twenty. A seventeen-year-old school-leaver from Tasmania would have had little hope of being accepted by a top Cambridge College.

King's is a famous college in Cambridge, perhaps the most prestigious of them all. Giblin soon made himself at home and developed a love of the place that he retained throughout his life. At the end of his three years at Cambridge he was awarded a second-class honours degree majoring in mathematics; a good result, but not an outstanding one. He had also made a lot of friends, particularly among Cambridge literary circles, including Goldsworthy Lowes Dickinson. This was Giblin's first connection with the Bloomsbury group, that coterie of literary intellectuals and artists who originated in Cambridge, but found their home in the Bloomsbury quarter of London near the British Museum. Taking his years in London and Cambridge together, he had spent six years at university – a long period by the standards of the time – and received a very broad education that would equip him for a career as an academic, administrator or teacher.

Interestingly, in view of his later eminence in the field, Giblin did not study economics at Cambridge, nor did he have any connection with the Cambridge economics fraternity. This was a lost opportunity because Cambridge was the major seat of economic learning in the world at that time. The great figure was Alfred Marshall, whose book *Principles of Economics* remained the standard text for 50 years, and was still required reading when I studied economics in the 1960s. Ten years after Giblin, another great Cambridge economist, John Maynard Keynes, entered King's College. In later years, Giblin did reconnect with Cambridge economics and with Keynes, and with Bloomsbury.

But his major achievements at Cambridge were not academic, but sporting. He rowed for King's and played rugby for King's, for Cambridge and, most astonishingly, for England. Giblin, a product of Tasmania where Australian Rules football dominated and where rugby was barely known, became good enough at the game to play for England on three occasions. In 1896, he was part of an English team that defeated Wales 25–0, but then lost to Ireland 4–0. He played again in 1897, when England defeated Scotland 12–3. Giblin was a big man for his time, standing six-foot tall and weighing 14 stone (89 kilos). His size and strength made him an excellent forward. For much of his time at Cambridge he associated with the 'hearties', who were mainly interested in rugby, rowing and beer (he was something of a connoisseur of the local brews himself). But his lasting friendships were with men on the literary, artistic and academic side of the university. After he formally left Cambridge, he returned to visit his literary friends there whenever an opportunity arose.

Having completed his degree at the age of twenty-four, he seems to have been unsure what his next step should be. While making up his mind, he remained in England for a further 18 months, taking various teaching and tutoring jobs to earn some money, and returning to Cambridge when he could. Even though there were good career prospects open to him in England and Australia, Giblin chose a totally unexpected course – he decided to go to Canada and join the Klondike gold rush.

Gold had been discovered in Yukon Territory in Northern Canada at the junction of the Yukon and Klondike rivers. The world learned about the discovery in 1897 and the Klondike gold rush commenced. Giblin, together with an Australian-born, English-educated friend from Cambridge, Martin Grainger, joined the gold rush, travelling by cattle boat to Wrangell, Alaska, a common starting point to the Klondike. Gold rushes are events where it is important to arrive early and stake a claim, as there is very little left for the latecomers. Unfortunately, Giblin and Grainger were latecomers as they did not arrive on the scene until the spring of 1898.

They realised there was no point in going north into Yukon Territory, so instead they travelled north-east along the Stikine river into Cassiar country in northern British Columbia. This had been the site of an earlier gold rush, and they thought their chances were better there than in the Klondike. Although they staked a claim and attempted to work it, they did not find any gold and soon ran out of money. They needed to find enough money to live on and provide supplies to get them through the harsh winter when no work was possible. They found jobs working for the Hudson Bay Company, rowing a supply boat 280 kilometres up and down the Dease River. This was very hard work as it had to be completed before the river froze over. They then spent the winter staying in a log cabin and supplemented their food supplies by hunting moose.

Although Giblin and Grainger survived the winter in good shape, many other miners did not. The government of British Columbia became aware that a number of miners in isolated log cabins were snowed in and starving, many of whom were suffering from scurvy. Giblin and Grainger joined a search party organised by the government to rescue the miners. Travelling by dog teams over frozen lakes, they brought them back to safety. When the leader of the rescue party was injured, Giblin took over his role. This was hazardous work, and again they relied on hunting success for food supplies.

The one and a half years that Giblin spent in Canada on this occasion is described in detail in an essay by the Canadian Charles Camsell, who worked with Giblin at the time. It is one of the essays in the book of tributes, *Giblin: the Scholar and the Man*, edited by Sir Douglas Copland and published in 1960, ten years after Giblin's death. The experience demonstrated Giblin's physical toughness, bravery and capacity for leadership, but he had not achieved what he set out to do, which was to find gold, and so he decided to return to Australia. The only way he could do this was to work his way back on a ship, which he did, qualifying as an able seaman in the process. He arrived in Tasmania in early 1900 at the age of twenty-seven, but his stay was brief, probably only a few months.

Giblin then entered a period of his life where records are scarce. There is no full-length biography of Giblin, but we can follow most of his life from two useful published sources, plus surviving letters. The first is the book of tributes to him mentioned above, and the second is a more recent book written by three economists – William Coleman, Selwyn Cornish and Alf Hagger – called *Giblin's Platoon*, which covers the contributions that four Tasmanian economists, led by Giblin, made to the growth of Australian economics. But the published material is of little help in understanding the period between 1900, when he briefly returned to Australia, and 1909 when he first ran for parliament in Tasmania. Fortunately, the surviving letters to his sister Edith allow us to piece together the main outlines, if not the exact dates.

By April 1900, he was on a ship back to Canada to re-join Grainger and to continue to look for gold in British Columbia. This episode lasted for three and a half years, and was a much more serious attempt to establish a commercially viable gold mine than the earlier attempt. Unfortunately, we do not have a firsthand account of it as we do of the earlier episode, so it has been ignored in the published material. But eight letters to his sister, mainly sent from Thibaut Creek, British Columbia, survive from this period and they show how slow and difficult the process was. At one stage they attempted to sell the mine and there is even an account in one letter of Giblin becoming bankrupt.

> I am engaged in that doubtful process – the repudiation of debt. Now that winter is coming to its end, I file my schedule. And with this sixpence in the pound make free to wipe off old debts.

I wonder how many of the politicians and government officials who later sought his economic advice knew they were dealing with a former bankrupt.

But his letters, as usual, do not give a lot of information about his own activities; they mainly cover his views on books, music and cooking, plus discussions of family developments back home in Tasmania. We do not, for example, find out how much, if any, gold he found. In fact, we learn more about his reading than his mining, including the fact that he is able to read old editions of *The Times* of London, several of which contain what he calls "Morrison's account of the Peking business". This refers to the Boxer Rebellion and the siege of the Legation, and is one of the only two occurrences I have found where one of this book's subjects refers to another.

At the beginning of 1904 he finally gave up on Canada, but instead of returning home, Giblin returned to London. The one surviving letter from him in this period shows that he still had some Canadian mining matters to clear up, but his main interest, as told to his sister, was in literary affairs. He spent a lot of time searching for rare books and met with literary luminaries such as Hilaire Belloc and Edward Garnett. But it was with the latter's young son, David, better known as 'Bunny' Garnett, who later became a member of the Bloomsbury group, that Giblin formed the closest bond. He also met Joseph Conrad by accident in a park. But we know from other information that there was something else that occupied his time, and again we find his life taking a totally unexpected direction.

He had become absorbed in the practice of Jiu-Jitsu, the ancient Japanese martial art that is now mainly known by its offshoot, Judo. He practised it with two Japanese experts, and together they established a school in London to train others. In his 1953 memoir, *The Golden Echo*, Bunny Garnett reflected:

> They fitted up a gymnasium in the basement of a house in Gordon Square, where they gave lessons and held exhibitions. At the latter, Giblin sometimes took the part of the heavy man who could be thrown and reduced to helplessness by a Japanese half of his weight.

Gordon Square in Bloomsbury, incidentally, was the central living and meeting place of the Bloomsbury group.

His interest in Jiu-Jitsu resulted in a book, *The Game of Jiu-Jitsu*, written by Taro Miyake and Yakio Tani, edited by L.F. Giblin and published by Hazell, Watson and Viney. This, his first published work, was not released until 1906, although it was probably written in 1904 or early 1905.

The next episode in his life followed shortly after. There is a letter written by Giblin in May 1905 from a boat near Samarai in British New Guinea, but it does not say what he is doing there. Fortunately, we know from another source what it was. Professor Earp, in the Copland volume says:

> Giblin, in 1904 I think, on a visit to England heard from me that Lord Stanmore wanted a man to take charge of a coconut plantation in the Solomon Islands, a dangerous job, since the natives in those days were notoriously ferocious. Giblin took the

job and seems to have had no difficulty with the natives, but a virulent local fever forced him after a year or two to go home.

Other sources said he went home after a few months. Whatever the details, I think that sometime around 1906, Giblin finally returned to Tasmania and started the process of settling down.

He had been away from Australia, apart from one brief return visit, for 16 years, and had done many different things. But his life had been directionless; there had been no logical connection between one episode and the next. He was thirty-three years old and had very little to show for it. We know that he was healthy, strong, well-educated and that he had a wide variety of interests, mainly in the arts. He loved literature and his best friend in England was the novelist and poet E.V. Lucas. As well as enjoying the established writers of his day such as Meredith, Borrow, James, Stevenson and Kipling, he was impressed with the up-and-coming E.M. Forster, and had a special interest in the Icelandic Sagas. He was also fond of music and live theatre, and he liked hiking, cricket, sailing and cooking. Copland, who knew him well, wrote: "He was particularly devoted to young people of the 'teenager vintage', and had the best knowledge of books for the 'teenager' of any man I had ever met." Professor Earp wrote that "Throughout his life he [Giblin] took an affectionate and eager interest in the progress and happiness of younger people, men and boys alike. Often, for example, he had the sons of friends and relatives stay with him." He was a very distinctive individual – complex and non-conforming from early on, if not yet an eccentric.

But even though he had settled down, it would still be another 15 years before he finally found the calling for which he is now recognised, so we must follow his progress year by year. Now back in Tasmania, Giblin did a very Tasmanian thing – he established an apple orchard, which he retained for the rest of his life. He also returned to teaching in order to earn his living, and he spent much of his spare time hiking in the Tasmanian wilderness. These activities might have been enough to keep most people satisfied, but not Giblin. He needed more, so he turned to politics.

Tasmanian politics at the time was dominated by two major parties: the Conservative Party, which was in office, and the Labor Party in opposition. There was a small party in the middle called the Liberal–Democrat Party, and this was the one that Giblin joined. He stood as a candidate in the 1909 election, but was easily defeated, as were other Liberal–Democrat candidates, and the party was largely disbanded. If he was to get anywhere in Tasmanian politics, he would have to choose one of the major parties, so he chose the Labor Party.

This was not surprising as Giblin had no Tory instincts and had spent a lot of time among working men as their equal. At times he described himself as a socialist, but never defined what that meant. He even grew a beard, which he referred to as his "socialist beard". But he was not a typical Labor man in other respects. For example, his main preoccupation was his opposition to government borrowing and spending on unproductive capital works. Also, in 1909 he had joined the Army Intelligence Corps as a citizen-soldier. Placing a high priority on defence and public finance was not a mainstream Labor position.

In 1913 he stood as Labor candidate for the seat of Hobart and won. He did not get chosen for the ensuing Labor Cabinet, but was an influential adviser to the Treasurer Joseph Lyons (later prime minister of Australia when he changed to the conservative side of politics), and he was elected a member of the Federal Executive of the Labor Party. However, a promising career in politics was cut short by the outbreak of the First World War. Giblin volunteered for service in early 1916 at the age of forty-three, and so relinquished his seat in parliament at the 1916 election.

We tend to think that willingness to volunteer for the First World War was something that nationalist, patriotic and politically conservative men did enthusiastically, but Labor men less so. But there were plenty of volunteers from Labor ranks, and it was a Labor prime minister, Andrew Fisher, who proclaimed that we would stand beside the mother country "to the last man and the last shilling". And it was another Labor prime minister, Billy Hughes, who was the chief advocate for conscription. Ted Larkin, a promising Labor member of the New South Wales parliament and well-known sportsman, volunteered the day war was declared, even though he was married with two children (he was killed on the first day of the Gallipoli landing).

Because of his age, position and education, Giblin could easily have been given a staff position away from the front line, but he chose to join a normal line unit – the 40th Battalion of the Third Division, comprised entirely of Tasmanians. They reached England in the summer of 1916 and first went into battle near Armentieres in April 1917, in which Giblin was wounded. Soon after, he returned to the front in the Battle of Messines in June, where he was shot through the thigh while leading his troops in an assault. He was awarded the Military Cross for bravery and sent back to England for medical attention.

After recuperating and a fortnight's leave, he was back in Belgium in September for the Third Battle of Ypres, and took part in the infamous Passchendaele campaign, where most of his battalion were killed or wounded. Only 100 out of the original 600 men were able to march back to safety.

In 1918 he was granted three weeks' leave in England, and in July he married Eilean Burton, who at thirty-three was 12 years younger than him. They had probably met briefly before the war when she spent some time in Tasmania, and were reunited in England during the war. Eilean Burton was an unconventional and determined woman, who is the subject of a recent biography, *Eilean Giblin: a feminist between the wars* by Patricia Clarke. Although coming from an affluent family and possessing a private income, she considered herself a socialist and a feminist, was a trained carpenter, and was quite eccentric in her dress. The marriage between these two very unconventional people lasted the distance, although they were frequently apart and there were no children.

Soon Giblin was back in France to take part in the great offensive of 8 August 1918, which Ludendorff described as "Germany's blackest day". In a night attack in late August during the Battle of Bapaume, Giblin was wounded for the third time and sent back to England, and so took no further part in hostilities.

By the war's end, he had been promoted to major and had won a Distinguished Service Order to go with his Military Cross. In the terminology of the time, he had had a "good war" in that he had survived, been promoted and twice decorated, but it had been a close-run thing; most of his battalion did not return and he had been wounded three times. Giblin was an unusual officer; no one could accuse him of being an enthusiast or a jingo; he regarded the whole thing as an unfortunate necessity, and he was a strong opponent of conscription. In an Anzac Day speech to schoolchildren after the war he said:

> It is an appalling wastage. Our 60,000 dead were nearly one

in five of our young men between twenty and thirty who were of a decent standard of health and strength. The permanently disabled make another two of every five. The damage to our manpower for any useful purpose is very grave, and the loss is greater than the numbers.

Interesting examples of Giblin's complex character were shown during his several interludes in England during the war. In 1917, while recovering from injuries sustained in the Battle of Messines, he paid a visit to Charleston, a house occupied by the Bloomsbury *ménage à trois* of Bunny Garnett, Duncan Grant and Vanessa Bell. Garnett and Grant were conscientious objectors required to perform agricultural labour, and Giblin wanted to see how they were getting on. It shows another side of Giblin's character that this big, strong outdoor man who had been a miner, a lumberjack, a footballer and a seaman would have anything in common with these sheltered aesthetes, but he did. Even more surprising is that this battle-hardened officer should show such interest in the welfare of two conscientious objectors. In a later visit in 1918, accompanied by Eilean, Giblin met them again and this time succeeded in his objective of meeting John Maynard Keynes, who was staying with them at the time.

Giblin's military service did not end with the Armistice on 11 November 1918 because there was still the massive task of getting the troops home. He stayed in France until July 1919 supervising the departures, which had been delayed because there were not enough ships available for such a large-scale operation.

In December 1919, at the age of forty-seven, Giblin was appointed government statistician for Tasmania. From today's perspective, it seems strange to appoint him to head an agency for which he had no professional training or previous experience. At this time he described himself in *Who's Who* as "miner, boatman, teamster, sailor, cook, lumberman, schoolmaster, fruit-grower, labour agitator, soldier, member of parliament." But by then, he was an important man in Tasmania; a returned war hero with a Cambridge mathematical education, a former member of parliament, and no doubt politically well connected.

An alternative question is why Giblin was happy to take a job that, at first sight, seems safe, sedentary, unexciting and out of character with his life to that point? One explanation is that he was evidently becoming interested in economics. His desire to meet Keynes when in England is evidence of this, as is one of his letters from France in which he reported reading a book called *The Purchasing Power of Money* by Irving Fisher. As well, the role of statistician was a very important one at that time; they were not just compilers of statistics, but were often called upon to be the chief economic adviser to the government. Until the 1930s, the Australian Government did not employ economists; the Treasury was staffed by accountants and the central bank by commercial bankers. If a government, state or federal, wanted economic advice, it turned either to its statistician or to one of the professors of economics in the universities (of whom there were only about half a dozen). So being government statistician, even of a state as small as Tasmania, did open up interesting challenges as well as opportunities.

Giblin's first major task was to prepare the Tasmanian case in negotiations concerning federal state financial arrangements. By the time he took up his role as state statistician, Tasmania accounted for only five per cent of Australia's population, compared with the more than 30 per cent when his great grandfather had arrived in 1827. It was not that Tasmania had not grown, but that it had grown so much slower than the mainland. Tasmania's income per head was also lower than the Australian average, and it expected to receive extra funds to compensate for this disadvantage. The Federal Government collected all tariff and excise revenue, which it then distributed to the states in a way that was supposed to take account of their respective needs. It is not surprising that Tasmania had a keen interest in these negotiations, or that Giblin went to such lengths to plead their case, but he did a lot more than that. Over the course of the 1920s, in a number of papers, he developed a criterion for distributing the revenue on the basis of what he called the state's taxable capacity, or what is now called the principle of fiscal equalisation.

It is not necessary to go into the details of this system, or to examine the body of statistical evidence that supports it, other than to say that it gradually supplanted the earlier methods that had been tried. By the mid-1930s it was the established method of dividing federal revenue among the states, and is still in use today. Also, in 1926 Giblin first proposed the establishment of an independent body of three commissioners to carry out the necessary calculations and provide a recommendation to parliament. In 1933 the Commonwealth Grants Commission was established by the federal government, led by Prime Minister Joseph Lyons, by now on the conservative side of politics as leader of the United Australia Party. Giblin was appointed as one of the three founding members. It was essentially the same structure that Giblin first outlined in 1926. If Giblin had achieved nothing else in his career, the establishment of the Commission and its use of the fiscal equalisation criterion for distributing Commonwealth grants to the states, would be enough to give him an honoured place in the history of Australian economics and public administration.

The other economic issue that exercised Giblin's mind in the 1920s was the level of the Australian tariff on imports. Australia had a high level of tariff protection at this time, and Prime Minister Bruce thought it might be too high or increasing too fast. While not an advocate of free trade, he and many others were conscious of the indirect costs imposed on the economy by high tariffs. There is no doubt that placing a tariff on a particular industry allows it to increase its price and profitability, but it also increases prices to consumers, and if other industries use its product as an input, it reduces their own profitability. It is a major task to measure and compare the benefit to the industry receiving the tariff with the cost to consumers and other industries.

In 1927, the government gave a group of five economists this task; Giblin and another Tasmanian economist, Professor Brigden, were the main authors of the ensuing report. The report, called *The Australian Tariff: An Economic Inquiry*, was published in 1929 and caused a lot of controversy in economic and political circles in Australia, and received some attention overseas. It is chiefly remembered today for advancing what became known as the 'Australian argument' for tariff protection. This argument does not claim that the structure of the Australian tariff improves the level of national output, but that it improves the distribution of income.

Giblin's interest in economics was essentially practical and determined by the issues facing the Australian economy at the time. He had little interest in theory, and none in publishing learned papers for their own sake. So it was something of a surprise when he was offered a chair at Melbourne University. It was not just an ordinary chair, but an endowed research chair, the only one of that type in Australia – the Ritchie Professorship in Economics.

So in 1929 at the age of fifty-seven, Giblin moved from his beloved Tasmania to Melbourne University, whose academics were at first taken aback by his strange presence. His appearance is well summarised in the *Australian Dictionary of Biography* entry by Neville Cain, who describes him thus:

A large sagging figure of quiet presence, the head close cropped, the cheeks high, the attire eccentric – homespun trousers and jacket, improvised tie, stout boots dubbined rather than polished – and the mouth clamping an ancient pipe.

(For the benefit of the 90 per cent of the population who, like me, didn't know what the word 'dubbined' meant, it refers to the practice of rubbing animal fat into your boots to keep the leather supple and waterproof.) Giblin also made a practice of cutting the lapels off his suits because he thought they were an unnecessary affectation. All accounts of him describe his appearance as unconventional, strange or eccentric.

Giblin's inaugural lecture at Melbourne University, when printed, became his best-known claim to fame as an economist. In it he presented his version of the economic concept known as the 'multiplier', nearly two years earlier than the version published by R.F. Kahn, a protégé of Keynes, which became an important part of Keynes's *General Theory of Employment, Interest and Money*. Giblin looked at the case where there was a large reduction in the price of rural exports, which led to an equal reduction in farmers' income, but that was not the end of the story. In the next round, farmers reduced their spending, and this reduced the income of those supplying farmers, who in turn reduced their spending and so it went on. But it didn't go on indefinitely; the size of the multiplier could be calculated as the sum of a geometric progression whose size depended on how much of the change in income was saved, spent on imports, or taxed.

There is no suggestion that Kahn or Keynes copied the idea from Giblin, and there are several other economists who have a claim to having independently discovered the concept in one form or another. But Giblin's analysis was original and important.

Giblin settled into the final stage of his life as a professor and government adviser just as the Great Depression was starting. Although it occupied much of his time and energy during the 1930s, I do not propose to delve deeply into it. Giblin was closely involved with several proposals aimed at countering the Depression and returning the country to prosperity, the best-known of which was the Premiers' Plan. With the benefit of hindsight, this plan and the various others put forward would have to be judged as contractionary and not very helpful. The most that could be said was that some plans were less harmful than others. Giblin, at least, was aware of the danger of contraction, and was prepared to partially offset these contractionary effects with a depreciation of the currency and with some monetary expansion.

The most contractionary proposal was the one put forward by Sir Otto Niemeyer. It is another reminder of how Australia still looked to Britain for help, that early in the Depression the Scullin Labor government turned to Niemeyer, the Deputy Governor of the Bank of England, for advice. His advice was to balance the budget by expenditure reductions and tax increases, maintain the parity of the Australian pound and avoid monetary expansion. This was about as contractionary as you could get, but it was taken seriously by the government, and Niemeyer's prestige and position were used against those economists whose proposals contained expansionary elements, such as Giblin and Copland.

Giblin was by now a very busy and influential man nearing the end of a successful career. As well as occupying the best chair of economics in the country, he was a member of the Commonwealth Grants Commission and a board member of the Commonwealth Bank, which was the central bank as well as a commercial bank. But before his retirement, he had one more pleasant task to complete – a sabbatical in 1938. It is no surprise that he chose King's College Cambridge for this purpose.

Giblin was welcomed back, appointed a Supernumerary Fellow of King's College and housed in Keynes's rooms. He resumed contact with Keynes, who was recuperating at his farm from a heart attack. He also looked up other old friends with varying degrees of success; he spent a week with Garnett, but E.M. Forster, despite his close association with King's, where he was later made a Fellow, did not set foot in Cambridge during Giblin's stay.

Giblin returned to Australia and shortly after retired from Melbourne University in 1939. But this was not the end of his career as an economic adviser. The Second World War had started, and at the age of sixty-six he was appointed chairman of a new body – the Financial and Economic Committee. This was a small think tank within Treasury set up to advise Cabinet on economic matters connected with the war. It consisted of Giblin, Roland Wilson, Leslie Melville, Douglas Copland, James Brigden and H.C. Coombs; it was the 'Brains Trust' of Australian economics.

When the war ended, Giblin's final task was to write a book on the history of central banking in Australia. This was the only book he wrote on economics, and he completed it while living in Sydney for three years while his wife remained in Hobart. But he was in failing health due to the onset of bowel cancer and he died in February 1951 at the age of seventy-eight. Tributes flowed from all those who knew him in economic, academic and government circles in Australia and, of course, King's College Cambridge.

Giblin had led a varied, adventurous and ultimately successful life, but he was still something of an enigma. Although widely admired and respected, I wonder how many friends and colleagues really understood his complex character. To my mind, he was really three different people, the first two well documented, the third merely hinted at.

The first side of Giblin's character was the one for which he is best known – the thoughtful, practical and wise economic policy adviser that he became in his mature years. Although not very academic in his approach, he had sufficient command of his subject to make several important advances to our understanding of the Australian economy. He impressed the people around him with his calm and constructive approach. Economists looked up to him, and non-economists also appreciated his qualities. Sir Paul Hasluck, later foreign minister and governor-general, recalled it was a privilege to work "close to this great Australian, sagacious, humorous, kindly to persons, devastating to humbug".

The second side of Giblin's character was the tough outdoors man – the footballer, lumberjack, miner, seaman and soldier. He was physically strong and tough enough to endure the most difficult circumstances. Camsell relates that in Canada, Giblin often went out in the coldest conditions that the Canadians avoided, to show that he could take it. He also made some very hazardous trips that could easily have ended in disaster. His bravery was shown again in the war. His period in action was only from April 1917 to August 1918, yet he managed to get himself shot three times in separate operations. He clearly must have been one of those officers who believed in leading from the front; majors don't normally have to do that. Both in Canada and in the war, it is almost as though he liked putting himself in life-threatening situations.

The third aspect of Giblin's complex character is harder to come to grips with because it seems so incongruous. It is the one that the two published works about him have tiptoed around, dropping various hints, but not clearly enunciating their views. This is also, to some extent, true of Patricia Clarke's biography of his wife. I had no idea of this side of Giblin when I started this essay. As my understanding increased, I then had to decide whether I would confront the issue explicitly, or be content with gentle hints as my predecessors were. I decided not to censor myself; I hope this was the right decision.

It is clear that Giblin was strongly attracted to boys and young men and the literature about boyhood. This is something he had in common with some of his literary friends in King's College and Bloomsbury. It is also why he made the effort to keep up these friendships, and why he sought to connect with E.M. Forster. Today, his obsession with boys would be seen as a form of pederasty. Whether it ever took physical form we will probably never know. I am inclined to give him the benefit of the doubt on the grounds that some of the men he was close to when they were boys continued to be his friend and admirer when they reached adulthood.

Coleman et al. leave this question up in the air. They include a footnote early in their book pointing out that Giblin's friend

> Lowes Dickinson is most remembered today for his early apologia for homosexuality which included the words "For those who like young men, Cambridge, especially King's, is ideal". Throughout his life Giblin did, literally, like young men. The extent to which he liked them in the more specific Dickinsonian sense is little more than conjecture.

The same authors also reinforce the point made by Copland about Giblin's interest in children's stories. They report that a journalist from the *Bulletin*, interviewing Giblin's wife after his death, recorded the "extraordinary number of children's books that Giblin owned, the most numerous being titles by Arthur Ransome, the author of boys' school holiday adventures that were first published when Giblin was aged fifty-eight."

For most of his life Giblin showed no romantic interest in women, although he did marry at forty-five. But the marriage was an unusual one in that they spent more time apart than together. Patricia Clarke, who closely analysed their letters concluded that "it appears a union between two compatible people, considerate and adaptive towards each other, but with no indication of intimacy or endearment".

In the Copland volume there is an interesting essay by Professor Richard Downing, Giblin's protégé, successor in the Ritchie chair and ardent admirer. Everything in the essay extolls Giblin's virtues to an almost fulsome extent, but at the end of the chapter Downing chose to include the full text of a letter Giblin wrote to E.M. Forster, but never posted. It is a rather embarrassing fan letter, and one hinting at a shared but secret interest. It adds nothing to Giblin's reputation. You wonder why Giblin wrote it in the first place. Having not posted it, you wonder why he kept it, and finally you wonder why an admirer such as Downing chose to have it published. I have come to the conclusion that it was Downing's not very subtle way of revealing the third side of Giblin's character. The letter reads:

> Dear Morgan Forster
>
> This impertinence springs from your Henry Thornton article, which like all you write nestles in my mind as very little contemporary stuff does. It's a queer family in which you are for me a member – the sagas, Hamlet and the sonnets, some of Miss Austen, and a good deal of Meredith, the later Beethoven and 4th Symphony of Sibelius.
>
> You may have heard my name. I spent most of last spring and

summer at King's; they very amiably made me a supernumerary fellow. In visiting England and Cambridge, I had rather counted on meeting you, and Wedd was confident you would be sometime in Cambridge. In default, I even thought of invading your Surrey fastness, but a sense of decency was reinforced by lack of time at the last. Still I would like to tell you baldly – and leave it at that – how pre-eminently you have been my refreshment these last thirty years.

There is another contemporary who gets home a good deal on a narrower field – Forrest Reid, and it was in your *Abinger Harvest* that I first found anyone else who seemed really to care about his work and think it important. (I have since found traces of another. Last spring I was housed for a few days at All Souls in a man's rooms lined to the limit with books, and by chance – half instinct, one likes to think, hit immediately on a complete collection of Forrest Reid. Most were now out of print. He even had one more than I had, which of course I read before sleeping.)

That's all and more than enough. It is in fact my first offence of this kind in 66 years. Call it dotage. It will harmonise with second childhood if I adopt the small boy's friendly ending –

Love,

L .F. Giblin

Apart from the embarrassing way of signing off, the third paragraph is the most telling. Forrest Reid was a friend of E.M. Forster and, although he is hardly known today, all references to him that I could find make a similar point, which is best summarised by Professor Paul Goldman of Cardiff University as "His fiction essentially deals with nostalgia, memory, dream and the internal world of the young male adolescent, and for this last feature he has become somewhat pigeon-holed as a gay writer". Incidentally, further evidence that Downing wanted people to understand this aspect of Giblin's character came to light in 1975. By this time Downing was the chairman of the ABC, when he made a very controversial public defence of the ABC's decision to broadcast a program where three pederasts set out their views without any censure.

I could have included more evidence of Giblin's great interest in boys, but I don't want to labour the point. I suspect that Giblin's friends and colleagues knew about this aspect of his character, but did not think it important. Contrary to modern opinion, there was quite widespread tolerance in intellectual and artistic circles to differences in sexual preferences, even apparently extending to those whose main interest was in boys and youths. The predominant view would have been – why should we hold this against such an outstanding man, loyal friend and wise counsellor?

In concluding my assessment of Giblin, I have to return to his remarkable versatility. He was a good enough mathematician to graduate from Cambridge, good enough a sportsman to represent England at rugby, good enough at politics to get elected to parliament, good enough a soldier to get promoted to major and twice decorated for bravery, and good enough at economics to be appointed to the best chair in Australia. He was probably also quite a good farmer, seaman and teacher. The one thing that he achieved little success at was gold prospecting. But it took this complex man forty-seven years to work out what he really wanted to do, and even then the decision was made for him by the Tasmanian government's offer. He then spent the next 30 years making a very valuable contribution to Australia's economic development and, in so doing, reached the top of his profession. Even in an era where the gifted amateur was more valued than today, his achievement was remarkable. He was the most important economist in Australia in the three decades from 1920 to 1950, and the one whom governments were first to approach for advice. He was looked up to by his peers, and even the ambitious Copland regarded him as the natural leader of the profession.

Giblin makes an appearance in each of the three volumes of Garnett's autobiography. In the last volume, *The Familiar Faces*, Garnett says of Giblin:

> He stayed a week with us at Hilton. It was my closest and longest contact with a man I had loved and admired since I was four years old and who was the most splendidly all-round man I have ever known.

Another of his qualities was his modesty and lack of interest in badges of honour or worldly success. He was unconcerned that some people were put off by his eccentric appearance. Also, it must be assumed that he rejected the honours that would have been offered to him. His colleagues and followers such as Copland, Wilson and Melville were knighted, so it is likely that the same honour was available to him if he wanted it. But he did not miss out on recognition altogether. In his later years, his colleagues contributed to a fund to have his portrait painted by William Dobell, which now hangs in Melbourne University. After his death, he received further acknowledgement in the book of tributes edited by Copland and in the naming of Giblin Street and Giblin Place in Canberra, plus the Giblin libraries at the Universities of Melbourne and Tasmania. In 1958, the annual Giblin Lecture was instituted, which brings me to my only connection with him in that I delivered the 2001 Giblin Lecture.

John Peter Russell self portrait 1886/87. Musée d'Orsay, Paris/Musée de Morlaix

7

JOHN PETER RUSSELL
Artist and Engineer

I first became aware of John Peter Russell about 50 years ago during my youthful enthusiasm for art. He was known for his close association with the French impressionists, and was reputed to have offered his collection of French impressionist paintings to one of Australia's state galleries, but was turned down by a philistine director. The first of these claims is true, but fortunately the second is not.

After leaving Australia, Russell spent most of his adult life in France, first in Paris, then in Brittany. He was one of the few people who formed an easy friendship with the intense and difficult Vincent Van Gogh. He was also close to Rodin and Matisse, and met with some of the impressionists, including Monet. Being independently wealthy, he was able to lead a glamorous life in Paris before moving to Brittany. Although he took his painting seriously, he did little to promote himself and exhibited rarely. His reputation as an artist and the prices of his paintings have risen appreciably since his death.

Russell's grandfather, who was an engineer in Scotland, migrated to Australia in 1830. Two of his sons – John and Peter – followed the family tradition and, in time, they established a successful engineering business in Sydney that became the foundation of the family fortune. The business manufactured everything from cast-iron building decoration in Sydney to railway bridges, rolling stock, and even a gunboat for use in the Maori Wars. The brothers were very different. Peter was an outstanding engineer and businessman, and was the real founder of the firm. John was more interested in sailing and adventure. He spent 12 years as a trader in the South Pacific, China and Japan before returning to Sydney in 1855 to join his brother in the firm.

In the same year, John Russell married Charlotte Ann Nicholl, the daughter of an English sculptor who had migrated to Australia. They had four children, the oldest of whom was born in 1858 and named John after his father and Peter after his uncle. So as not to be confused with his father, John, he was called John Peter by his family, although in adult life he referred to himself as John Russell and signed his paintings as either John or John P. Russell. Decades after his death, when interest in his paintings increased, the organisers of his exhibitions revived the use of the name John Peter Russell in order to distinguish him from the Regency period portraitist John Russell. I will refer to him as John Peter during his upbringing and Russell for the remainder of his life.

John Russell senior was a man of strong views and expected his son to follow in his footsteps. John Peter was sent to boarding school at Goulburn, nearly 200 kilometres south of Sydney, and when he was finished his father encouraged him to spend some time, as he had, as a trader in the Pacific. Russell family reminiscences record that John

Peter then spent nearly a year on a sailing boat trading between Tahiti, China and Japan. During this time he developed a love of sailing, and the first stirring of his artistic interests began to show when he returned with a collection of Eastern artefacts, Japanese prints and two ancient Samurai swords.

The next step in John Peter's development, as decreed by his father, was for him to train as an engineer. At the time, this was best done by becoming a 'gentleman apprentice' in a leading engineering firm. At the end of 1876, aged eighteen, he moved to England and spent three years at Robey and Co. in Lincoln, emerging as a qualified engineer before returning to Australia. With his engineering background, he retained an interest in constructing things throughout his life. He was good with his hands, and later contributed to the construction of his house, made pieces of furniture and built three boats. He was a very physical, practical man like his father, but his interest in art continued to grow. Perhaps this side of his nature came from his mother and his maternal grandfather, the sculptor. In any event, he took up the genteel art of watercolour painting seriously while in England.

In Australia, the brothers' engineering firm – P.N. Russell and Co. – thrived, so much so that Peter Russell was able to retire to England and look after their affairs there. John Russell remained in Australia to manage the company, which he did with great energy and determination. But a series of strikes and other industrial action annoyed him to such an extent that he closed the company in 1876, and also retired to England with the considerable proceeds of the firm. So the two brothers, having made their fortunes in Australia, returned to England to live the life of moneyed gentlemen. This was not uncommon during the nineteenth century.

Back in Australia in 1879, John Peter received the news that his father had died in England. This not only released him from his father's control, but bequeathed him a large inheritance. In the first biography of Russell by Elizabeth Salter, *The Lost Impressionist*, she says the capital value of the inheritance was 50,000 pounds, and Ann Galbally in her biography, *The Art of John Peter Russell*, confirms this assessment by recording that it generated an annual income of between 2000 and 3000 pounds. These were enormous sums of money for the time.

At the age of twenty-two, John Peter had just about everything you could ask for. He was a tall, strong, good-looking man in excellent health and totally independent. He had no father to order him around and no dependents to support. Because of his inheritance, he never needed to work a day in his life for a wage or salary, and he never did. He didn't even have to undertake the work of investing his money: this was done by the Permanent Trustee Company, which paid a generous monthly allowance into his bank account.

He now had the choice of following what he was trained for, which was engineering, or what he was most interested in, which was painting. The decision was an easy one, and by January 1881 he was back in England and enrolled in the Slade School of Art attached to University College London. He spent the next seven years in London and then Paris training to be an artist, but his training was not continuous – there were several breaks for travel, painting tours and a return to Australia. During his time in London he and Tom Roberts, who was studying at the Royal Academy, became friends, a friendship that lasted for most of their lives. Russell made friends easily wherever he went, and kept up many of these friendships even when he was living in different countries.

After three terms at the Slade, Russell returned to Sydney for the best part of a year, suggesting that he had not yet made up his mind about where he wanted to live. While in Sydney he completed a number of paintings and showed them in the Art Society of New South Wales exhibitions in September 1882 and March 1883. In all there were over 30 paintings including portraits and landscapes, using both oils and watercolours. They were well received by local critics, but few survived, not least because all those in the first exhibition were destroyed when the gallery burned down.

Russell returned to London and re-enrolled at the Slade in early 1883. Later that year, he and Roberts and two others made a tour of Spain to paint and to see firsthand the paintings of Velasquez and Goya. One painting from Spain by Roberts was exhibited at the Royal Academy the next year, but nothing from Russell painted during that trip survives.

The biggest influence on Russell's painting during his London years was his teacher at the Slade – expatriate Frenchman Alphonse Legros. He was a painter of international standing who had exhibited widely, including at the Paris Salon in 1857, the Salon des Refuses with Pissarro, Cézanne and Manet in 1863, and at the second Impressionist Exhibition in 1876. Thus, Legros and his pupils, including Russell, would have been aware of the growing influence of impressionism.

It first acquired that name from Monet's painting of the same name in the first Impressionist Exhibition of 1874, eight years before Russell enrolled at the Slade. So we might expect a keen young painter such as Russell to quickly embrace this progressive new movement, but he didn't. That does not mean that he opted for a formal academic approach; it would be a mistake to think there were only two choices. There was already a rich artistic tradition of non-academic painting in France before impressionism arrived. Artists such as Corot, the

Barbizon School painters like Millet and Daubigny, realists like Courbet and, of course, Manet, could never be called academic, refined or polished. They chose everyday subjects, sometimes painted quickly outdoors on small canvases, and did not try to smooth out their spontaneous brushstrokes.

In Russell's London years it is very hard to classify him into any distinctive school of painting, although the best paintings from that period that survive are portraits and figure studies, not landscapes. Ann Galbally summarises it best:

> During these years in London, Russell's tastes were very much those of his peer group. He was not interested in the radical extremes of art – the exclusive aesthetes or the dedicated out-of-doors painters. He chose a middle path ... his teacher's insistence on the importance of draughtsmanship and form was to make Russell's eventual decision to adopt Impressionist colour painting such a protracted experience.

Paris, not London, was the centre of the art world, and Russell moved there in 1884 at the age of twenty-six. The three and a half years he spent in Paris were to be the most exciting, pleasurable and productive period of his life. He enrolled at the Atelier Cormon, one of several private art schools in the city. Like Legros, Fernand Cormon was neither an impressionist nor an academician, but was heavily influenced by Millet, realist co-founder of the Barbizon School. Although the students were instructed by their teacher, Cormon only attended twice a week, so they learned as much from their fellow students as from him. The best-known fellow student when Russell arrived was Henri Toulouse-Lautrec, but many others also went on to successful careers as painters.

Russell settled in easily as he was naturally gregarious, and he soon became a popular member of the school. He acquired lodgings and a studio in Montmartre near the school, which became a meeting place for his friends. Although he socialised with his artist friends, he could not be described as a bohemian. For a start, his wealth set him apart from the other artists, many of whom were living a very precarious existence. He was also as much physical as intellectual or artistic; he established a boxing club, and he rowed and sailed boats on the Seine, as well as riding his horse in the Bois de Boulogne. But he took his painting seriously, and stayed at the Atelier for three years.

In early 1885 he met the love of his life, Anna Maria Antoinetta Mattiocco, known as Marianna. She was a tall, beautiful Italian who had moved to Paris with her two musician brothers, and probably had worked as a model for Russell's sculptor friend Bates. The story that she was Rodin's favourite model at the time is apocryphal, as I will explain later. She became Russell's mistress, a term that can have many different meanings, but in this case it meant they lived together virtually as man and wife (which they later became). In November 1885 Marianna gave birth to their first child, a son called Jean Paolo.

Early in 1886, a new student arrived at the Atelier Cormon who was to become its most famous alumnus. His name was Vincent Van Gogh. After a failed career working for an art dealer, then as an evangelist, Van Gogh turned to painting. His whole career as a painter covered only ten years, the first five in his native Holland and the last five in France. Van Gogh's stay at the Atelier Cormon was also very brief – three months – and his time in Paris working with Russell was only two years, although they corresponded when they went their separate ways.

To say that Van Gogh was difficult to get on with would be an understatement. He was intense, opinionated and argumentative, especially when he had been drinking. He made a few friends, but usually the friendships did not last; he fell out with almost everyone who tried to help him. Throughout his career as an artist he was supported by his endlessly patient brother – art dealer Theo Van Gogh. Many of the students at the Atelier Cormon avoided him and some thought he was slightly mad, but Russell did not object to him and, in fact, formed a professional and personal friendship with him. Marianna, on the other hand, thought he was frightening. One thing Russell and Van Gogh had in common was that they were older than the other students – Russell was twenty-eight and Van Gogh thirty-three when they met. Another link was that they probably conversed in English, in which Van Gogh was fluent. Their later correspondence was all in English.

Van Gogh's largely self-taught and very personal style of painting was clearly not impressionist. He preferred hard outlines and bold, fluid brushstrokes, whereas the impressionists preferred the rounded, softening effects of light and small, drier brushstrokes or dabs. By the time Van Gogh arrived in 1886, impressionism was being overtaken by younger artists with their newer approaches, and this suited him.

It is clear from Van Gogh's letters to Theo that he was attracted to Russell and counted him as a friend. Stephen Naifeh and Gregory White-Smith, in their massive recent biography of Van Gogh, sum up the friendship in the following rather florid account:

> As in Antwerp, Vincent was forced to seek companionship at the margins of the class, among the handful of foreign students. Fortunately for him, the leader of this tiny band was a genial English speaker a long way from home: an Australian painter named John Peter Russell. Son of a South Seas adventurer and arms manufacturer, Russell had everything Vincent envied: money, friends, standing, and a striking blonde Italian girlfriend, Marianna. (Rodin, for whom she modelled, called her "the most beautiful woman in Paris.") ... Russell frequented fashionable

nightspots like Le Chat Noir, often driving his own horse and carriage. On weekends he promenaded in the Bois de Boulogne or sailed his yacht on the Seine ... Vincent joined the crowd drawn to Russell's easy hospitality.

Russell, accompanied by Marianna and their son, then spent the summer in Belle Île, an island 14 kilometres off the coast of Brittany. On this first visit, he loved the isolation, rugged scenery and simple peasant society so much that it became a very important part of his life. They rented a house on the rugged Atlantic coast and Russell painted, rode and sailed. On one occasion he spotted an older painter outdoors at his easel. It was none other than the foremost of all the impressionists – Claude Monet. He too was attracted to the rugged coastline of Belle Île and produced a number of paintings of it. He and Russell got on well. In a letter to his partner, Alice Hoschede, Monet wrote:

> He's nice, and in the evening we took a walk together and this evening I'm dining at his house, so I hope to eat well as he's quite well set up here and they have their own cook.

This accidental meeting with Monet, which lasted about a fortnight, is one of the few occasions I can find where Russell met with any of the great names of impressionism (the others being Pissarro, Sisley, Renoir and Degas). He did associate with several of the lesser names such as Armand Guillaumin, but most of his dealings were with younger painters who could be broadly classified under the post-impressionist label.

Russell returned to Paris in late 1886 and painted the portrait for which he is best known. It was the portrait of Van Gogh that now hangs in the Van Gogh Museum in Amsterdam. It is almost a formal portrait with the respectable-looking figure emerging from a dark background. Its most striking feature is the treatment of the eyes, which are looking sideways, hinting at something slightly sinister or disturbed. The painting was widely admired, especially by Van Gogh himself. Russell gave the portrait to him, but Van Gogh insisted on giving something of his own back in exchange. As a result, Russell acquired a lithograph of an old man and an early oil painting of three pairs of old shoes. Van Gogh was also painted by Toulouse-Lautrec and Gauguin, and he painted 20 self-portraits during his two years in Paris. Does this suggest self-obsession, or was it, as he explained, simply because he could not afford models, so he had to paint himself? Even though Van Gogh soon left the Atelier Cormon, he and Russell continued to meet on occasions during the remainder of the two years he spent in Paris.

In late 1886 and early 1887, Russell, Marianna and son headed south where they met with Marianna's parents in Italy and continued on to Sicily where Russell produced some paintings that were much admired by Van Gogh. However, tragedy struck when their infant son died, and so they returned quickly to Paris. In July 1887, a second child was born – a daughter called Jeanne Marianna. Shortly after, they returned to Belle Île for two months, this time buying a piece of land for future use. When they returned to Paris, Russell painted some landscapes that were starting to show some influence of impressionism and of his friend Van Gogh. Three scenes of the Seine, which now hang in Australian public galleries, mark his movement towards this approach.

For Russell, 1888 was an eventful year. In February, he married Marianna, and decided to celebrate by having a bust sculpted of her by the sculptor he most admired Auguste Rodin. He was aware that Rodin was very selective about accepting commissions from people he did not know, so he had to arrange for someone to make

Russell's portrait of Vincent Van Gogh, 1886. Van Gogh Museum, Amsterdam.

the introduction. Fortunately, one of Russell's friends – the painter Achille Cesbron – knew Rodin well and the commission was accepted. Rodin created a bronze bust of Marianna, and a silver one was later produced, which is now in the Louvre. Rodin was impressed by Marianna's beauty and used her face in several later works depicting classical women such as Minerva and Pallas. Russell and Marianna got to know Rodin well during the production of the bust, and it was a friendship that lasted for many years. It was during this time that Rodin is said to have made his much-repeated remarks about Marianna's great beauty.

The other big event during 1888 was Russell's decision to leave Paris and live permanently on Belle Île. It was a turning point for him and one that puzzled some of his friends. First, he was turning his back on Australia and the English-speaking world in which he was brought up. Second, for someone so naturally gregarious, it was a big step to remove himself from Paris, with its nightlife, clubs, restaurants and other entertainment, to an environment that had none of these attractions and where he had almost nothing in common with the local inhabitants. And third, while still planning to be primarily a painter, he would be moving to a place completely cut off from artistic influence.

This third aspect is not as strange as it seems. Most of the leading French painters of this period forsook the Paris art scene and moved to the country. Monet went to Giverny, Pissarro to Pontoise, Sisley to Moret-sur-Loing, Cézanne to Aix-en-Provence and Gauguin eventually to Tahiti. The other artist who made the move at the same time as Russell was Van Gogh, who moved to Arles in Provence, a much sunnier and cheerier place than bleak and windy Brittany. Although Russell and Van Gogh were now about 1000 kilometres apart, their friendship continued until the latter's death in 1890.

By late 1888, the Russell family had moved into their new home above the bay at Port Goulphar on Belle Île, in which they were to live for the next 20 years. Russell designed the building that came to be known as 'Le Chateau de l'Anglaise'. It was more of a mansion than a house, having many bedrooms and reception areas, a studio, a workshop, stables, accommodation for the servants and terraced gardens. No expense was spared, and for the first time Russell's considerable income was put under strain. Russell enjoyed making things, including some of the furniture for the house and, over the course of 20 years, three sailing boats. These boats were used to sail around the island or to the mainland, and to take visitors for stimulating and occasionally dangerous pleasure trips. Russell was a generous host to the frequent visitors to the chateau, and through them he kept in touch with developments in the world of French art.

Over the next two years, Russell in Belle Île and Van Gogh in Arles kept in touch. Van Gogh sent seven letters to Russell, of which three survive, and Russell sent three to Van Gogh, of which only a fragment remains. Van Gogh also made a number of favourable references to Russell in his letters to Theo. Van Gogh congratulated Russell on leaving Paris, praised his Sicilian paintings, and gave his views on various aspects of art. He was keen to form a group of artists to exhibit together and encouraged Russell to join. Van Gogh was aware that Russell was considering building a collection of French paintings for the Art Gallery of New South Wales. In a letter to Russell he said, "If you should go to Paris, please go and take a canvas of mine at my brother's if you still stick to the idea of someday getting together a collection for your native country." Another Van Gogh aim was to help Gauguin, and he asked Russell to buy one of Gauguin's paintings. Unfortunately, the purchase did not take place. In one letter Van Gogh included 12 drawings. In a letter from Russell to Van Gogh, he invited him to come and stay at Belle Île. Van Gogh declined the offer because, as he wrote to Theo, he couldn't afford the fare.

What should we make of the friendship between Russell and Van Gogh? One writer suggests that Russell found Van Gogh 'cracked but harmless' and indulged him because he had a taste for 'artistic eccentricity'. But there was more to the friendship than that. Ann Galbally, who wrote a book about their friendship called *A Remarkable Friendship: Vincent Van Gogh and John Peter Russell* shows that Van Gogh's views on art were taken seriously by Russell, and they helped to change his painting style, particularly in his use of colour. Russell's decision to paint a portrait of Van Gogh and his later invitation for him to stay at Belle Île show a clear respect on his part. But it wasn't an equal friendship; Van Gogh was somewhat in awe of Russell because of his imposing physical presence, his wealth and his wife. He also hoped to cultivate Russell as a patron, both for himself and for his fellow artists, so he was the one asking for favours.

In fact, Russell did buy a number of paintings by his fellow artists, but not by artists who today would be seen as in the first rank. His collection included paintings by Achille Cesbron, Louis Anquetin, Armand Guillaumin and Émile Bernard. Despite Van Gogh's offer from Arles to exchange paintings and to take one of his from Theo's gallery, there was no Van Gogh painting in Russell's collection (other than the early painting of old shoes). In all, Russell did have 12 drawings given to him by Van Gogh, eight of which he sold in Paris in 1920, three of which he left to his daughter, and one he gave to Matisse (see later). Nor did Russell buy a Gauguin, despite Van Gogh's urging. Both Van Gogh and Gauguin were desperately short of money, so a purchase by Russell would have been a godsend to them. With the benefit of hindsight, Russell missed a golden opportunity to acquire a priceless art collection at a time when it would have been easy to do so.

Russell was thirty when he went to live permanently at Belle Île. He soon settled in, but returned to Paris from time to time and kept a residential studio there. His family continued to grow. In all, Marianna gave birth to 12 babies between 1885 and 1898, of whom six survived. As well as daughter Jeanne, who had been born in Paris, there were five surviving boys – John Sandro, Cedric, Harald Alain, Siward, and the youngest, Lionel, who was born in 1898. The children were educated at home in Brittany and tutors were hired from England.

Russell was seen by the locals as the *seigneur* of the district, or in English as the lord of the manor. His coachman's daughter later wrote a memoir of life on Belle Île in which she said;

> It was generally considered that Mr Russell, a red-bearded giant, well over six foot tall, was the most important person of the district. His wife, Marianna Mattiocco was an Italian, tall and very beautiful. They were a superb couple with a private income … They lived in grand style with many servants, an English governess for the children, a cook, a maidservant, a gardener and a coachman.

Russell's painting continued to evolve towards a style that was clearly impressionist, but it took a long time. It was not until the late 1880s – nearly 15 years after the first Impressionist Exhibition – that his paintings could truly be labelled as impressionist. He finally overcame his desire for fine draughtsmanship and clearly delineated outlines, and replaced it with subtle variations in colour to reflect the effects of light. He was also prepared to use much brighter colours than in his earlier paintings. The painter he now most resembled was

Monet. Partly this was because both had painted Belle Île, and Russell was clearly influenced by Monet's earlier examples. Similarly, Monet later produced a series of influential paintings of the bay at Antibes. Russell twice took his family with him to Antibes and chose to paint some of the same landscapes as Monet. So in the years at Belle Île, Russell turned into a type of impressionist, but one whose primary interest was colour purity and intensity.

One of Russell's first guests at Belle Île was the Australian painter John Longstaff (later Sir John). As a result of Russell's reference, he was able to study at the Atelier Cormon. But Russell's most illustrious guest, who stayed there twice, was Rodin. They had got to know each other well following the commission of the bust of Marianna, they occasionally dined together when Russell was in Paris and continued to correspond until Rodin's death in 1917. Rodin had a high opinion of Russell as a painter, and Russell turned to him for advice whenever he doubted his own ability. Rodin wrote, "I rank you high in my estimate as a painter and you owe it to yourself to do likewise." He also encouraged Russell by adding, "I also have found art difficult. You'll overcome the difficulties as I have done and it is in doing so that we artists achieve happiness."

Another visitor was the young Henri Matisse, who visited Belle Île in 1895, 1896 and 1897. Of all the artists who Russell met, Matisse was the one he most influenced. Matisse became very close to Russell, and Hilary Spurling, in her two-volume biography of Matisse, refers to him as "Russell's young protégé". Matisse himself said that it was Russell who introduced him to the impressionist theories of light and colour. Russell in turn thought highly of Matisse and gave him one of the Van Gogh drawings. Matisse was an impressionable young man at this stage and quickly adopted impressionism. Spurling writes, "For

Matisse, the influence of Russell, Monet and Pissarro was crucial, but short-lived". On his return to Paris, Matisse surprised his friends by painting in an orthodox impressionist manner for a time, before moving onto the style for which he later became famous.

Throughout the 20 years at Belle Île, Russell seems to have painted mainly for his own satisfaction, and rarely exhibited. He exhibited four paintings in London in 1891 and four in Paris in 1895. He next exhibited ten years later in 1905, but showed only one painting. He then exhibited at the Salon des Indépendants in Paris in the four years between 1906 and 1909, showing 18 paintings. In the 47 years between his first exhibition in Sydney and his death, he only exhibited his oil paintings ten times and showed a total of 38 paintings. It is true that he also submitted six paintings to the Société National des Beaux-Arts exhibition in 1902, but they were rejected. At no stage in his career did he ever have a one-man show. In my reading of the four biographies of Russell – the one by Salter, the two by Galbally and the most recent one by Wayne Tunnicliffe, *John Russell: Australia's French Impressionist* – I cannot find a mention of him ever selling a painting in his lifetime.

Russell's idyll at Belle Île came to an end in 1908 when Marianna died at the age of forty-two. She had been operated on in the previous year, and is thought to have died of cancer. Her death meant that Russell no longer enjoyed his time at Belle Île, which he associated so much with her and their happy marriage. He sold the chateau for a fraction of what it had cost him to build, and sent his younger sons to boarding school in England. Then, according to his daughter Jeanne, before leaving he made a huge bonfire of his paintings. This sounds very dramatic, but my guess is that he only burned the ones he regarded as not worth keeping. We know that a large body of his

Belle Île work survived his departure from the island, and it is this work that was the basis of his subsequent reputation.

Then, at the age of fifty, he and Jeanne moved to Neuilly in Paris so that she could further her career as a singer. Later they moved to Italy so that Jeanne could receive further tuition. Russell continued to paint, but now almost exclusively using watercolours. In Italy, a fellow student of Jeanne's – the American Caroline de Witt Merrill – became a close friend of the Russell family. She was an opera singer whose career was suffering due to encroaching deafness. In 1912, at the age of fifty-four, Russell married the thirty-two-year-old Caroline with his daughter's blessing. They remained in Italy, where in July 1914, just as the First World War was about to break out, Caroline gave birth to Russell's sixth son, Hereward. During the War, Russell, Caroline and Hereward moved to England, where he helped the war effort by making equipment including, among other things, invalid chairs. All five of Russell's grown-up sons enlisted in the British Army and all survived the war, but not without injury.

After a period of painting in Italy, Russell decided to return to Australia to help his son Siward establish himself as a farmer. Before he left, he sold the paintings and drawings he had acquired from other artists, including the Van Gogh drawings he still had. His own paintings were left in the care of Jeanne and her husband, but with the intention that they later be distributed to other members of the family. In 1921, Russell, Caroline and Hereward left Genoa and sailed to Sydney with Siward.

I found Russell's decision to return to Australia a surprising one because he had been away so long and become so thoroughly European. It is not clear whether the move was intended to be permanent or whether, once Siward was settled, they planned to return to Europe. I suspect it was not intended to be permanent. Russell was very much the patriarch of the family and derived much pleasure from their company. Although somewhat domineering, he was devoted to all his children, and took a strong interest in their welfare. He had been living in Europe for well over 30 years, had become out of touch with Australia, and all of his adult children were thoroughly European. They were bilingual English/ French, had never even visited Australia, and were settled in either France or Britain.

Russell's arrival in Australia went largely unnoticed. Although he still had a few Australian friends that he had made in Europe, plus a few relatives, he had no reputation as an artist and no one in the Australian art world was much interested in him. That did not disturb him as by this time he had given up all hope of being recognised as a serious artist. He still painted watercolours for enjoyment, but did not exhibit them. The Russell family moved into rented premises at Rose Bay on Sydney Harbour while they looked for a farm for Siward. After about a year they concluded that there was nothing suitable, so they decamped to New Zealand.

They ended up at Brigham Creek on the North Island. Here they found an orchard that Siward, with his father's help, could develop into a viable farm. All four lived on the property in a shack with a leaking roof for three years. It is hard not to wonder whether Russell ever dwelt on the contrast between his life as a wealthy boulevardier in Paris in the 1880s with his present position on a small farm in rural New Zealand. If the contrast did disappoint him, he never showed it, but his children and their spouses must have wondered how it all ended up this way.

Russell, Caroline and Hereward returned to Australia in 1925 and settled in Watsons Bay on Sydney Harbour. As so often was the case, he found a need to be close to the water and to boats. He was able to buy a small house on the waterfront and construct a harbour for his boat. The work of building the harbour, terracing and planting a garden, and remodelling the house satisfied his need for creative work and took the place formerly occupied by his painting. He worked at these projects right up to his death from a heart attack in April 1930 at the age of seventy-one. Caroline took Hereward back to her home in the United States, so that none of Russell's seven children had any connection with Australia. While most of his descendants are scattered across England, Scotland, France, the United States and New Zealand, several grandchildren did eventually end up in Australia.

What should we make of his life? It had most of the ingredients we associate with success and happiness – a carefree and glamorous lifestyle in the early years, wealth enough to indulge his passion, a happy marriage and a supporting family, plenty of opportunity for travel and many stimulating friends. But in some respects it was a bit of a disappointment. At twenty-two he had everything that anyone could hope for, yet in the end he died in obscurity. Despite the modest circumstances in which he lived his last years in Australia and New Zealand, he did not die poor. He left an estate of 41,973 pounds, a substantial sum in 1930, to be divided among his wife and children.

To the outside observer, the great disappointment must have been that his life's work was not appreciated in his own lifetime. Surprisingly, this does not seem to have worried him because at no stage in his career did he ever seem to have promoted himself. It is hard not to conclude that his career as a painter might have been more successful if he had had less wealth, and been forced to exhibit more frequently and rely on the sale of his paintings for part of his support.

But this is not the end of the story: any account of Russell's life must record the events after his death. In this respect, he is different to the other people covered in this book. They achieved a measure of fame in their own lifetimes, but have since been largely forgotten. Russell, on the other hand, despite living an extremely interesting life, never achieved or sought fame in his own lifetime and died unnoticed. It was not until more than 30 years after his death that he started to be recognised as an artist of substance. This is the one thing he has in common with his friend Vincent Van Gogh, although the latter's posthumous recognition came quicker.

The first retrospective exhibition of Russell's work was mounted by the Wildenstein Art Gallery in London in 1965, 35 years after his death. Australian art dealer Joseph Brown then scoured Europe and began collecting as many of Russell's paintings as he could find to bring back to Australia. He held exhibitions in Melbourne in 1968, 1969 and 1977. Russell's paintings then found their way into the auction houses and into Australian public galleries, and their prices soared.

While the majority of the Australian art world agreed with the favourable reassessment of Russell, not all did. Some, like writer and cultural critic Max Harris, felt that Russell's revival owed more to his colourful life and friendships with Van Gogh, Monet, Rodin and Matisse than to the inherent merit of his paintings. There is something in this claim; his close link with French impressionism made him unique among Australian artists and is emphasised in the titles of books about him such as *The Lost Impressionist* and *Australia's French Impressionist*, and the fact that a whole book was written about his brief friendship with Van Gogh. The French connection certainly added an element of exoticism and glamour to his story.

Although it helped, there was more to Russell than that. You only have to look at his best oil paintings from Belle Île and Antibes to realise that his unique handling of vivid colour meant he was not just another impressionist. He had developed his own approach so that his paintings are readily recognisable. Yet it certainly was unusual that a painter who never saw himself as anything more than a committed amateur should be elevated to such an exalted position.

In Australia, the National Gallery has the biggest collection of his works, and he is also represented in all the state galleries. The largest collection of his paintings worldwide is in the Musée de Morlaix in Brittany (part of the Louvre), which has 18 of his paintings and the bust of Marianna by Rodin, all left to the museum by his daughter, Jeanne. Recent exhibitions of Russell's work include *Matisse, Russell and Monet at Belle Île*, mounted by the Art Gallery of New South Wales in 2002, and *Australia's Impressionists* at the National Gallery in London in 2012, which featured only four painters: Roberts, Streeton, Conder and Russell.

By far the biggest and best exhibition is the recent one put on in 2018 by the Art Gallery of New South Wales, *John Russell: Australia's French Impressionist*. Its accompanying book of essays of the same title, edited by the curator of the exhibition, Wayne Tunnicliffe, is the best account of his life and work now available. The exhibition and book, plus an ABC documentary, have revived interest in Russell to such an extent that he now hardly qualifies as someone who has been forgotten.

The paintings most in demand by collectors are the oils he painted during his residence at Belle Île. His watercolours are not as highly regarded. The highest price achieved so far is A$1,800,000 for the painting *Boys on the Beach*, sold by Sothebys in 2007. This depicts two of his sons on the beach at Belle Île. There are two other paintings of his sons playing on the beach that are better known and more frequently reproduced, but they are in public galleries. Were they on the auction circuit, they could well command higher prices. Another painting, *Belle-Île-en-Mer* (1904), was auctioned in 2008 for A$1,560,000. Ann Galbally has compiled a catalogue of Russell's surviving works and it runs to 517 pieces including oils, watercolours, pastels and drawings – not a bad achievement by someone who was reluctant to exhibit and is known to have destroyed some of his work.

What of the claim I mentioned at the beginning of this essay – that Russell offered a collection of French impressionist paintings to an Australian public gallery, but it was rejected? This claim still rears its head from time to time. As recently as 2001, John McDonald wrote, "His [Russell's] attempts to install works by French impressionists in an Australian public collection were rudely rebuffed." A more accurate summary of this widely quoted episode is provided by Robert Hughes in his book *Art in Australia*, where he records, "There is a rumour, current only since the late 1940s, which no records substantiate, that he offered a handsome collection of paintings by Van Gogh, Cézanne, Seurat, Monet and others to the Art Gallery of New South Wales, and that the trustees refused it." Hughes is correct; this widely spread rumour has no basis in fact.

Gilbert Murray aged twenty five in 1891.

8
GEORGE GILBERT AIME MURRAY

Scholar and Worker for Peace

Gilbert Murray was a central figure in English cultural and intellectual life for more than 50 years. From his base as a professor at Oxford, he branched out into the theatre, domestic politics and international affairs. While primarily a scholar and prolific writer, he became an outstanding example of what we would call today a public intellectual. Indeed, in the first half of the twentieth century he became a household name and was probably the best-known Australian in England, although Melba was more famous worldwide. He led a charmed life, and even managed to marry into the British aristocracy.

No account of Gilbert Murray's life would be complete without also saying something about his equally brilliant – but very different – brother, Hubert. So, on a couple of occasions I will divert from Gilbert's story to follow Hubert's life, which culminated in him becoming the founding father of Australia's involvement in Papua New Guinea.

The Murray family first arrived in Australia permanently in 1827. Gilbert and Hubert's grandfather, Old Terence Murray, despite being an Irish Catholic became a captain in the British Army, and so he was entitled to a free grant of land in New South Wales. The land he received was in sheep country around what is now Canberra. His son, Terence Aubrey Murray, although only seventeen at the time, also received a neighbouring grant of land, which he later expanded. When his father died in 1837, Terence Aubrey became the owner of two properties covering 20,000 acres. One of the properties was called Yarralumla, which in time became a suburb of Canberra and the name of the Governor-General of Australia's official residence.

Terence Aubrey Murray became a wealthy pastoralist and an important and much-admired man in the district. When representative government was granted to the Colony of New South Wales in 1843, he was elected to the lower house of parliament. He prided himself on being neither Whig nor Tory and took little interest in party politics. Gilbert wrote that, with his Irish background, his father tended to be suspicious of the establishment and sympathetic to those he thought were suffering from oppression or injustice. Others recorded him, however, as being equally interested in protecting the rights of the landed gentry. In religion he was broad-minded and took no part in the sectarian rivalries that were common at that time.

Terence Aubrey's first marriage produced three children, but his wife died in 1857 after giving birth to the third. He married again in 1860, and this marriage was the one that produced the two brilliant sons. Hubert (christened John Hubert Plunkett) was born in December 1861 and Gilbert (christened George Gilbert Aime) about four years later in January 1866. Both boys were baptised as Catholics, but their father didn't see the need to attend the ceremony. His second wife, the boys' mother, was Agnes Ann Edwards, an Englishwoman who had migrated to Australia to become governess to the children of the Chief Justice of New South Wales. She was a trained teacher and came from an interesting family herself; a first cousin was W.S. Gilbert of Gilbert and Sullivan fame. She was a Protestant, so the marriage ceremony was held twice, once by Catholic rites and then by Anglican ones.

Shortly before Gilbert's birth, Terence Aubrey found himself in financial trouble. A combination of drought and excessive borrowing meant that he had to sell his two properties to repay his debts. He was no longer a member of the landed gentry, and so had to rely mainly on his parliamentary position to support his family in reduced, but not poor, circumstances. He was then made President of the Legislative Council of New South Wales and was knighted in 1869. Despite his reduced circumstances, Sir Terence Murray saw himself as a gentleman of substance, and the family held a high social position. Both he and his wife were educated, widely read, and expected their sons to attain high educational achievements, in which the boys did not disappoint.

The family lived in Darling Point and Rose Bay on Sydney Harbour, and the boys were at first educated locally at day schools. In 1873, when Gilbert was seven years old, his father died, which was a severe blow to him and his brother as they both greatly admired their father. Their mother, by now Lady Agnes Murray, stepped into the breach and opened a school for girls, which flourished and supported the family comfortably.

At the age of nine, Gilbert was sent to a boarding school at Moss

Vale, south of Sydney. In his book *An Unfinished Autobiography*, Gilbert writes at length about his schooling there and later at another school in Mittagong. Even though he describes it in a matter-of-fact way and does not adopt a disapproving tone, the thing that stands out from his account is how rough and tumble he remembers his early life to have been. This is not what we expected to hear from the gentle scholar, but we must remember it was written 70 years after the events. Even before going to school, his father, who was a physically strong and impressive man, taught him to box and shoot a rifle. At school he reports being involved in fights, at one stage six fights in a quarter of a year. He lists them all. I find it hard to believe that 70 years after the events he could still remember each schoolyard fight, so we should treat all these reminiscences with caution.

We cannot doubt, however, that he was an excellent student and regularly topped his class. He also reports that from an early age he tended to support the underdog "and be 'agin the government' whatever the government might be". He and his family were "keen on the protection of animals, children, foreigners, heretics, unpopular minorities and the like … Only gradually as we reached positions of responsibility did we get to see that there was something to be said for the authorities, and that mostly they were doing their best".

Hubert, being older, entered Sydney Grammar School at the age of ten and completed his secondary education there. He grew to six foot three inches tall, played rugby for the school and trained at boxing at a local gymnasium. He also excelled academically and Gilbert looked up to his older brother. But Hubert had a prickly personality and did not make friends easily because of his attitude of superiority and aloofness. Gilbert said that Hubert always resented criticism and restraint, and was impatient with human stupidity.

In 1877, Lady Agnes Murray sold her girls' school in Sydney at a good profit and left for England with Gilbert, now eleven years old. Hubert stayed in Sydney, cared for by family friends for two years until he completed his schooling before joining his family in England. Gilbert's secondary education took place at Merchant Taylors, a fee-paying day school in London. His studies were concentrated on languages, principally Latin and Greek, but also French, Hebrew and, of course, English. He was an outstanding student and his main love was Greek. He also took an interest in politics, read John Stuart Mill and Herbert Spencer, and became a supporter of Gladstone and Home Rule. Not surprisingly, in his final year he won a scholarship and several other awards that fully financed his years at St John's College, Oxford.

Gilbert entered Oxford in 1884 at the age of eighteen. Hubert had to spend a year at an English school in order to qualify for Oxford. He then had his entry delayed by a further year because of some impertinent answers he gave in the entrance examination. He spent that year in Germany. As a result, Hubert, although four years older than Gilbert, only preceded him at Oxford by a year.

The two brothers then spent a few years together at Oxford; Gilbert at St John's College and Hubert at Magdalen College. This was the last time they were to live together in the same city, and almost the last time in the same country. Their experiences at Oxford were rather different. The one thing they had in common was they were both academically gifted and both took out first-class honours degrees. Hubert was bigger, more physical and more interested in sport than Gilbert. He rowed, played rugby and boxed, and tended to associate with the 'hearties', who were interested in those things, rather than with his intellectual peers. In Gilbert's autobiography he claims that Hubert won the All England Amateur Heavyweight

Boxing Championship, but the records do not support this claim. As we will see as the story unfolds, Hubert and Gilbert had very different approaches to life, to religion, to military service and to drinking. Despite their differences, they remained good friends and regularly corresponded during the rest of their lives when they lived apart.

Another important difference between them was in respect to social skills. Hubert, as we have seen, had very little. He was impatient, sensitive to criticism, had no 'small talk' and made no effort to cultivate friends. As a result, he had few. Gilbert, on the other hand, was good with people, well liked, and made friends easily. This may seem surprising in someone who was what we would call a 'swot', a teetotaller and a puritan. But it is clear that throughout his life he made a large number of friends, had many admirers, and was an accomplished networker.

When Hubert graduated from Oxford, he became a member of the Inner Temple, the oldest and richest of London's Inns of Court. He passed his bar examinations and was called to the bar in London, but instead he returned to Australia, where he was admitted to the bar in Sydney. The two brothers then lived in different countries for the rest of their lives.

Gilbert meanwhile continued with his studies at Oxford and soon gained a reputation as the outstanding classical scholar of his undergraduate generation. In his first year he won prizes for Greek and Latin against competition from second and third-year students, an unprecedented achievement. The list of prizes he won is too long to record here, suffice it to say his reputation as a classical scholar reached beyond Oxford even while he was still an undergraduate. He was, as you would expect, a prodigious worker, although he did find some time for liberal causes in college debating and essay societies.

He also wrote a novel, *Gobi or Shamo*, which was published two years after he graduated.

In 1888, he was awarded a first-class honours degree in Classical Moderations (Greek and Latin languages) and Greats (classical literature, history, philosophy, archaeology and linguistics). His academic achievements were so outstanding that he never considered any other career than that of a classical scholar. He immediately sat for a prize fellowship at New College Oxford (the name 'New' was given to it in 1379 when it was founded) and won it. The fellowship paid 200 pounds per year for seven years; a good start, but someone of Gilbert's ability could do better.

In 1887, Gilbert and several friends had met Rosalind Howard, who became the Countess of Carlisle when her husband became the Earl of Carlisle. She was a strong-willed aristocrat with liberal sympathies who was president of both the British Women's Temperance Association and the Liberal Women's Association. Gilbert was invited to their ancestral seat of Castle Howard in Yorkshire, where he met the Howard family. This magnificent palace is chiefly known today as the setting for the 1981 BBC TV series of Evelyn Waugh's *Brideshead Revisited*. These visits allowed Gilbert to meet and then fall in love with the Countess's eldest daughter, Lady Mary Howard. Initially there was some hesitation on her part, but in time she returned his love. The fact that her mother was enthusiastically behind the union helped to bring them together. But then Gilbert hesitated, because he doubted that his humble fellowship gave him the income or status to be a suitable son-in-law to the Earl of Carlisle.

In 1889 at the age of twenty-three, Gilbert was appointed Professor of Greek at the University of Glasgow. Not surprisingly, this was a controversial appointment and was opposed by those who objected to his youth and to the fact that he had hardly written anything of substance. It was an appointment based on promise rather than achievement. As an aside, about 50 years later the English classical scholar and later Conservative politician Enoch Powell was appointed Professor of Greek at Sydney University at the age of twenty-five. Greek scholars, like mathematicians, must mature early. The chair in Glasgow paid a handsome salary plus the use of a large house. Perhaps, more importantly, it gave Gilbert the prestige and dignity of being a professor, a title more valued in Scotland than in Oxbridge.

Later that year, in November 1889 and still only twenty-three, Gilbert married Lady Mary Howard, who then became Lady Mary Murray, the name she retained for the rest of her life. As well as the income from Gilbert's chair, the couple also enjoyed Lady Mary's considerable dowry, her annual allowance and frequent gifts from the Countess. They were able to live in comfort in Glasgow during term, and spent summers at the various houses owned by the Howard family. There were always plenty of servants and nurses for the children they later had. Although Lady Mary shared the same political views as her mother and Gilbert, there was more than political compatibility that drew the couple together. The surviving letters show that the marriage was also the result of romantic love and physical attraction. It was a successful marriage and Lady Mary strongly supported Gilbert's work throughout her long life.

Gilbert had achieved what many aspire to, but few attain – he had reached the heights of his profession, achieved complete economic security and made a happy marriage – all by the age of twenty-three.

His time in Glasgow was dominated by a heavy teaching load plus examinations and academic administration, although he still managed to find time for research and began his lifelong interest in the Greek dramatist Euripides. Over the course of his life Gilbert was a prolific writer, so it came as a surprise to find that in the decade he spent in Glasgow he produced very little academic research. His one published work was a book, *A History of Ancient Greek Literature*, published in 1897. It was well received and used as a textbook well into the 1920s. Gilbert saw himself as more than a scholar; his ambition was to be recognised as an important man of letters, even a poet. Just as in his Oxford days when he had written a novel on the side, in Glasgow he diverted his attention to writing two plays in English, *Carlyon Sahib* and *Andromache*. These were circulated among his friends and eventually found their way onto the London stage after he left Glasgow.

All his life he was prone to overwork, which caused periodic bouts of illness. On one such occasion in 1892 at the age of twenty-six, he was advised by his doctor to take an ocean voyage for rest, so he took the opportunity to make his first and only return visit to Australia. We know little about that trip, other than he was disappointed with what he regarded as Hubert's heavy drinking and the company he kept. One of Hubert's drinking companions was Edmund Barton, who later became Australia's first prime minister, but whose drinking habits earned him the nickname 'Toby Tosspot'. Even more disappointing was to learn that his father had also been a heavy drinker. To the teetotal Gilbert, this was almost the worst family news he could receive. But what Gilbert regarded as heavy drinking might be regarded by others as normal social drinking. In view of their later achievements, neither Hubert nor Barton could have been drunkards.

While they lived in Glasgow, Lady Mary gave birth to three children, Rosalind in 1890, Denis in 1892 and Agnes in 1894. Two other children were born later when they returned to England, Basil in 1902 and Stephen in 1908. In his biography of Gilbert, Francis

West describes the children's upbringing:

> Although the children were brought up with nurses, maids and cooks, although they were regularly taken to the great Carlisle houses – Castle Howard, Naworth Castle, Palace Green – under the watchful eye of the Countess, they were not expected to acquire any taste for luxury or high living, any more than they were to display religious tendencies. Both Murrays carefully watched for such ominous signs in their children from an early age, but their actual contact with their daughters and sons was not extensive when the children's basic needs were looked after by servants.

After a decade in Glasgow, Gilbert felt exhausted and resigned his chair to return to England, to spend some years as a gentleman of leisure and further his literary ambitions. While Gilbert's life in Glasgow had been stable and prosperous, Hubert's back in Australia had been a struggle and seemed to leave him dissatisfied. From his return in 1886 until about 1891 he was in private practice as a barrister, but he did not receive enough briefs to properly support his family. As a result he had to borrow money from Gilbert and Lady Mary. To succeed, a barrister needs the social skills to cultivate a network of clients, solicitors and law officials and so build a practice. Hubert, as we have seen, was too impatient and aloof to do this. So he left private practice and was appointed Crown prosecutor. This job enabled him to support his family, but he felt that it was not sufficiently challenging for someone of his ability.

He then did two things that were completely contrary to his brother's beliefs, but do not seem to have ruined their friendship. In 1897, he reconverted to Catholicism, which re-affirmed his Irish heritage. At about the same time he became an officer in a militia regiment – the New South Wales Irish Rifles. When the Boer War broke out in 1900, by which time he was a major, he volunteered for service and spent a year fighting in South Africa. Meanwhile in

London, Gilbert was a very vocal opponent of the Boer War. Not that Hubert was ever enthusiastic about the war either; rather, it seems he volunteered to get away from what he regarded as his humdrum existence in Sydney. By the end of the war he was a lieutenant-colonel in the Australian Army and a major in the Imperial Army.

He returned to Sydney and his job as Crown prosecutor, but was still restless. In 1904 he applied for, and was chosen as, Chief Judicial Officer in British New Guinea. To the legal fraternity of Sydney this was a strange decision. If his Sydney legal work had not challenged him enough, how could the primitive legal system of British New Guinea do so; and if life in Sydney was disappointing, how could the shanty town of Port Moresby be any better? They assumed this was just another example of his wish to escape and could not have known that it would lead to him finding his life's work.

As mentioned, Gilbert and his family returned from Scotland to England in 1899, where they lived in a large house in Surrey provided by the Countess. They remained there for six and a half years, during which Gilbert held no academic position or regular employment. It gave him the time and freedom to pursue his literary interests without giving up his academic research completely. Although on the surface he was a gentleman of leisure, he worked as hard as ever. His main activity was to translate Greek tragic dramas, mainly those by Euripides, into English, have them published, and then performed on the stage. Instead of using literal translations, he chose to render the Greek into rhyming English poetry suitable for the stage. This meant he became part-scholar, part-poet and part-dramatist.

During these years he translated *The Frogs* by Aristophanes, and four plays by Euripides: *Hippolytus, Bacchae, Trojan Women* and *Electra*. All these were published and were commercially successful as books. More importantly, each of the four plays by Euripides plus a fifth, *Medea*, were staged professionally in London and in the regions. Gilbert became part of the English theatre scene, mixing with actors, directors and fellow dramatists such as Sir James Barrie and George Bernard Shaw. Shaw based a character in his play *Major Barbara* directly on Gilbert. The character, Cusins, is a professor of Greek specialising in Euripides. To make it clear he is referring to Gilbert, he had one of the other characters say, "Cusins is a very nice fellow certainly: no one would ever guess he was born in Australia". Later, Shaw had Cusins proclaim:

> Let me advise you to study Greek. Greek scholars are privileged men ... Other languages are the qualifications for waiters and commercial travellers. Greek is to a man of position what the hallmark is to silver.

My reading of the play suggests that Shaw was good-naturedly sending up his friend Gilbert by portraying him as a man proclaiming high principles, but who could be very pragmatic if it was to his advantage.

Gilbert had brought classical Greek drama to a wider audience, something no other classical scholar had achieved. He also found time to start a serious piece of classical scholarship in which he was to edit the definitive Greek edition of the works of Euripides from the various manuscripts found in European libraries.

After his years of 'freelancing' in Surrey he decided he was ready to resume his career as a classical scholar, and in 1905 accepted a fellowship at New College, Oxford. This allowed him to complete his edition of Euripides in three volumes, and to write another book, *The Rise of the Greek Epic*, based on a series of lectures he gave at Harvard in 1907. These further enhanced his reputation as an outstanding Hellenist and led to his appointment in 1908 as Regius Professor of Greek at Oxford University. This chair was the pinnacle of Greek scholarship in the English-speaking world. It was created in 1541 by Henry VIII and, being a Regius chair, the appointment was made by the King on the advice of the prime minister, not by university authorities.

From today's perspective it is hard to appreciate just how important the educated world viewed the study of Greek a century ago. It was a compulsory prerequisite for entry into Oxford and Cambridge, and for some other universities as well, including Glasgow. Many educated people could read Greek, and many others read Greek literature in translation. The Regius Professorship of Greek at Oxford was a position of great influence and its incumbent was assumed to possess exceptional wisdom. One of Gilbert's predecessors as Regius Professor was the famous Master of Balliol, Benjamin Jowett (pronounced Joe-wit if what follows is to rhyme), who was commemorated in the lines:

> First come I. My name is Jowett.
> There's no knowledge but I know it.
> I am the Master of this College.
> What I don't know isn't knowledge.

So we come to the halfway mark in the lives of the Murray brothers. In 1904, at the age of forty-two, Hubert took up his position in New Guinea that was to occupy him for the rest of his life. In 1908, also at the age of forty-two, Gilbert became Regius Professor of Greek at Oxford, a position he retained until retirement, and that enabled him to branch out into the wider political sphere.

Gilbert was not an 'ivory tower' academic concerned only with his reputation among his peers. While the Euripides volumes in Greek were aimed at classical scholars, most of his published work was aimed at a wider audience. He saw himself as a public educator, proselytiser and all-round intellectual. His translation of *Oedipus Rex* by Sophocles was performed in 1911, despite efforts to censor it, and it became his best-known work. In 1912 his lectures at Columbia were published as the book *Four Stages of Greek Religion,* and at the same time he accepted a position as editor of *The Home University Library* series of books covering all academic subjects and aimed at the general reader.

There is not enough space to follow Gilbert's academic career year by year. Suffice it to say that it was hugely successful, and he became known as the greatest Hellenist of his generation in the English-speaking world. Honorary doctorates were bestowed on him and he was in high demand to give public lectures. His output of published papers and books was enormous and continued right up to his death, even though his non-academic work took up increasing amounts of his time. As best I can count, he produced 33 books of English translations of Greek works or text editions in Greek. In addition, there were 20 books dealing with Greek literature, religion, education, history and philosophy. And then there were all the books on contemporary political issues. In 1960, a year after his death and 21 years after his retirement from Oxford, his publisher, George Allen & Unwin Ltd., still had 21 of his books in print.

If you look up the index of the State Library of New South Wales, or any other long-standing public library, you will be surprised by how many of his books they contain: in this case 134 books. If we eliminate multiple editions of the same book, we come up with 61 individual books written by Gilbert. It is hard to believe anyone could have written so many serious books, and raises the question as to how much deep scholarship went into each one. What is even more remarkable is that in the second half of his life, his academic career played a secondary role to his interest in political affairs. And it is the latter that made his name so familiar to the British public.

Gilbert had always been interested in politics. As a young man he adhered to the classical liberal or Whig tradition. He opposed imperial expansion, supported Home Rule for Ireland, female suffrage, workers' rights and other liberal causes. His views on philosophy were utilitarian, he was agnostic in religion and a believer in humanism and progress. He was public spirited in his outward life and prudent in his personal life; he was a teetotaller throughout his life and a vegetarian in his later years.

Gilbert was a lifelong member of the Liberal Party and associated closely with its radical wing. He also supported a wide variety of other causes including opposition to the Poor Law, encouraging university education for women, and he was a member of the Society for Simplified Spelling, of which he became president. He was a great supporter of causes, a frequent signer of petitions and an inveterate joiner of committees too numerous to mention. He was several times offered Liberal Party preselection for winnable seats, but turned the offers down. Later he stood five times as Liberal candidate for the seat of Oxford University, but lost each time. His political friendships were mainly with people on the progressive side such as Shaw, H.G. Wells and particularly Bertrand Russell, with whom he remained friends for 50 years.

The coming of the First World War was a massive challenge for Gilbert's beliefs: he termed it the "Ordeal of a Generation". In July 1914, when he was forty-eight years old, he became aware that war was a possibility, and his first instinct was to oppose it, which he did by signing a declaration in favour of British neutrality in the event of war between the Powers. But when war broke out, he parted company with his radical friends and supported Britain's involvement. He was in the Strangers' Gallery of the House of Commons when Sir Edward

Grey, the foreign secretary, delivered his famous speech explaining the government's position. Gilbert was persuaded by the clear logical case that Grey enunciated and supported the government the next day when it declared war after Germany's refusal to respect Belgian neutrality.

As usual Gilbert did not keep his views to himself, but explained his support for the war in a booklet called *The Foreign Policy of Sir Edward Grey*. This methodically set out the arguments for and against British participation before concluding that the case for resisting German aggression was overwhelming. In his view there was only one country that desired war and territorial expansion, and that was Germany. For those who had thought of him as a pacifist his views came as a shock, but Gilbert said he had never been a pacifist, although he had pacifist friends. His views brought him into public conflict with Bertrand Russell, who also published his position – which was the opposite of Gilbert's. Surprisingly, their friendship endured despite the public conflict.

Gilbert also decided to make a direct personal contribution to the war effort. In late 1914 he joined the Oxford Volunteer Training Corps and attended regular drills and exercises, rising to the rank of corporal. Just what this group of over-age part-timers meant to achieve is not clear as Britain was never under threat of invasion in the First World War (the BBC sitcom *Dad's Army* comes to mind). His abilities were put to better use by the government when they sent him on goodwill tours to Sweden and the US, ostensibly to lecture on the classics, but also to put forward Britain's views when possible. As the war progressed he lost some of his enthusiasm for it, particularly when Lloyd George replaced Asquith as prime minister. He opposed conscription and the government's policy towards conscientious objectors, some of whom he helped to obtain lighter sentences.

Like many people who were horrified by the huge loss of life in the war, his thoughts soon turned to finding ways to prevent this ever happening again. The quest for an international peacekeeping body became his preoccupation for the rest of his life. In 1918 he became chairman of the League of Nations Union (henceforth referred to as the Union), a position he held for the next 20 years. In this capacity he became the voice of the League of Nations (henceforth known as the League) in Britain.

The Union was a British pressure group headquartered in London, with a membership of 400,000 paying members dedicated to supporting the League in Geneva. It was not part of the British government, but what would be termed today a non-government organisation (NGO), whose role was to educate the public and mobilise support for the League and its ideals of collective security, international arbitration of disputes and multilateral arms limitations.

Gilbert was never a full-time official of the League, nor a member of the permanent British delegation there. He was still employed on a full-time basis at Oxford, and all his work for the Union was voluntary. In fact, his first official connection with the League in Geneva was when he was invited by Field Marshal Smuts, Prime Minister of South Africa, to be on the South African delegation to the Opening Congress in 1921. He then was invited to attend on an occasional basis by the British government in 1924, from which he branched out in 1928 to become chairman of one of the League's committees – the Committee for Intellectual Cooperation. This took him to Geneva several times a year, but his main work was in London for one or two days a week as chairman of the Union, and at Oxford as Regius Professor of Greek. His capacity for work was extraordinary; in effect he was doing two full-time jobs. When the Vice-Chancellor of Oxford University questioned his ability to fulfil his duties there, Gilbert resolved the problem by using the family wealth to finance another academic position in Greek in order to lighten his load.

The Committee for Intellectual Cooperation was mainly a 'talk shop' for prominent intellectuals who were already internationalist in outlook, and so could set a good example for their fellow citizens to help to overcome any overly nationalistic attitudes. It also did some more practical work in standardising copyright for written material and promoting the rights of inventors, plus organising meetings for the exchange of views of museum curators, library experts and directors of education. This work was taken over by UNESCO after the Second World War. But the committee is now chiefly remembered for its impressive membership, which included physicist Madame Curie, philosopher Henri Bergson, composer Bela Bartok, novelist Thomas Mann, poet John Masefield and the most illustrious name of all – Albert Einstein.

Gilbert worked tirelessly in London to promote British support for the work of the League. As well as chairing the weekly meetings of the Union, he wrote pamphlets, books and letters to editors and gave public lectures throughout the country. In addition to influencing public opinion, he used his wide contacts in parliament to influence British government policy in support of the League. It was not an easy task because there was much public and government scepticism about the League's chances of maintaining peace. Churchill, not surprisingly, did not have any faith in the Union's position, when he said in the House of Commons in 1932, "What impresses me most about them is their long suffering and inexhaustible gullibility".

It is easy to accuse Gilbert of naivety in that he continued to support the League through its difficulties in the 1930s. But his fundamental position was based on a realistic assessment of the situation. In 1921 in his book, *The Problem of Foreign Policy*, he bluntly stated his position that a war of revenge by Germany was inevitable in his lifetime unless a collective solution was found to prevent it. Whether the League, with its emphasis on disarmament, was the best collective solution is another matter.

The League's biggest problem was its membership. It got off to a bad start when the United States declined to join despite the fact that President Woodrow Wilson was its most influential supporter. Germany too was not a member because it was initially not invited. In 1925 it was invited and accepted, but in 1933, with Adolph Hitler now Chancellor, it pulled out. Other countries to pull out included Japan, Italy and Spain.

The League's first big test came in 1931 when Japan invaded China and occupied Manchuria. The League was powerless to stop it, or to retaliate with penalties such as trade sanctions. In 1935 Italy invaded Ethiopia, then known as Abyssinia, and again the League could not do anything about it. Similarly, the League could do nothing but watch as Germany reoccupied the Rhineland and invaded Austria, Czechoslovakia, and eventually Poland, which led to the Second World War. This spelled the end of the League; it had lasted less than 20 years.

Gilbert retired from Oxford in 1936 at the age of seventy, and his work with the League ceased by 1940. The Union continued in much-reduced form throughout the Second World War until it was absorbed into the United Nations Association in 1945, with Gilbert as vice-president. But these events did not stop him from working at his usual pace. He continued to translate Greek poetry and drama and to write on political subjects. He published at least ten books on Greek subjects and about half a dozen on political issues after he retired from Oxford. In addition, he continued his interest in extrasensory perception and psychic powers. His interest and research in these areas went back to before the First World War, and continued right up to 1952 when, at the age of eighty-six, he became president of the Society for Psychical Research.

Throughout his life, Gilbert had strong views on many subjects and took every opportunity to communicate them to as wide an audience as he could. He made frequent use of newspapers and radio to do this, and so became widely known beyond academic and political circles. He first broadcast on the BBC in 1925 when it was still a monopoly with a huge audience, and he was still broadcasting in 1956. Overall he made over a hundred broadcasts by himself, as well as being a regular on the *Brains Trust* program. At its peak, this program had an audience of 12 million listeners, and this made him a household name in Britain. Another British institution that he made use of was the letters page of *The Times*. Almost 300 of his letters were published there, a total only exceeded by George Bernard Shaw. His last letter appeared in July 1956.

In May 1957, Gilbert died at the age of ninety-one, eight months after Lady Mary's death. He was lucid until the end and had been working until a few months before his death.

Before turning to an assessment of Gilbert's life and work, it is time to conclude the story of Hubert. We left him in 1904, when he had just been appointed Chief Judicial Officer of British New Guinea. To everyone's surprise, and probably his own, he remained there for the rest of his life and gained international respect as an enlightened colonial governor.

The island of New Guinea was divided into three parts when Hubert arrived in 1904. The western half was occupied by the Dutch, and the eastern half was divided into two. The northern part was occupied by the Germans and called German New Guinea and the southern half, which included Port Moresby, was called British New Guinea, but placed under the sovereignty of Australia. In 1905 it was renamed the Territory of Papua, but remained under Australian administration. It was still called the Territory of Papua when Hubert became governor in 1908 (his formal title was Lieutenant Governor, but there was no rank of governor), so Hubert was clearly in charge of the Territory. He led Papua from 1908 until his death in 1940, an unprecedented tenure for a colonial governor. Unlike other colonial governors, he did not retire to London or Sydney after his term of office expired, but stuck it out to the end.

Throughout his long period as Governor of Papua New Guinea, his main challenge was to balance economic development against the need for protection of the native population. There was no set of policies that would please everyone, and each issue was seen as a conflict between the white settlers and the needs of the native tribes. Overall he did a difficult job as well as anyone could have in the circumstances. As he got older his approach evolved towards giving more emphasis to native protection and he created the post of government anthropologist. His views gained a wide audience in Australia and London through his reports, lectures and the two books he wrote, *Papua or British New Guinea* in 1914, and *Papua of Today* in 1925. His achievements in Papua New Guinea were recognised by the Australian Government when he was knighted in 1925.

Looking back at Hubert's life, the most interesting question is – why did he find fulfilment in the harsh and primitive conditions of Papua, when he couldn't in Sydney, Oxford or London? I can think of two explanations. The first comes from what we already know of his somewhat prickly personality. He did not like taking orders or touting for work, nor did he look up to anyone. In Papua, he was not only the boss, but he was physically and intellectually superior to those around him. His academic, athletic, legal and military accomplishments meant even his critics had to acknowledge his superiority. The second attraction of the job in Papua was that he liked the physical and outdoor aspects of it – the frequent expeditions by boat, on horse or foot into the remoter parts of the island. He would never have been content with purely a desk job.

In returning to Gilbert's life, it is time to make an assessment of his place in the world. In doing so, I will concentrate on three aspects. Was he as famous in his lifetime as I have suggested; what was his relationship with Australia; and what were his lasting lifetime achievements?

I will start by quoting the Australian diplomat Sir Walter Crocker, who was in Oxford in the 1920s. He is reported as saying he "was disappointed that Gilbert Murray, the Regius Professor of Greek and perhaps the most famous Australian of his time, expressed no interest whatever in Australia". The first part of this quote calls Gilbert "the most famous Australian of his time". That is a big claim – Melba has a much better claim to that accolade – but Gilbert certainly was famous, particularly in Britain. He was offered a knighthood in 1912, which he declined, largely at Lady Mary's insistence. Why was she so insistent? A likely, but slightly cheeky explanation is that while they were known as Professor and Lady Murray, she was clearly a member of the aristocracy, but if they became Sir Gilbert and Lady Murray, people might think she was just a woman who happened to marry a bloke with a knighthood. In 1941, he accepted the much higher honour of the Order of Merit, of which there are only 20 holders at any time. He was therefore one of the nine Australians to have received that honour in the past 100 years. The others in chronological order are Samuel Alexander, Sir Frank Macfarlane Burnet, Sir Owen Dixon, Howard Florey (later Lord Florey), Sir Sidney Nolan, Dame Joan Sutherland, Robert May (later Lord May) and John Howard.

An even greater honour came his way when he died. His ashes were buried in Poets' Corner in Westminster Abbey and 1500 people attended his funeral service in the Abbey. I think he is the only Australian to have been buried in Westminster Abbey, although several others have had memorial plaques placed there.

The second part of Sir Walter Crocker's quote says that Gilbert expressed "no interest whatever in Australia". There is some truth in this statement in that Gilbert only returned to Australia once. But Gilbert was proud to be an Australian; he was always recognised as an Australian and often regaled his friends with stories, usually exaggerated, about his Australian boyhood. In his short memoir, *An Unfinished Autobiography*, he devotes 48 of the 80 pages to his Australian memories. On four occasions he gave broadcasts on the BBC about Australia. Two were titled *Calling Australia*, the third was *Australians in Britain* and the fourth was *Australia and Civilisation*. In 1953, a book was published in England called *A Sunburnt Country*. It was a collection of essays about Australia by Australian writers living in Britain, such as Martin Boyd, Russel Braddon, Chester Wilmot, George Johnston and Colin MacInnes. Gilbert, who wrote the foreword to the book, is described as the "President of the Society of Australian Writers in Britain". I think it is fair to say that he was still interested in Australia, but his work did not involve any direct contact with Australia. His prominence in British intellectual circles, however, reflected well on Australia.

The three great causes that were dear to his heart, and to which he devoted his life, were liberalism as embodied in the British Liberal Party, Hellenism, and the League of Nations. It may be a harsh judgement, but it is hard to avoid the conclusion that they all proved to be lost causes. Perhaps this is not surprising from someone whose life was centred on Oxford – long known as the home of lost causes.

Gilbert's liberalism was referred to by his son-in law, the historian Arnold Toynbee, as "aristocratic liberalism". Gilbert recognised he was in the privileged class by marriage, and was prepared to give up some of these privileges to help those beneath him. But he didn't much care for those beneath him taking matters into their own hands, hence his lack of interest in the Labour Party. In fact, Lady Mary, aristocrat though she was, joined the Labour Party in old age, whereas Gilbert, after nearly a lifetime of membership of the Liberal Party, voted Conservative in 1950 at the age of eighty-four. Before we conclude that his liberalism was a lost cause, we should recognise that the actual policies he supported were not lost causes; they were all put into effect – Home Rule for Ireland, female suffrage, university education for women, the old-age pension, etc. But as for the Liberal Party itself, its fortunes declined immediately after the First World War and by 1922 it wasn't even the official opposition. From that point onwards it has been a small centre-party with little power.

As a classical scholar, Gilbert was primarily an educator who spread an appreciation of Greek drama, poetry, religion and history to a wide audience. Some academic purists questioned his lack of commitment to pure research and his failure to publish much in learned journals. But his approach and his dedication to Hellenism helped to keep interest in the subject alive longer than it would have without his efforts. It was a losing battle, however, and he was realistic enough to recognise this. He even supported the decision to make the study of Greek no longer compulsory at Oxford. His view was he only wanted to teach students who wanted to learn, not those who were forced to. Nowadays, Greek and Latin are tiny compared to their role in the university curriculum of a century ago.

The League of Nations, as has already been established, did not achieve its objectives and lasted for less than 20 years. But it did lead to the United Nations, which is still going 70 years after its founding, and those 70 years have been a period of relative peace, unlike the first half of the twentieth century. What role the United Nations had in this outcome I leave to others to decide.

Perhaps because of these disappointments, the name Gilbert Murray is now rarely mentioned. But we should still remember his achievements as a scholar and a tireless worker for peace. As an academic, his career was outstanding whether judged by his immense output of scholarly publications or by his teaching. He was a popular lecturer, generous mentor, and former students even commented on his beautiful voice. His contribution to political debate in England covered almost 50 years of writing, public speaking and private persuasion for which he was duly honoured in his lifetime. We should also recognise his many personal qualities – his tolerance, his ability to make and keep friends, his charm and his capacity for hard work. He appears to have shown malice to no one, and it is hard to find a serious criticism of him as a person. The worst that could be said of him is that he tended to make the mistake of thinking everyone was as reasonable as he was.

Snowy Baker as a young man.

9

REGINALD LESLIE (SNOWY) BAKER

Sportsman and Showman

The name Snowy Baker crops up often enough in the history of Australian sport for him to have become something of a legend. His fame was based on his prowess at a wide range of sports, and he has been called 'Australia's greatest all-round sportsman'. A number of writers have repeated the claim that he excelled at 26 sports. I was keen to find out what exactly lay behind this claim. Could anyone really have excelled at 26 sports? This had to be an exaggeration, but was there enough substance behind it to still qualify him as our greatest all-round sportsman?

As I delved into it, I discovered that he was involved in some of the most fascinating events in our sporting history, and that some of the characters he mixed with were as interesting as he was. Also, somewhat to my surprise, his life was not only about sport, but he spent the greater part of his life as an entrepreneur, promoter, actor and filmmaker, both in Australia and later in Hollywood.

Unsurprisingly, the nickname 'Snowy' was due to his blond, almost white hair. This was attributed to some distant Germanic ancestry on his father's side although his father, George Baker, came from Protestant Irish stock. He arrived in Australia as a child in about 1850 and married in 1879. His wife, Elizabeth Jane Robertson, was Sydney born, and they settled in Bourke Street, Surry Hills, now an inner suburb of Sydney, but then surrounded by a lot of open space. George Baker was what we would now call a fitness fanatic. He rode his horse and took a long walk each morning before work, but his main sport was boxing, at which he trained regularly and competed in local competitions.

George and Elizabeth Baker had six children. Snowy, the third son, was born on 8 February 1884. From an early age, he imbibed his father's strong message that he should be physically active, build a strong body and excel at sport. George Baker's encouragement was not wasted and all his sons excelled at sport. Incidentally, Snowy Baker did not like his nickname; although he used it professionally, he preferred his friends to call him Reg. Henceforth, I will follow his wishes and not refer to him as Snowy, but call him by his surname Baker.

The first sport that we hear of Baker mastering is horseriding, where he accompanied his father whenever he could. By the time he was halfway through primary school he could ride confidently on the various horses his father provided. But his real claims to sporting excellence in the first part of his life from school to young manhood were his achievements in swimming, boxing and rugby union.

He first attracted attention as a swimmer. The turn of the century was an exciting period for swimming, as Australian swimmers first won medals at the Olympic Games and experimented with the various strokes that were evolving. The first Australian swimmer to win Olympic gold medals was Freddie Lane at the 1900 Paris Olympics. He won gold in the 200 metres freestyle and the 200 metres obstacle race. Both events were held in the River Seine, and in the obstacle race competitors had to swim under and around moored boats, climb aboard some and then dive back into the water. Not surprisingly, this event did not last long on the Olympic agenda.

The main achievement in the evolution of swimming strokes was the development of the Australian crawl. Until then, most swimmers used breaststroke or a hybrid called the Tudgen stroke, but there were also experiments with other styles. Most writers on the subject date the Australian crawl's introduction from the late 1890s, when a young boy from Samoa with an English father and a Samoan mother arrived in Sydney and used the stroke in a local competition. The boy, Alick Wickham, explained that he had been taught the stroke by his father, who had learned it from the natives of Samoa. Australian swimmers soon learned to use it and the first significant milestone was in 1899 when Dick Cavill, from a famous swimming family, won the New South Wales 100 yards championship using it. Eventually it spread around the world, and is still the only stroke used in freestyle events. Interestingly, Freddie Lane had not yet adopted it in his two Olympic victories in 1900.

During his childhood, Baker spent a lot of his leisure time swimming in the pools around Sydney Harbour, and at the age of fourteen he took it up competitively when he joined the East Sydney Swimming Club. He was soon the best schoolboy swimmer in New South Wales, specialising in the 100- and 200-yard freestyle. He also competed in club championships and finished second to Freddie

Lane in the club's handicap competition. Although Baker continued to improve, he could not beat Lane and had to be content with being a member of the winning relay team with Lane, Wickham and others who broke the Australian record on several occasions. The Australian record was also the world record, but the event, which involved the five members of the relay each swimming a 100-yard leg, was unique to Australia, and was soon replaced by the more familiar four-member relay. Baker also represented his club at water polo and took up diving, but mainly to amuse the crowd at swimming carnivals.

One sport that Baker dabbled in while at school, but did not pursue seriously, was cricket. He was a student at Crown Street Public School in Surry Hills, which boasted both Monty Noble, a future Australian cricket captain, and Victor Trumper, Australia's most illustrious batsman, as ex-students. Many years later Baker explained, "After being at school with Victor Trumper and Monty Noble, I always had an inferiority complex about cricket." It is doubtful if all three were at the school at the same time because Noble was 11 years older than Baker, and Trumper six years older. Nevertheless, for a small school this was an amazing concentration of sporting talent in such a short time.

When Baker left school he was able to get a job as an office junior at the Colonial Sugar Refinery (CSR) and he remained in this job until he left for England five years later.

At about this time he took up boxing seriously. Amateur boxing during this period was regarded as a normal sporting activity suitable for men from all walks of life. It was sometimes called the 'noble art', just as horse racing was called the 'sport of kings'. Baker's father had seen nothing disreputable about it, so it was acceptable for his son, just as it was acceptable for English gentlemen as we will see later.

Boxing's fall in respectability came later when professionalism began to dominate.

Baker was five foot eight inches tall, about average for men of that time, and very strong, agile and well-coordinated. He started his career as a lightweight, but then moved up and fought as a middleweight for most of his career. He took boxing seriously, and at his father's suggestion was coached by the best boxing coaches available, so he quickly matured. Ever confident, he entered the 1902 New South Wales Amateur Boxing Championships at the age of eighteen. He won the lightweight title at his first attempt, a remarkable achievement for a teenager.

At the same time as his boxing career was developing, Baker was playing a lot of rugby union with a local club. In 1903 he was recruited to play for the prestigious Eastern Suburbs Rugby Club, and went straight into their first team as halfback. At the end of the first season he was selected to play for New South Wales against Queensland. He played in the three interstate matches, which were all won by New South Wales, and his reputation as a rugby player rose.

But better things were to come. In 1904, Baker was chosen to play scrum-half for Australia against the visiting Great Britain team. Although Australia was easily defeated 17–0 in the first test, Baker was chosen again for the second test. Another comfortable British victory of 17–3 meant new blood was needed for Australia so Baker was dropped for the third test, which ended his involvement in international rugby. Again, Britain had an easy victory, 16–0. The Australian rugby team was struggling to reach international standard at this time; as well as being beaten by Great Britain, it had also lost heavily to New Zealand in the previous season. As Baker's rugby ambitions faded, his boxing progress continued. In 1904, he moved up a division and won the middleweight title at the New South Wales Amateur Boxing Championship.

He kept up a vigorous sporting schedule with boxing, club rugby and his new interest – rowing, which helped him to build strength and stamina for boxing. He easily defended his New South Wales middleweight title in 1905. In Greg Growden's biography, *The Snowy Baker Story*, he relates how, when presenting the gold medal to Baker, Sir Francis Suttor MLC said that when he was minister for public instruction he had attempted to get boxing taught on a compulsory basis in the schools because he thought "every boy in the country should learn the art", but he was overruled in parliament by the "Wowsers".

So, at the end of 1905 when he was twenty-one years of age, Baker already had an impressive list of sporting achievements that would easily qualify him as a great all-round athlete. He had played rugby for Australia, was the holder of the New South Wales amateur middleweight boxing title, and was a member of a swimming relay team that held the world record for that event. In addition, he had played water polo, rowed at club level, given diving displays at swimming carnivals and was a very good horseman, although not a competitor in racing events or gymkhanas.

Into this busy schedule, Baker also managed to join the Royal New South Wales Lancers, a part-time military regiment. The Lancers, being a cavalry regiment, attracted well-off and well-connected members of Sydney society, an opportunity that the upwardly-mobile Baker valued. It also offered new and exotic avenues for him to show his sporting prowess, such as tent-pegging (where a galloping rider uses his lance or sword to pick up a small ground target), mounted tug-of-war (surely the horse should get most of the credit in this event) and wrestling on horseback.

I am conscious of the claim that Baker excelled at 26 different sports and have tried to count them all up. So far we have rugby, boxing, swimming, diving, water polo, rowing, riding, and then if we add tent-pegging, mounted tug-of-war and horseback wrestling, we are still only up to ten sports. This is an impressive achievement, particularly as he was working full-time, but it is a long way short of 26.

By this time, Baker had become something of a celebrity and his exploits were written up regularly in the sporting press. His sporting efforts were increasingly concentrated on boxing, where he was virtually unbeatable in amateur events. First, he won the Australasian middleweight crown in Brisbane by knocking out his opponent from New Zealand. Then he returned to Sydney and won the New South Wales middleweight and heavyweight titles. With his reputation spreading across Australia, he was invited to fight for the Victorian titles in Melbourne. His presence was expected to increase public interest and crowd attendance. He didn't let the organisers down, and again he won the middleweight and heavyweight titles, even though the finals took place on the same night.

It is hard to believe that someone who had started as a lightweight only a few years earlier could now be winning heavyweight titles. By 1906, when he was doing so, he was still only twenty-two years old, but his weight had increased to 11 stone, 12 pounds (75 kilograms), still very light for a heavyweight by modern standards. We have to remember that these were amateur fights and that some of his opponents, particularly in the heavyweight division, were journeymen or outright plodders. He was very keen to test himself against better boxers, but to do so would require him to fight overseas.

Fortunately, by now his reputation had spread abroad and he was invited to compete in the 1907 England Amateur Boxing Association Championships. He accepted the invitation enthusiastically and resigned his job at CSR. He had become well known in Australian sporting circles by this time and well connected, so he had no trouble in organising a fund to finance his overseas trip. But events did not turn out as expected.

He left Australia at the end of 1906, intending to compete in the British Championships in March 1907. On the way his ship stopped in Aden (then an important port, now a minor city in the Yemen) and Baker and friends went ashore for a drink. While his friends drank beer and whisky, Baker, who was a teetotaller and obviously a novice traveller, drank two glasses of water. His health soon deteriorated and by the time he reached London he had a high fever. This was diagnosed as enteric fever (Salmonella enterica) and was probably caused by the water he drank in Aden. He was hospitalised and ordered by his doctors to have three months' complete rest. He recuperated in Ireland, but missed the 1907 championships.

After recovering, he decided to try again for the 1908 championships. While waiting, Baker and an Australian friend and fellow swimmer, Theo Tartakover, entered swimming contests in Scotland and throughout Europe, but Baker did no serious boxing. Again fate was against him, as he contracted pneumonia shortly before the 1908 boxing championships and had to withdraw. The whole overseas trip had been a huge disappointment as he had had no chance to test himself against the British boxers. His money was running out, and he prepared to return to Australia.

His luck then changed when he received a very welcome letter from the New South Wales Swimming Association. The letter said that as the 1908 Olympic Games were to be held in London, would it be possible for Baker and Tartakover to remain there until mid-year and represent Australia in swimming (diving was added later). For Baker, this was a great relief and honour, although he later learned that he would have been in the Olympic team anyway because he had been chosen for boxing on the strength of his Australian titles. Thus, Baker found himself in the very unusual position of representing his country in three events at the one Olympics.

It is worth spending a little time to understand how these early Olympic Games were organised. First, they were nothing like modern Olympics in that there were fewer countries competing, and so the Games were a lot smaller. Second, there was not much money behind it, and visiting teams were often tiny and not very representative. This gave the home team an enormous advantage, much more so than in recent Olympics. For example, the United States won 237 medals in 1904 when the Games were held in Saint Louis, but only 47 in 1908 in London. An even more extreme example is Great Britain, which only won two medals in Saint Louis, but 146 in London. The host country could field as many competitors as it liked, even in team events. As a result, Great Britain won all the medals – gold, silver and bronze – in team events such as hockey, polo and tug-of-war.

Australia had no Olympic Committee as there is today, to choose the best representatives from each sport. Instead, each sporting association, such as swimming, athletics, boxing, rowing, would do what it could afford to do, which was often very little or nothing. In most sports Australia was represented by athletes who were already in England, or those who could afford to pay their own way, whether or not they were national champions in their event. In the first modern Olympic Games in 1896, Edwin Flack, an Australian accountant on an assignment in London for Price Waterhouse, paid for himself to go to Athens. He competed in athletics and tennis, but could hardly be said to have represented Australia as it did not yet exist as a nation. Flack won gold in the 800 and 1500 metre races. He competed in the 800 metres final in the afternoon after playing and losing a doubles tennis match in the morning.

Part of the legend about Baker being Australia's greatest all-round sportsman is that he was the only person to ever represent Australia in three sports at the one Olympics: swimming, diving and boxing. But he was not anywhere near internationally competitive in the first two sports – he was only chosen because he was already in England. In diving he came last in his heat and didn't make the final, and in swimming he did not even enter any individual event, but was part of the four-man relay team that came fourth.

The big success for Australia was that it won the gold medal in rugby. This was only possible because Australia's national rugby team – the Wallabies – happened to be in England at the time playing tests against Great Britain. In the final they faced Great Britain, represented by the championship county team Cornwall, not by the national team. Australia easily defeated them 32–3. Another big success was the seventeen-year-old swimmer Frank Beaurepaire, who had scraped enough funds together to buy a steerage passage to England, where he stayed with relatives to save money. He won a silver medal in the 400 metres freestyle and a bronze in the 1500 metres. He was a better swimmer than Baker, but shared something in common with him. Both, when they retired from sport, became entrepreneurs. Frank Beaurepaire, later Sir Frank, became Lord Mayor of Melbourne, and established the large Australia-wide tyre retailing firm that still bears his name.

While the swimming and diving events in June were a wipeout for Baker, the boxing was not held until three months later, by which time he was able to get fully fit. And there can be no doubt that he was a much better boxer than a swimmer or diver; he held Australian titles in boxing, which he did not in swimming or diving. There were five weight divisions in boxing and so 15 medals to be awarded. Boxers from Great Britain won 14 medals, with Baker being the only non-British medal winner. Great Britain's success was not surprising, as only four countries entered the boxing events: Great Britain entered 32 boxers, France seven, Denmark two and Australasia one. The United States, which is traditionally the strongest boxing nation, did not enter any boxers.

All matches were fought over three rounds, and the three heats and the final were held on the same day. Baker won his three heats against British boxers, two by knockouts, but even so had only one hour to recover between the third heat and the final. His opponent in the final, Johnny Douglas, had an easier passage to the final with only two bouts – both of which he won by a knockout – and a bye. The final was fiercely fought with Baker, realising that tiredness would hamper him in the later rounds, going for a knockout in the first round. Douglas was able to resist this, and his greater fitness began to tell. The fight went the distance with Douglas winning narrowly on points. But Baker's performance was widely praised in the British and Australian sporting press and he returned to Australia with his silver medal, a homecoming hero.

His opponent, Douglas, was a classic example of the English gentleman sportsman. He came from a wealthy family, did not need to work, and could devote himself to his sporting interests. Australians got to know him better through his other sporting interest – cricket, when he captained the English team in the 1924 tour of Australia. Being an amateur cricketer, as all English captains had to be at that time, he was referred to by his initials as J.W.H.T. Douglas. Australian cricket crowds, irritated by his slow batting and amused by his four initials gave him the nickname 'Johnny Won't Hit Today' Douglas.

When Baker arrived in Australia late in 1908, he was welcomed back by crowds when the ship berthed and by a civic reception in the city. His photograph showing his impressive physique, good looks and distinctive blond hair was reproduced widely. He was only twenty-four years of age, and people assumed there were many sporting triumphs yet to come. Many people of wealth and importance sought him out and he revelled in the attention. He knew how to promote himself and he did so unashamedly.

One of the first important people to gain his confidence was the biggest boxing promoter in Sydney, Hugh D. McIntosh, known as 'Huge Deal' McIntosh. He had originally made his money through a chain of pie shops, but then went on to build the boxing stadium at Rushcutters Bay. This was the premium venue for boxing in New South Wales, so he effectively controlled professional boxing in the state. It was an extremely popular sport, attracting big crowds and enticing boxers from America and Europe as well as the locals. It was also a very profitable business, but there was much resentment about McIntosh's power, and his business principles were regarded by some as being on the shady side. His business needed something to make it more respectable and remove any suspicion that the outcome of fights might be being rigged. McIntosh's solution was to hire Baker as the permanent referee for each fight.

Until now, Baker had spent his time in the relatively genteel world of amateur sport, especially amateur boxing. Now he had to make the transition to the world of professional boxing. Although most of its participants were honest toilers, there was a fringe element of touts, spivs and urgers who were eager to infiltrate the game, and the big promoters were ruthless in maximising their share of the gate receipts at the expense of the boxers. Baker seems to have had no trouble in moving from being a boxer in the amateur world to being a referee, and later a promoter, in the professional world.

McIntosh soon pulled off his greatest coup when he staged the world heavyweight boxing championship in his stadium in Sydney at the end of 1908. Tommy Burns, a Canadian, was the self-proclaimed world champion, but there was a very powerful and much-feared challenger in Jack Johnson, the first great black heavyweight. Most heavyweight boxers avoided fighting Johnson, some because of his race, but others because they knew he would beat them. McIntosh paid Burns a huge sum to defend his title in Sydney, but it didn't take much to entice Johnson. Baker was chosen to referee the fight, but Johnson would not accept him because he was too close to the Burns camp. In the event, McIntosh, who had never refereed a fight before, ended up refereeing the world heavyweight boxing championship himself. A massive crowd turned up and press came from around the world, including the world's best-known sporting writer, Jack London.

Johnson was far too strong for Burns and could have won quickly, but he strung it out for 13 rounds, all of which he won easily. Burns was in severe distress, but the incompetent McIntosh only stopped the fight when the police threatened to intervene. Johnson's victory was a big event in the history of boxing, and a shock to the white supremacists who controlled the sport in America. It is interesting that although he was the best boxer in the world, Johnson could not get a shot at the title in America or Europe, but he could in Australia. This was the only time a world heavyweight boxing championship was held in Australia, and it was arguably the most important in the history of boxing. McIntosh made a fortune from the gate receipts and film rights, and could have retired on the strength of them. Instead, he continued to organise fights at his stadium with Baker as his permanent referee.

Baker's life then took an unexpected turn. At the beginning of 1909, at the age of twenty-five, he retired from all competitive sport. There is no suggestion that injury forced him to do so, and no explanation was given. In the three sports where he excelled – boxing, swimming and rugby – sportsmen are usually competitive through to their early thirties. The only explanation I can come up with for such an early retirement is that he needed to make some money. Rugby and swimming were entirely amateur, so there was no hope of making money there. Boxing was a possibility if he turned professional, but that was both financially and physically risky. Whatever the reason for his action, it meant his sporting career was confined to a seven-year period between the ages of eighteen and twenty-five. But he had become famous enough in that short time to launch himself into a business career whose marketing approach was based on the prominent use of his name.

Also in 1909, Baker met and soon married Ethel Rose Kearny, a widow 12 years older than him with two daughters. There was a sporting connection as she was an accomplished horsewoman, and her late husband had represented Victoria in tennis. Now with a family to support, Baker looked for ways to supplement the modest income he received as a boxing referee. His first new business initiative was to open a gymnasium in central Sydney with that old boxing advocate, Sir Francis Suttor MLC, giving the opening address. With Baker's fame, extensive sporting contacts and heavy advertising, it was well patronised and financially successful.

At the beginning of 1912, Baker added to his business interests by launching a fitness magazine called *Snowy Baker's Magazine*. Its aim was to "furnish informative articles on all manly health-giving pastimes", and it gave advice on a range of health issues. In the magazine's view "Poverty, misery, crime and destitution are the products, primarily of physical unfitness". It offered helpful hints on such issues as how to overcome stammering – the solution was to read aloud. It also advised against the wearing of hats: "baldness and nervous headaches are encouraged by too constant use of the hat." Women were also given advice, such as to avoid wearing high heels. Using a homespun version of the Lamarkian theory of evolution, it claimed "they will permanently destroy the bone structure of the feet and upset the delicate balance of the natural functions. It is a later generation that probably suffers most, unfortunately, so severe and exacting is hereditary". The magazine also advertised Baker's own patented medicine, *Snowy Baker's Embrocation*. It advised readers to "keep a bottle handy because it overcomes rheumatism, banishes lumbago, knocks out stiffness and extracts pain from bruises".

While he was launching these new businesses, Baker remained heavily involved in boxing, not only refereeing matches, but in promoting them as well. Meanwhile, McIntosh was tiring of fight promotion and wanted to move upmarket by becoming an entertainment impresario. This required him to buy the Tivoli theatre group and sell the Sydney Stadium. Baker arranged finance and bought the stadium from him. Although Baker's gymnasium and magazine had been doing well, it was difficult to believe he would have had the financial resources to buy something as expensive as the stadium. The suspicion was that McIntosh still retained a share, and that another big investor, John Wren, was also a part-owner.

Wren controlled boxing in Melbourne, and a lot else. He ran the Collingwood Football Club, controlled legal and illegal betting in inner Melbourne, was influential in the Catholic Church, owned three race courses, a newspaper and a theatre. He was more prudent than McIntosh, but still a figure who inspired suspicion and resentment because of his widespread influence and secrecy. He was the figure whom author Frank Hardy set out to discredit in his controversial book, *Power Without Glory*, but Baker also rates a mention in the book under the name of Snowy Bacon.

I don't think there is any doubt that Wren and McIntosh were still the main owners of the stadium business, while Baker was the frontman and minority owner/manager. In typical style, he tried to disabuse the public of this perception by renaming Sydney Stadium 'Snowy Baker's Stadium'. Soon the business purchased stadiums in Brisbane, Melbourne and Adelaide, and the combined group was called Stadiums Ltd. This was further evidence that there must have been big money behind the project. The Brisbane venue was called 'Baker's Olympic Stadium' and claimed to be the largest building in Queensland. By now Baker was still only twenty-nine, but running a large Australia-wide business.

In order for the business to succeed, he had to be able to attract boxers who were good enough to draw the crowds. Many of the boxers came from America, Britain and Europe and some were serious contenders for world titles, although there was a lot of confusion and ambiguity about who held what title. Baker also needed to encourage local boxers and was always on the lookout for a local who could beat the highly-credentialed imports and so put in a claim to be world champion. Soon that boxer came along in the form of the Maitland blacksmith, Les Darcy.

Darcy is still an Australian folk hero, the subject of at least four biographies, although it is hard now to remember the huge public support there was for this unassuming, clean-living and superbly talented boxer. His legend was like that of Phar Lap, with which he shared several experiences. His boxing career was extremely short, with his first fight at seventeen years of age and his last at twenty. While still living in Maitland, he fought in Sydney six times for three wins and three losses. Baker then arranged for him to move permanently to Sydney, to be coached and to train seriously. Thereafter he won 22 fights in a row, mainly by knockout, against increasingly experienced and highly-rated local and imported American middleweights. Darcy also fought heavyweights and won, although one – Harold Hardwick – knocked out two of Darcy's teeth before he was knocked out himself. Darcy gained a huge following, ensured full houses whenever he fought, and was Stadium Ltd.'s greatest asset. By general consensus, he was by far the best middleweight in the world. Baker called him the middleweight champion of the world, but Darcy could not be recognised as such until he defeated a couple of American contenders, which experienced boxing judges, both here and in the US, felt he could easily do.

There were a number of promoters who were keen to take Darcy to America; some with credible schemes, some less so. Even McIntosh had been hatching a plan to get Darcy to America on his terms. But the most insistent was an American called Jack Kearns, who nearly pulled it off. He is mostly remembered now from a quote about him by an associate who said, "When you first meet Jack, you are inclined to dislike him, but when you know him for a while, you really get to hate him."

Darcy's tragedy was that his boxing peak coincided exactly with the First World War. If he had been born a few years earlier, he would have achieved all his boxing goals before the war started. If he had been born a few years later, he would have been too young to serve. All his big boxing triumphs occurred between February 1915 and September 1916. At this time, Australia was in the grip of the First World War and patriotic fervour was high after the Anzacs first went into battle at Gallipoli in April 1915. A lot of the population felt that Darcy should have been fighting for his country, rather than staying at home making money fighting in the ring. Others felt that Darcy in the trenches with a rifle would be no better than any other soldier, but in the boxing ring he was unique; surely some other way could be found to use his boxing talent to help him and the war effort.

Darcy was in a near impossible position. Obviously he would have preferred to continue boxing, make a lot of money, help his large family, and then if the war was still going, enlist. He tried to find a way to do this, but it was not possible. Despite Baker's best efforts he could not get good opponents for him to box in Australia, and Darcy couldn't go to America because single males of military age were denied passports. Even if he had wanted to enlist he needed his mother's permission because he was still under twenty-one, and she would not give it. Baker, who was still only thirty when the war started, was found unfit to serve because of a back problem caused by a car accident in March 1915.

Darcy then did something very rash. In October 1916, he stowed away on a tramp steamer headed for Chile, and then took another ship to America. This outraged a large section of the Australian population who called him a shirker, a money grubber and now a law breaker. A number of people wrote to America expressing their disapproval of Darcy's action, which had the effect of reducing his boxing opportunities there. Baker was one of those, and was particularly incensed because Darcy had broken his contract with Stadiums Ltd. when he left without notice.

The result was that Darcy's American fights were cancelled by state authorities. Less famous Australian and English boxers still plied their trade in America, but Darcy never got to box there. In April 1917, six months after he left Australia, he died suddenly from septicaemia (blood poisoning), caused by infected teeth damaged in the Hardwick bout.

The tragedy of his early death caused a huge outpouring of public sympathy in Australia; all was forgiven and he was now viewed as a martyr. Those, like Baker, who had criticised him for going to America, were now the subject of public vilification. Of course, they had nothing to do with his death; that would have happened whether he'd stayed in Australia or left. Nevertheless, for the first time Baker became very unpopular with the Australian public and was not welcome at Darcy's huge funeral in Maitland. In due course he was able to salvage his reputation with the public at large, but it took a personal appearance at a public inquiry in Maitland to establish his innocence and even so, many boxing fans never forgave him.

Baker's next big problem was that boxing was starting to lose its appeal and attendances were falling. The death of Darcy had cast a pall over the whole sport. Baker could not get good boxers to replace him and the public became sick of watching sub-standard fights. In early 1918, Stadiums Ltd. closed its doors and Baker had to look for new ways to supplement his income. He had half-expected this, and it didn't take him long to find a way.

He realised there was money to be made from films, which were rapidly increasing in popularity. More and more cinemas were opening, and attendances rising. Films were relatively cheap to make at that time because, being silent, they were very simple, could be made in a month or two and there were no film stars to command high salaries. Baker put himself forward as an actor and financial partner and soon found a filmmaker with an attractive project. The film was called *The Enemy Within* and was made while the war was still going. It was basically a piece of pro-war, anti-German propaganda. Baker didn't just act in it, he starred in it, and the film was moderately successful and profitable. Baker was not much of an actor, but he was very good at stunts, like jumping off a galloping horse onto another one, diving from heights and participating in numerous chases and fight scenes. The poster promoting the film said "He performs the stunts which other actors can only fake. See his terrific fight against four men, his 80-foot dive into the harbour, his leap from the flying cars". This was the man who had recently been found physically unfit for military service.

With the success of this film behind him, Baker decided to set up his own filmmaking company, not surprisingly called Snowy Baker Films. He visited Hollywood, met various famous actors including the biggest name of all – Charlie Chaplin – plus various producers and directors, then returned to Australia with great plans. He also imported an American director, a screenwriter and an actress, and used them to make a further four films over the next 18 months. The films were *The Lure of the Bush, The Man from Kangaroo, The Shadow of Lightning Ridge* and *The Jackaroo from Coolabong*.

The films were all very similar. Baker starred in each one and though his acting hadn't improved, he found more and more stunts to perform involving boxing, swimming, diving and horseriding on his famous

Charlie Chaplin left and Snowy Baker right in Hollywood in the 1920s.

horse, 'Boomerang'. He was setting himself up as a sort of cowboy hero along the lines of the Hollywood star of the time, Tom Mix. These films were mainly set in the Australian bush and extolled the virtues of the uncomplicated rural, manly life. A favourable review in the newspaper *The Referee* (owned by McIntosh), gives the flavour:

> There are brushes with bushrangers, encounters with wild Aboriginals, a kangaroo drive, musterings of cattle and sheep, a shearers' shed in action, a shearers' 'ball', some attractive little scenes of farmyard life, also possums and native bears [sic] are seen moving in trees.

Although the films made money, it was becoming more difficult as so many competitors entered the industry. As well, Baker's films were seen by the public and critics as too American, which they were because they had all been made with ambitions for distribution in America. As usual, Baker was pursuing other money-making schemes at the same time as his filmmaking. One was to sell acting lessons through his gymnasium, and another was to bring out another patented medicine – this time it was 'Snowy Baker's Unfailing Liniment'. He was also, throughout this time, a sporting correspondent for *The Evening News* newspaper. But his opportunities to make money in Australia were drying up, so in August 1920 at the age of thirty-six, accompanied by his family, he left Australia to try to make his fortune in Hollywood. His career as an actor and filmmaker in Australia had lasted about three years.

Baker's departure from Australia was permanent, apart from three brief return visits. He lived the rest of his life in Los Angeles, where he worked in various capacities in the movie, entertainment and hospitality industries. His main aim in going to Los Angeles was to break into the Hollywood film industry. He started by re-shooting some scenes from his Australian films to make them more suitable for American audiences. He also renamed them, so *The Man from Kangaroo* became *The Better Man*, and *The Jackaroo from Coolabong* became *The Fighting Breed*. They must have had some success because he then went on to star in a further six films: *The Last Race, Sleeping Acre, The Empire Builders, Fighter's Paradise, White Panther* and *The Sword of Valour*. These films are now referred to as B-grade movies, and copies of all but the last have disappeared.

Movie roles started becoming harder to find, so Baker turned to Vaudeville. He used the rope-spinning and whip-cracking skills he had acquired for his movie roles in a stage act to fill the gaps between movie roles. But soon there were no film roles at all. As his biographer Growden puts it:

> Just as Snowy had discovered in Australia, there are only so many stories you can base around a person who can't act, but can ride horses, crack a whip and perform wild stunts. Slowly, but surely, the movie studios stopped contacting the Baker household.

Fortunately Baker found a new career, which he pursued for the rest of his life. It was less glamorous than acting, but at least it kept him in touch with the movie world. He became equestrian director of the Riviera Country Club in Santa Monica, a luxurious club frequented by many of the best-known actors and directors in Hollywood. The club boasted every athletic facility available, including an outstanding golf course and five polo fields. Baker ran a regular polo competition in which players such as Will Rogers, Walt Disney, Gary Cooper, Spencer Tracy, Leslie Howard and others competed. Under Baker's direction, the Riviera Country Club hosted all the equestrian events at the 1932 Los Angeles Olympics.

He still did occasional work as a stuntman in movies, and taught sporting skills to actors. He taught Douglas Fairbanks fencing, and a young Elizabeth Taylor how to ride a horse for her role in the film that made her famous, *National Velvet*. He also, less plausibly, claimed to have taught Rudolph Valentino to kiss. From 1928 onwards he wrote an 'American Letter' column for *The Referee*, which kept Australian readers up to date on American sport and entertainment gossip, and kept his name in the public eye in Australia.

Baker settled into these roles on the fringe of Hollywood and seems to have been satisfied with this more stable lifestyle. His wife and stepdaughters were also happy with it, and the family remained close. He was seen as the Australian who everyone in Hollywood knew. At an event associated with the Los Angeles Olympics, he was introduced by the master of ceremonies thus: "Ladies and Gentlemen, it is now my pleasure to introduce the very popular equestrian director of the Riviera Country Club and Australia's greatest all-round sportsman – Snowy Baker." Clearly his self-promotion had worked well in America.

In 1946, Baker was relieved of his duties at the Riviera Country Club, and stepped down to be chief instructor at the less glamorous Beverly Hills Saddle Club. After a few years there his health gradually deteriorated and he died in 1953, at the age of sixty-nine, from cerebrovascular disease (a stroke).

I am aware that I have dealt lightly with the last 30 years of Baker's life. This is because it adds nothing to his record as a great sportsman, and it is only in this respect that he is still remembered. Growden reports that in 1946 the Australian magazine *Sporting Novels* asked its readers to nominate the all-time best Australian sportsman. The top five in order were Darcy, Bradman, Baker, Lindrum and Trumper. In 1957 they conducted the survey again, and the order was Bradman, Darcy, Landy, and then Baker. So there is no doubt that the legend of Baker as a great sportsman survived beyond his death. In fact, he has frequently been lauded as Australia's *greatest* all-round sportsman. It appears on the cover of Growden's biography, Harry Gordon in his book *Australia and the Olympics* repeats it, and the Australian Olympic Committee has it on their website. It is treated as a fact – like Landy was the first Australian to break the four-minute mile or Bradman had the highest batting average – but it should really only be viewed as an opinion. The claim rests primarily on two supporting statements – that he was the only sportsman to represent Australia in three events in one Olympics, and that he excelled at 26 sports.

We have already established that the first claim, while true, is largely an accident of timing in that he happened to be in England in 1908. Under modern selection practices, he would only have been chosen for boxing and not for swimming or diving. The second claim that he excelled at 26 sports is also widely quoted, but has never been substantiated. Who first made this claim? Who would have been able to count them other than Baker himself? In my reading of Baker's life I can't get past a dozen sports, and even then I am counting some that are hardly championship class, such as teaching fencing to actors, or playing polo with them. Gordon, in his brief description of Baker, also lists him as a champion wrestler, gymnast and track athlete, but none of these are mentioned in Growden's much bigger and more detailed biography. Wikipedia says he excelled at cricket, but Growden quotes Baker himself saying he didn't. The most extreme claim comes from the Sport Australia Hall of Fame, which says "he competed at either State or National level in twenty-nine different sports". It then goes on to list them, but only gets to 13, three of which – athletics, hockey and yachting – are not mentioned in Growden's biography. The truth is that no one has kept count of, nor verified, the individual sports, so we have to regard the claim that he excelled at 26 (or 29) sports as pure hype.

I am not doubting that Baker was a very talented all-round sportsman who competed at international level in four sports during his brief career. But is he entitled to be called *the greatest*? Again, who first made this claim? Was it the result of a thorough investigation of all the other sportsmen who might have a claim? I haven't done such an investigation either, but even among Baker's contemporaries, there are some versatile sportsmen – the aforementioned Harold Hardwick, for example. He was a quiet and modest man, but was New South Wales state swimming champion at 100 yards, 220 yards and one mile. At the 1912 Olympic Games, he won bronze medals for the 400 and 1500 metres and a gold in the four by 200 metres relay. He held the New South Wales and Empire amateur heavyweight boxing titles and also boxed professionally (including against Darcy). He was a member of the Eastern Suburbs Rugby team that won the Premiership in 1913 and played for New South Wales. He also participated in gymnastics, water polo and life-saving. Victor Richardson, as well as captaining Australia at cricket, captained South Australian at Australian rules, played baseball for Australia and golf for South Australia, won the South Australian tennis title, and also played lacrosse and basketball. More recently, Mike Cleary represented Australia in rugby union and rugby league and won a bronze medal in athletics at the 1962 Commonwealth Games. There may well be other sportsmen who have a claim as good as Baker's or Hardwick's or Richardson's or Cleary's. I don't know enough to judge, but it is not obvious to me that Baker's claim to be the greatest is any stronger than the others. W.F. Mandle in the *Australian Dictionary of Biography* sums it up well:

> His stature as an athlete depends largely on the enormous range rather than the outstanding excellence of his activities; it was as

an entrepreneur-showman, publicist and businessman that he seems in retrospect to have been most important.

In most of the other essays in this book I have described the lives of people whose exploits have been underestimated and as a result they have been largely forgotten. Baker is different in that, for a time, his reputation was greater than his achievements warranted. Nevertheless, no one could doubt that he led an interesting and varied life. The third phase in California was something of an anticlimax, but it kept him and his family in comfort. He was survived by his wife and stepdaughters, and he left them a reasonable inheritance. The other two main characters in this essay did not fare nearly as well. McIntosh gambled on one-too-many huge deals and died a pauper in England. Darcy, as we know, died at twenty-one years of age, but left a sporting reputation far greater and longer lasting than Baker's.

Frederick Septimus Kelly in London in 1908.

10

FREDERICK SEPTIMUS KELLY

Concert Pianist, Composer and Oarsman

When I first read of Kelly about 15 years ago in a biography of Rupert Brook, I was slightly taken aback by the author's description of him. He described Kelly as "an Australian-born Oxford 'hearty' who had thrice won the Diamond Sculls at the Henley Regatta". I wondered whether it was fair to call him a 'hearty', which is the term the English use to describe a jovial sporting type, much as the Americans use the term 'jock'. Following some quick research, I soon realised there was much more to Kelly than that. He was primarily a concert pianist and classical music composer who also happened to be an outstanding oarsman. He led a fascinating life in Edwardian England and seems to have met many of the most interesting people of that era. But, like so many of that generation, the advent of the First World War changed everything.

Frederick Septimus Kelly came from a very prosperous Australian family. His father, Thomas Hussey Kelly, had migrated from Ireland in about 1860 at the age of thirty. He had a rapid rise in the Sydney business world, first as a wool and produce broker, then in the metals and mining industries. He became managing director of the Sydney Smelting Company and was a major shareholder and director of such established companies as Burns Philp and Co., Tooth and Co., and the Colonial Sugar Refinery, among others.

He married an Australian woman, Mary Ann Dick, in a Protestant ceremony shortly after arriving in Australia and they had seven children, four of whom survived them. The family lived in a mansion called Glenyarrah in Double Bay on Sydney Harbour. The oldest son, Thomas Herbert Kelly, known as Bertie, was followed by another son, William Henry Kelly, and a daughter, Mary, known as Maisie. Frederick Septimus Kelly was born in May 1881 and, as his second name indicates, was the seventh child and was always known in family circles as 'Sep'. This is the name I will use in the family phase of his life, although in later life he acquired the other nickname, 'Cleg'. He was almost never called Frederick or Fred.

Apart from work and education, the family had two other main interests. Living next to the harbour enabled them to own boats, to sail, to row and to become members of sailing clubs. But even more important to the family was music, and this meant mainly classical music. Playing music, not just listening to it, was a big part of family life in the days before radio or recorded music. Bertie was a violinist, Maisie a singer and pianist, but Sep eclipsed them all by being a child prodigy as a pianist and budding composer.

In 1893 the family, by now very wealthy, sailed to England and the three boys were enrolled at Eton to finish their secondary education.

It was the practice in Australia, as it was in England, for rich parents to send their children to boarding school, but to send them to one in another country was unusual. It illustrated once again the esteem with which established English institutions were held in Australia. The parents returned to Australia and Thomas Hussey Kelly continued to expand his business interests. Bertie finished at Eton, took a degree at Magdalen College Oxford, then returned to Australia and followed his father in business, while continuing to play the violin in an amateur orchestra and chamber music quartets, as well as helping to establish the Sydney Symphony Orchestra. William Henry Kelly also returned to Australia and went into politics, winning the federal seat of Wentworth in 1903 and holding it until 1919 for the Liberal (later Nationalist) Party. Sep and Maisie remained in England.

We don't know how Sep felt at Eton, separated from his parents at the age of just twelve. It must have been difficult, but at least he had his two older brothers there as well. His frequent return visits to Eton after he left show his affection for the school, so he must have regarded his time there as of value to him, possibly even enjoyable. In addition to a normal academic education, he was able to increase his proficiency as a pianist under the school's musical director, Dr Charles Harford-Lloyd. While at Eton, he composed a number of pieces for piano and voice, the sheet music for which can still be viewed in his original scores. He also took up rowing and became good enough to be chosen as stroke in the school eight. In his final year at Eton, he won the Nettleship Music Scholarship awarded by Balliol College Oxford.

Balliol is one of the most prestigious Oxford colleges, and his time there was a busy one as he juggled his two great interests – rowing and music – with his academic study of history. As a rower, he was a member of the Oxford crew in the Oxford–Cambridge Boat Race and so was awarded his Blue. As a musician, he continued his piano tuition and performed at the Oxford University Musical Club, of which he was president. He also started to compose music seriously, and one of his Oxford pieces, *It is Not Dawn Till You Awake*, was later published and performed. Given the time and effort he put into his rowing and his music, it is not a great surprise to learn that his academic results suffered and he graduated in 1902 with a fourth-class degree (I didn't know they went that low). But, in line with the usual Oxbridge practice, this was turned into a Master of Arts degree in 1912 following the payment of a small fee and the lapsing of at least 21 terms after graduation.

Another reason for his poor academic result was that his studies were interrupted by one or more return visits to Australia sometime between 1899 and 1901. We don't know the exact reason he returned, but it roughly coincides with the death of his father in 1901, followed shortly after by the death of his mother in 1902. Did he return to make a final visit to his ailing parents? Quite possibly. What we do know is that his father left an estate of 259,000 pounds, which was an enormous sum of money in 1901. After his wife's death, we can assume it was divided among the four surviving children. Even a quarter of the estate was enough for each of them to live a life of luxury without the need to ever take paid employment. This permitted Sep from the age of twenty to indulge in the lifestyle of a wealthy Edwardian English gentleman, a subject to which I will return. But before doing so, we need to follow his exploits as an oarsman and then his further continental education as a pianist and composer.

While still competing as a rower, towards the end of his time at Balliol he started to concentrate on sculling. For the non-initiated, he moved from pulling one oar in a team of rowers to pulling two oars in his own boat. This move was uncommon, and probably reflected his Australian background. In the last three decades of the nineteenth century, sculling was a hugely successful sport in Australia. It was organised on a professional basis for big prizes and attracted large crowds and even larger bets. There was a world professional championship run on a similar line to boxing in that the champion could be challenged, and if the challenger won the contest, he would become the new world champion. World championship races were held in England, Australia, Canada and the US depending on who was competing. The writer Scott Bennett, in a book on Henry Searle, one of the greatest Australian world champions, wrote:

> Between 1876 and 1907 the world title was held by seven Australians for twenty two of the thirty one years. These men – Trickett, Beach, Kemp, Searle, McLean, Stanbury and Towns – were demigods and they had the adulation of crowds wherever they went.

Kelly would have grown up in this environment, which would explain his high regard for sculling, but he was not likely to enter into the rough and tumble of the professional world. Being a gentleman with a private income, he was able to scull as an amateur and compete at the high temple of rowing and sculling at the Henley Royal Regatta.

Although the best professionals were faster than the amateurs, as conceded by the rowing writers of the time such as Frank Beddington in his 1908 book, *Boating and Boat Racing*, they had no hope of competing at Henley. The definition of amateur adopted by Henley in 1879 debarred anyone "who is or ever has been by trade or employment for wages a mechanic, artisan or labourer". An additional clause was added in 1886, which excluded any person "engaged in any menial duty". These clauses would have ruled out scullers like Bill Beach, the seven-times world champion, because he had been a blacksmith. In 1936, Henley's definition of amateur reached its final absurdity. As Richard Burnell in his book, *Henley Royal Regatta: A Celebration of 150 Years*, explains:

> An Australian eight, bound for the Olympic Games in Berlin, sought to enter for the Grand Challenge Cup. A most welcome occurrence one might think, for it was not often that crews from Britain's far-flung dominions were able to come to Henley. But, alas, this crew was composed of policemen, *ergo* "manual workers" by Henley reckoning. Their entry was refused and they went on their way to Berlin, perplexed and in considerable dudgeon.
>
> The proposition that a crew from Australia, competing in the Olympic Games, could be unacceptable at Henley Regatta was so grotesque that even the moguls of Henley and the Amateur Rowing Association at last realised that they could not remain forever out of step with the rest of the world.

In 1937, the offending references to manual labourers, mechanics, artisans and menial duties were deleted. A sign of how much things have changed is that in the six years between 1957 and 1962, the Diamond Sculls were won by the Australian Stuart Mackenzie, who listed his occupation as chicken-sexer. In 1997, all references to amateurism ended and now the regatta is open to all.

Even though they may not have been as fast as the professionals, there was still a large field of keen amateur scullers competing at Henley each year with the hope of winning the Diamond Sculls, an event that has been held annually since 1844. Kelly's first victory was in 1902 when he represented Balliol College. He then joined the fashionable Leander Club, which is situated on the Berkshire side of the Henley on Thames course, and won again in 1903 and 1905 in their colours. His winning time in 1905 of eight minutes and ten seconds stood as the record for 33 years until it was broken in 1938

Kelly during his time as champion sculler.

by the American, Joe Burke. Hylton Cleaver in his book *A History of Rowing* wrote: "Many think F.S. Kelly was the greatest amateur stylist of all time." It must have been his superior technique and stamina that brought him success as he was not a particularly big man and so could not rely on brute strength. He was less than six feet tall, and in his years as an oarsman he usually weighed about twelve and a quarter stone (77 kilos).

Although mainly remembered as a sculler, Kelly did not give up rowing and achieved success there as well. He was a member of the Leander eight, which won the Grand Challenge Cup at Henley in 1903, 1904 and 1905, as well as being in the crew that won the Stewards Cup for coxless fours in 1906. His final achievement as an oarsman was to be a member of the Leander eight that won the gold medal for Britain in the 1908 Olympic Games held in London and rowed over the Henley course. There were four rowing events at the Games, and the gold medal in each event was won by Britain from a very small field. The eights were contested only by Britain, Belgium, Canada, Hungary and Norway. In fact, it was probably no more difficult for the Leander crew to win Olympic gold than it was for them to win the Henley eights.

The fact that Kelly was born in Australia did not exclude him from the British team; he was a British subject by virtue of having been born in a British colony. In sport, the distinction between being Australian and being British hardly existed at that time. There were five cricketers who represented both England and Australia at test level before the First World War and, as we have seen, the Tasmanian Giblin played rugby for England in 1896 and 1897.

The 1908 Olympics, by which time Kelly was twenty-seven, marked the end of his career as an active participant in rowing and sculling.

It had been a successful sporting career, and he finished with a shelf full of trophies and an Olympic gold medal. He also became quite well known as a result of his sculling achievements, a reputation that opened doors to society, but did not help him build credibility as a serious musician. He continued as a member of the Leander Club, sculled for enjoyment, officiated at races and was a regular spectator at the Henley Royal Regatta, but his main focus moved increasingly to his music.

Soon after graduating from Oxford, Kelly enrolled at the Hoch'sche Konservatorium (Dr Hoch's Conservatorium) in Frankfurt, and attended from 1903 till 1908. He trained to be a concert pianist under Ernst Engesser and to be a composer under Iwan Knorr. Although most of his time was spent in Germany, he must have returned to England frequently as he was still winning sculling and rowing titles at Henley in 1903, 1904, 1905, 1906 and 1908. Unfortunately, we do not have a lot of information about this period as his diaries do not commence until late 1907.

The German musical world that Kelly entered in 1903 was divided between the conservative classical approach of Schumann and Brahms and the 'New Germans' exemplified by Wagner and Liszt. The Hoch Conservatorium was clearly in the first camp and Clara Schumann, the widow of Robert Schumann, and a prominent pianist and composer in her own right, was an important influence there. Kelly was comfortable in this environment; he was always seen as being on the conservative side of the music world, but he was prepared to perform modern composers such as Ravel, Debussy and Scriabin, and when he later became influential as an organiser of concerts he often chose modern works in addition to the classics.

His routine at the conservatorium consisted of four hours of piano practice each day plus private piano lessons from Engesser and composition lessons from Knorr. But it wasn't all work and study; sometime in late 1906, he travelled to China, Japan and Singapore. Another Australian who studied at the Hoch was Percy Grainger, who entered at the age of thirteen and had left by the time Kelly arrived. They later became quite good friends and played each other's compositions. Kelly's work, *Allegro de Concert Op.3* written in 1908, was dedicated to Grainger. It was an unusual friendship as Grainger was almost the exact opposite of Kelly – barely educated, poor and eccentric – but he became a much more famous figure in the world of music, producing a vast output during his long life and dedicating a museum to himself in Melbourne.

Kelly composed a number of pieces during the five years he was associated with the Hoch, several of which were later performed and published including *Cycle of Lyrics Op.4* and *Theme, Variation and Fugue for Two Pianos Op.5*, commenced in 1907 and 1908 respectively. When he returned permanently to England he was asked to serve on the committee of the London-based Classical Concert Society, of which he later became chairman. This added a third string to his bow; he was now an organiser of concerts as well as a pianist and composer.

Kelly was a frequent performer in concerts and in country houses with some of the best musicians of the time. He accompanied Pablo Casals, generally regarded as the century's greatest cellist, and frequently appeared with the Hungarian violinist Jelly d'Arányi and promoted her career whenever possible. But, as in his sculling, he was very much the gentleman amateur. He knew that if he was to advance in the music world, he would have to become professional. Obviously, he didn't need the money, but if he wished to be included in the important concerts at the major venues, he would need to be a professional. Interestingly, he chose to return to Australia to start his professional career as a concert pianist.

Kelly sent his Steinway to Australia in late 1910, and then travelled there via Germany, Venice and Egypt, where he took a boat up the Nile to Luxor during which he continued his daily piano practice on board. On the ship to Sydney he met John Lemmone, Melba's flautist, and composed a piece for him that later became one of his most-performed compositions – the *Serenade for flute, harp, horn and strings*. On reaching Australia, he took his time, staying with his brother Bertie at Glenyarrah and travelling widely as he prepared for his professional debut. His first performance took place in June 1911 at Sydney Town Hall, where he played Beethoven's *Piano Concerto no. 4 in G, op. 58* with the Sydney Symphony Orchestra. He then gave a series of six piano recitals in St James Hall, Sydney over July and August, in which he played a variety of music including some of his own compositions. When the season finished, he travelled through Northern Australia and Indonesia back to Europe. He had been away for a year.

Back in London, Kelly soon resumed performing, and between February 1912 and May 1914 he gave 14 concert performances. Some were piano recitals in small groups, but he also performed with the London Symphony Orchestra. He received some favourable reviews for his performances, but not enough to propel his career to new heights. He worried that he was viewed as a sportsman who dabbled in music, whereas he saw himself as a musician who had earlier dabbled in sport. He wrote in his diary: "Most of the critics seemed to be on their guard against being taken in by a sculler who has turned to music." One review that particularly irked him described his playing of Chopin as "too muscular". As in Australia, he included some of his own compositions in his repertoire, and these were well received. He was probably coming to the conclusion that his future in music was more likely to be as a composer than as a performer.

I have said all that needs to be said about Kelly as an oarsman, and much of what I intend to say about him as a musician. On his music, I make no pretence of being an authority, and what I have written relies on Therese Radic and Christopher Latham, both of whom are music specialists.

It is now time to move on to the aspect of his life that most interests me and encouraged my research. I am referring to his extraordinary lifestyle as a very wealthy young gentleman in Edwardian London. Between leaving Oxford in 1902 and enlisting in 1914, Kelly led a life of luxury in which he mixed with some of the most interesting and important people in English society, and where all doors seemed to have been open to him. And fortunately, we know a lot about it because he kept a detailed daily diary from 1907 to 1916, and unlike many other diaries, it is written in good English and easily readable handwriting.

The lifestyle of well-born young men with inherited wealth in Edwardian London immediately conjures up images of Bertie Wooster and his friends at the Drones Club. But life doesn't have to be as aimless as that just because you have inherited wealth. Charles Darwin had a large private income and never had to work for a living, yet he devoted his life to science, became the world's greatest biologist and changed our view of the world. On the spectrum from Wooster to Darwin, Kelly was much closer to the Darwin end, but if you didn't know of his achievements, a casual reading of his diaries could make his lifestyle seem more like Wooster's.

Life for him consisted of a succession of dinners at his club or restaurants, parties at country houses, concerts, theatre, golf, tennis and bridge. A high proportion of the people he mixed with were titled, even including a few members of European royalty. Of course, his musical activities as a concert performer, concert organiser and composer take up by far the largest part of the diaries as you would expect. And they show just how hard he practised and his capacity to find time, even at the end of a busy day, to work on his latest composition. Most of the names that appear in his diaries have a musical connection, but it is in the gaps between these musical references that we can get a glimpse of how he lived.

He had a substantial house called Bisham Grange at Marlow near Henley, which backed directly onto the Thames, and so was accessible by boat. He also maintained a flat in London and owned two automobiles. We don't know how many servants he employed, but his diaries refer to a housekeeper, a kitchen maid and a chauffeur. There were probably a lot more as he often had guests to stay at Bisham Grange. The clubs and restaurants of London provided the usual venue for his meetings with friends. Famous places such as Claridges and the Savoy Grill appear regularly in the diaries, plus many others that have ceased to exist. Kelly was a club man who always dressed for dinner, and although his club – the Union in Trafalgar Square – has gone, others he frequented such as the Garrick and Boodles are still going strong.

He had a wide range of friends with whom he met regularly, plus a number of acquaintances he met through his regular friends. His regular friends came mainly from the world of music or had a connection with Balliol College. For example, he knew a number of members of the Asquith family. Prime Minister Herbert Asquith and his son-in-law, Maurice Bonham-Carter, who was also his private secretary, were Balliol men. Kelly was close to Bonham-Carter, known by his friends as Bongie, as well as Logan Pearsall-Smith, Francis Henley and Patrick Shaw-Stewart, all Balliol men. He was a particularly good friend of Pearsall-Smith, the American poet, essayist and critic who wrote the words for several of Kelly's songs. At one stage Kelly dined with Bertrand Russell, a seemingly unlikely companion, but he was Pearsall-Smith's brother-in-law. On another occasion Kelly toured Rome and Florence with the art historian Bernard Berenson, but again the connection came through Pearsall-Smith because Berenson was another brother-in-law.

There were also many notable people whom Kelly met where it is hard to find the connection. For example, he met Sir Ian Hamilton, who later commanded the forces at Gallipoli, but well before that event. On his way back to Australia in 1910, Kelly met Lord Kitchener in Venice and spent a couple of days with him. On another occasion in 1909 he attended a party at the Admiralty given by Reginald McKenna, the First Lord of the Admiralty. Maybe these high military connections tell us something about how he would react when war was later declared.

He records in his diaries many other notable people he met at various dinners or parties. He met George Mallory, the mountaineer and Somerset-Maughan, the writer. Although Kelly was a keen reader, it is hard to believe he would have had much in common with either Edith Sitwell or Gertrude Stein, two other people he met through friends. Kelly did approve of another writer he met, the Australian poet Dorothea Mackellar. He also reports in January 1912, "When I got home I finished Gilbert Murray's translation of *Oedipus Rex*. It was somewhat of a surprise to me to find how much of it I could thoroughly appreciate." This is only the second occasion that one of the subjects of this book makes reference to another.

Some of his acquaintances were more exotic. In September 1909 at a yachting regatta in Dorset, he records spending time with minor European royalty. (The explanations in brackets have been added by me.)

> It rained all morning, but cleared up sufficiently for a foursome of golf at about 3.30 pm in which Prince Maurice [of Battenburg] and I beat Mrs Van Raalte and Prince Alphonso [de Bourbon]. The whole of the morning we played hide and seek all over the house which has about seven staircases, numerous passages and a basement ... Prince Leopold [of Battenburg] was nearly always one of the catchers as his stiff leg prevented him from running away ... Next day at lunch the Princess gave us some personal reminiscences of bomb throwing in Russia.

Other glimpses of his life can be found in his diaries, such as this entry for 13 November 1911:

> At 2.45 pm I walked to Cockburn and Campbell to order some wine and to Fribourg and Treyer to buy some cigarettes for my guests (I have not smoked since July 1909). I met Billy Vickers who walked with me down Piccadilly and told me he was married again and very happy. Mrs Popplewell came to tea with me and we discussed Winnie Parnell's musical affairs.

An indication of how well connected he was with the Asquiths is shown in the diary entry for 25 November 1913, when he records:

> Practice 10.15 am to 12.45 pm, 3 to 4 pm, 6.45 to 7.40 pm, 9 to 9.20 pm. My A Major, B Major and B Minor Monographs. I lunched with Hugh Godley at the Union and we walked into Maurice Bonham-Carter's study at 10 Downing Street through the Treasury to solicit a knighthood for Dr Harford-Lloyd [his old Eton music teacher] on his retirement from Eton next year. Maurice was not in so we left a note.

I could give a lot more examples from his diaries to show the comfortable, well-connected life that he lived, but there is not room. My main purpose has been to show what he had to give up when he enlisted in the First World War. We know that many young men from poor backgrounds – for example from rural Australia – enlisted because it allowed them to escape their dreary existence and travel abroad. But Kelly had to give up one of the most privileged and comfortable positions it is possible to imagine, and one with a real purpose through his dedication to his music.

Kelly's reaction to the declaration of war is best described in his diary entry of 5 August 1914, which is reproduced in full below. The explanations in brackets have been added by me. Unlike other volunteers who would have sought out the nearest recruiting office, Kelly again headed straight for Downing Street.

> The first news was of England's declaration of war on Germany, in consequence of which I decided to come up to London to see whether the territorials were in need of recruits. I travelled up by the 2.45 pm train from Marlow and, after leaving my bags at 29 Queen Anne Street [his London flat], I went to the Union Club where I saw Francis Henley who was on a similar errand. We went to Hugh Godley in the Treasury and made him take us in to 10 Downing Street where we asked Maurice Bonham-Carter for advice as to what Corps to apply. He advised the Inns of Court Corps and gave us a note to Lieutenant Field. During the ten minutes we were in Maurice Bonham-Carter's study, Lord Haldane [the Lord Chancellor] came in, Lord Kitchener [the Secretary of State for War] was just outside the door and Asquith [the Prime Minister] put his head in from a neighbouring room.
>
> Francis Henley and I went to 10 Stone Buildings, Lincoln's Inn, but were told to come back tomorrow morning, though they held out small hope of our being accepted in view of our complete lack of training. I spent an hour and a half at the Union Club

before walking back to 29 Queen Anne Street and then onto 49 Montagu Square where I dined with Francis Henley, Michael and Mrs Howard and Lady Mary Murray. Lady Dorothy is preparing for an event and had her dinner in the drawing room. After dinner we had a pleasant talk and Francis Henley played Schumann's Arabesque on the Sophonola(?) and invited me to play it afterwards. I also played Chopin's Nocturne in C Minor Op.48 no. 1. Lady Mary Murray seemed to me very thoughtful, clever and cultured. [She was the wife of Gilbert Murray.]

Kelly's decision to enlist did not involve any agonised decision making, nor was it a flamboyant, patriotic gesture. He simply assumed it was his duty to do so. As Therese Radic put it in her book *Race Against Time: the Diaries of F.S. Kelly*, "Kelly was the product of Empire: loyal to established values, King, country and class." Being a gentleman, he of course expected to be offered a commission; joining as a private would be out of the question. But commissions were not easy to come by for young men without any military experience, no matter how exalted their pedigree, prestigious their education, or close their access to 10 Downing Street. Even in England, the thought of a novice lieutenant commanding a platoon of 30 men, some of whom were hardened soldiers, was not easily accepted. After about five weeks and several rejections, he was finally offered a commission in a newly-formed and most unusual unit.

The Royal Naval Division (RND) was the brainchild of Winston Churchill, who was by now the First Lord of the Admiralty. Recognising that the Navy had more sailors than it needed, and that the war would be fought on land, he formed this division to fight on land alongside the army. It retained some naval traditions, such as ranks and drills, and even the permissibility of beards, but was under the operational command of the army. As soon as it was formed, it sought officers and was prepared to take outstanding applicants even if they had no military training. Thus, Kelly became one of a small group of brilliant young men who were offered commissions in the RND, by now known as 'Winston's private army'.

After months of training in England, Kelly was posted to the Hood Battalion of the RND and became one of an elite group of officers in that battalion, nicknamed 'the Latin Club'. His most famous fellow officer was the poet Rupert Brooke, but the group also included Arthur Asquith, the prime minister's third son; W. Denis Browne, the organist, composer and critic; Patrick Shaw-Stewart, academic and banker; Charles Lister, the second son of Lord Ribblesdale (and yet another Balliol man); and Bernard Freyberg, a New Zealander who later commanded the New Zealand Army in the Second World War, and went on to become their first local-born governor-general. Kelly was appointed sub-lieutenant and put in charge of the fifth platoon of B Company in the Hood Battalion.

In February 1915, the RND sailed to the Mediterranean en route to Gallipoli, spending time in Egypt and several Greek Islands on the way. Kelly formed friendships with his fellow officers during the two-month voyage and, like everyone else, was particularly impressed by Rupert Brooke. He wrote in his diary:

> I had a delightful talk about literature and poetry with Rupert Brooke after tea and again after dinner. He strikes me as being made of really fine stuff – both physically and mentally.

Brooke, still only twenty-seven years old (Kelly was thirty-three), was a published poet, a Fellow of King's College, Cambridge and had already travelled around the world. W.B. Yeats declared him "the most handsome man in Britain". His five sonnets, for which he is now best known, were published before he left England for Gallipoli. They seem to welcome the war as a relief from a boring and decadent existence, and an opportunity for heroism and sacrifice, as his first sonnet shows.

> Now, God be thanked, who has matched us with his hour,
> And caught our youth, and wakened us from sleeping,
> With hand made sure, clear eye, and sharpened power,
> To turn, as swimmers into cleanness leaping,
> Glad from a world grown old and cold and weary,
> Leave the sick hearts that honour could not move,
> And half-men and their dirty songs and dreary,
> And all the little emptiness of love!

The Edwardian period was one of the most secure and comfortable in history, yet a lot of clever young men looked forward to war, just as in the 1960s when economic security was at its peak, some naïve youths in the West embraced the idea of revolution. In the event, Brooke did not live to see action: he died of septicaemia from an infected mosquito bite on 23 April 1915, two days before the landing at Gallipoli. Kelly and his fellow officers buried him on the island of Skyros. His death had a big impact on Kelly and inspired what some believe was his most important composition. Brooke was an important poet, although his unquestioning patriotism was soon overtaken by events and turned most readers against him; yet his poems have never been out of print in the century since his death. What would he have written if he had lived to see how ghastly the war became, and how would he have reacted to the death of most of his fellow officers in pointless and failed attacks?

The Hood Battalion landed at Cape Helles on the Gallipoli Peninsula on 30 April, and Kelly was to stay there, with one interlude, for eight months. He took part in two fierce attacks on the Turks known as the second and third battles of Krithia. In the latter he received a bullet wound and was evacuated to Alexandria in early June to recuperate for a month. During this time he wrote what was to become his best-known work, *Elegy for Strings in Memoriam Rupert*

Brooke.

Kelly returned to Gallipoli in early July and remained there until 6 January 1916. Fighting continued, but in quiet periods he worked on another piece of music, his *Violin Sonata in G Major*, which has come to be known as the *Gallipoli Sonata*. He was one of the last three officers to leave, and his part in the evacuation was recognised by the award of the Distinguished Service Cross (DSC). He took his soldiering seriously, just as he had his sculling and music. His attention to drill, detail and discipline irritated some of his platoon, but according to Arthur Asquith, "he was as brave as a lion, aware and utterly contemptuous of all risks, he commanded the confidence and respect of all under his command." The whole Gallipoli campaign had been a failure and a very costly one. The RND incurred 7000 casualties, including 2500 dead out of a force of 16,000 men. Two of Kelly's close friends, W. Denis Browne and Charles Lister had been killed, so of the seven members of the 'Latin Club', only four returned from Gallipoli.

Kelly then had nine weeks' leave in England during which he seamlessly returned to his old pattern of life. There were frequent dinners with old friends and influential acquaintances such as the prime minister and his old commander, Sir Ian Hamilton. But, as before, most of his energy went into music – performing it, composing it and having his work published.

In May 1916, he was ordered to return to the Hood Battalion in France and promoted to captain. He looked forward to his new role, but did not know what part of France he was headed for. At first he was sent to the Pas-de-Calais region north of the Somme, where his unit was engaged in defensive duties in holding the line. This still involved danger from artillery and gas, but it was not as dangerous as attacking. In his diary for 1 July he reports:

> I got up in the morning and there was a distant rumble from the south like a seething cauldron, and when I got to 47 Division Headquarters they showed me the telegram to say that our big offensive had begun at 7.30 am and had penetrated the German trenches on a fifteen mile front.

That rumble was the first day of the Battle of the Somme, the most disastrous day in British military history and the start of a battle that lasted five months. For the time being, Kelly was still in the Pas-de-Calais, but that could not last.

On 4 October, the RND was transferred to the Somme proper. On 13 November, they took part in the Battle of the Ancre, the last big set-piece action of the Battle of the Somme. Here Kelly had to face the full horror of the First World War – being ordered to 'go over the top' and charge the German line of rifles and machine guns, knowing that his chance of survival was low. At 5.35 am, Kelly led his company in a charge towards the German trenches and was killed by a bullet to the head. When reading his diary for 1916, you had a feeling that this was going to happen. The lifespan of a junior infantry officer was short; there almost seemed to be an inevitability about his fate.

The day's objective had been captured by 6.05 am, but of the 25 officers and 535 other ranks who had crossed no-man's-land 20 minutes earlier, only four officers and 250 men answered the roll call on the captured objective (a piece of pock-marked, muddy ground about 300 metres wide and 800 metres deep).

Kelly is buried at Martinsart Cemetery in the Somme, a mile from where he died. Patrick Shaw-Stewart was killed in France a year later, so of the seven officers of the 'Latin Club' of Hood Battalion, only two survived the war – Bernard Freyberg VC and Arthur Asquith, who lost a leg.

So that was Kelly's life – 35 eventful years snuffed out by the First World War. Throughout the period covered by his diaries we know a lot about him: every piece of music he played, listened to or composed, every meal he ate, every event he attended and every friend and acquaintance he made. But there are some things we don't know and never will. Despite the detailed description of his daily life, he is still something of an enigma. Did this eminently eligible bachelor have any romantic or sexual attachments? The diaries are silent on the subject. Was it because there were none, or was it because he was too much of a gentleman to mention it? We do know that the Hungarian violinist Jelly d'Arányi fell in love with him and claimed after his death to have been his fiancée, but we don't know whether Kelly reciprocated her feelings. We know of his friendship with the pianist Leonard Borwick, and that they shared a flat at one time, but that was common practice.

Kelly's life held so much promise, but ended in an almost predictable tragedy. We are frequently reminded of the poets killed in the First World War, but as the English writer Hugh David put it:

> Little is now made of the fact, but the world of music suffered just as grievously. From the same generation as Brooke, Owen and Rosenberg, and every bit as promising, Brooke's friend the organist W. Denis Browne was killed in 1915. The composers George Butterworth and Frederick Kelly died in 1916, and Ernest Farrer in 1918.

How big a loss to the world of music was Kelly's early death? Chris Latham points out that by 1916, Kelly's musical output in quantity and quality was much the same as that of Ralph Vaughan-Williams at the same stage. Had Kelly survived the war he may have gone on to produce a body of work equal to that of Vaughan-Williams. Latham also comments:

Kelly composed his music in his head without referring to a piano, polishing the works until they were perfect, before he committed them to paper. There are very few corrections in his mature works, if any. There are very few drafts. As with Mozart, the pieces seemed to come into being perfectly formed, as if they already existed.

Kelly was still composing in 1916 on the Western Front. One unfinished piece that he did write down has now become known as *The Somme Lament*. There were also four other pieces he refers to in his diary that were still in his head at the time of his death.

How much richer would his legacy have been had he survived the war? His death was a major cultural loss for Australia and the world. As a result, little of his music was played after his death, and most of it was forgotten until recently. Now it is being revived, played at concerts and recorded. There is an excellent double-CD collection of his best work available from the ABC. Let us hope this revival continues. As we have seen in the case of John Peter Russell, a body of work may lay dormant for many decades before it is revived by a later generation. So may it be with Frederick Septimus Kelly.

BIBLIOGRAPHY

Ackland, Michael, *Henry Handel Richardson: A Life*, Cambridge University Press, Cambridge, 2004

Andrews, Malcolm, *Hubert Who?*, ABC Books, Sydney, 2011

Beddington, Frank, *Boating and Boat Racing: a practical modern work on rowing and sculling*, British Sports Publishing Co., London, 1908

Bennett, Scott, *The Clarence Comet: the career of Henry Searle 1866 – 1889*, Sydney University Press, 1973

Bevan, Ian, *The Sunburnt Country: Profile of Australia*, Collins, London, 1953

Bickers, Robert, *The Scramble for China: Foreign Devils in the Qing Empire 1832 to 1914*, Penguin, London, 2011

Blackmore, L.K., *Hawker – One of Aviation's Greatest Names*, David Bateman, Auckland, 1990

Bramson, Alan, *Pure Luck; The Authorised Biography of Sir Thomas Sopwith, 1888-1989*, Patrick Stephens, Sparkford, UK, 1990

Bown, Stephen, *The Last Viking: The Life of Roald Amundsen, Conqueror of the South Pole*, Aurum, London, 2012

Buckley, Vincent, *Henry Handel Richardson*, OUP, Melbourne, 1970

Burnell, Richard, *Henley Royal Regatta; a Celebration of 150 Years*, Heinemann, London, 1989

Clark, Axel, *Henry Handel Richardson: Fiction in the Making*, Simon and Schuster, Sydney, 1990

Clarke, Patricia, *Eilean Giblin: A Feminist Between the Wars*, Monash University Publishing, Melbourne, 2013

Cleaver, Hylton, *A History of Rowing*, Herbert Jenkins, London, 1957

Coleman, William, Cornish, Selwyn & Hagger, Alf, *Giblin's Platoon: The Trials and Triumph of the Economist in Australian Public Life*, ANU, Canberra, 2006

Cooksey, John and McKechnie, Graham (Ed.), *The Lost Olympian of the Somme*, Blink Publishing, London, 2015

Copland, Douglas (ed), *Giblin: The Scholar and the Man*, Cheshire, Melbourne, 1960

David, Hugh, *Heroes, Mavericks and Bounders: The English Gentleman from Lord Curzon to James Bond*, Michael Joseph, London, 1991

Davis, Wade, *Into the Silence: The Great War, Mallory and the Conquest of Everest*, Alfred Knopf, NY, 2011

Dundy, Elaine, *Finch, Bloody Finch*, Michael Joseph, London, 1980

Fenton, Peter, *Les Darcy: The Legend of the Fighting Man*, Ironbark, Sydney, 1994

Finch, George Ingle, *The Making of a Mountaineer*, with a memoir by Scott Russell, J.W. Arrowsmith, Bristol UK, 1988

Galbally, Ann, *The Art of John Peter Russell*, Sun Books, Melbourne, 1977

Galbally, Ann, *A Remarkable Friendship: Vincent van Gogh and John Peter Russell*, The Miegunyah Press, Melbourne, 2008

Gammie, Alexander, *George H Morrison D.D.*, James Clarke, London, 1928

Garnett, David, *The Golden Echo*, Chatto and Windus, London, 1953

Garnett, David, *The Flowers of the Forest*, Chatto and Windus, London, 1955

Garnett, David, *The Familiar Faces*, Chatto and Windus, London, 1962

Gibbs, Philip and Grant, Bernard, *Adventures of War with Cross and Crescent*, Methuen, London, 1913

Gillman, Peter and Leni, *The Wildest Dream: Mallory His Life and Conflicting Passions*, Headline, London, 2000

Gordon, Harry, *Australia and the Olympic Games*, University of Queensland Press, Brisbane, 1994

Green, Dorothy, *Henry Handel Richardson and her Fiction*, Allen & Unwin, Sydney, 1986

Grierson, John, *Sir Hubert Wilkins: Enigma of Exploration*, Robert Hale, London, 1960

Growden, Greg, *The Snowy Baker Story*, Random House, Sydney, 2003

BIBLIOGRAPHY

Hardy, Frank, *Power Without Glory*, Panther, St Albans, 1975

Hawker, Muriel, *H.G. Hawker, Airman: His Life and Work*, Hutchison, London, Facsimile of the 1922 edition

Hughes, Robert, *The Art of Australia*, Penguin, Sydney, 1981

Jenness, Stuart, *The Making of an Explorer: George Hubert Wilkins and the Canadian Arctic Expedition 1913–1916*, McGill-Queens University Press, Montreal, 2004

Jones, Nigel, *Rupert Brooke: Life, Death and Myth*, BBC Books, London, 2003

Latham, Christopher, *Sacrifice: The Lost Songbirds of the Somme: Les Rossignols Perdus de la Somme*, Canberra, 2016

Latham, Christopher, *Frederick Septimus Kelly; A Race Against Time*, Commentary on Double CD, ABC Classics, Sydney, 2016

Lo Hui Min, *The correspondence of G E Morrison: 1895–1912*, 2 vols, Cambridge University Press, 1976

Lomas, Graham, *The Will To Win: The Story of Sir Frank Beaurepaire*, Heinemann, London, 1960

Mason, Francis, *Hawker Aircraft since 1920*, Putnam, London, 1991

Maynard, Jeff, *Wings of Ice*, Random House, Sydney, 2010

Maynard, Jeff, *The Unseen Anzac: How an Enigmatic Polar Explorer Created Australia's World War 1 Photographs*, Scribe, Melbourne, 2015

McDonald, John, *John Peter Russell 1858–1930*, exhibition catalogue, Rex Irwin Gallery, 2001

McLeod, Karen, *Henry Handel Richardson: A Critical Study*, Cambridge University Press, Cambridge, 1985

McMullin, Ross, *Farewell Dear People*, Scribe, Melbourne, 2012

Monash, John, *The Australian Victories in France in 1918*, Hutchison & Co, London, 1920

Morrison, George, *An Australian in China: being the narrative of a quiet journey across China to Burma*, Earnshaw Books, Hong Kong, 2009

Montague, Richard, *Oceans, Poles and Airmen: the first flights over wide waters and desolate ice*, Random House, New York, 1971

Murray, Gilbert, *An Unfinished Autobiography*, George Allen & Unwin, London, 1960

Naifeh, Steven and White Smith, Gregory, *Van Gogh: The Life*, Random House, New York, 2011

Nasht, Simon, *The Last Explorer: Hubert Wilkins, Australia's Unknown Hero*, Hodder, Sydney, 2005

Noel, Captain J.B.L, *Through Tibet to Everest*, Edward Arnold, London, 1927

Palmer, Nettie, *Henry Handel Richardson*, Angus and Robertson, Sydney, 1950

Pearl, Cyril, *Morrison of Peking*, Angus and Robertson, Sydney, 1967

Purdie, Edna and Roncoroni, Olga, (ed), *Henry Handel Richardson: Some Personal Impressions*, Angus and Robertson, Sydney, 1957

Radic, Therese, *Race Against Time: the diaries of F S Kelly*, National Library of Australia, Canberra, 2004

Reade, Eric, *Australian Silent Films*, Lansdowne Press, Melbourne, 1970

Rewald, John, *History of Impressionism*, Secker & Warburg, London, 1973

Richardson, Henry Handel, *Maurice Guest*, Virago, London, 1981

Richardson, Henry Handel, *Myself When Young*, Heinemann, London, 1964

Richardson, Henry Handel, *The Fortunes of Richard Mahony*, Heinemann, London, 1961

Richardson, Henry Handel, *The Getting of Wisdom*, Heinemann, London, 1976

Rodway, George (ed), *George Ingle Finch's the Struggle for Everest*, Carreg, Ross-on-Wye, 2008. English translation of G.I. Finch, *Der Kampf um den Everest*, Brockhaus, Leipzig, 1925

Robertson, David, *George Mallory: Bibliotheca Himalayica*, EMR, Kathmandu, 1991

Rowe, Percy, *The Great Atlantic Air Race*, Angus & Robertson, Sydney, 1977

Russell, Bertrand, *The Autobiography of Bertrand Russell*, (3 vols), George Allen and Unwin, London, 1967

Salter, Elizabeth, *The Lost Impressionist: a Biography of John Peter Russell*, Angus and Robertson, London, 1976

Shaw, George Bernard, *Major Barbara*, Longmans, Green & Co., London, 1966

Spurling, Hilary, *The Unknown Matisse: Man of the North 1869–1908*, Hamish Hamilton, London, 1998

Stray, Christopher (ed), *Gilbert Murray Reassessed*, Oxford University Press, Oxford, 2007

Swanwick, Raymond, *Les Darcy: Australia's Golden Boy of Boxing*, Ure Smith, Sydney, 1965

Thomas, Lowell, *Sir Hubert Wilkins: His World of Adventure*, Arthur Barker Ltd, London, 1962

Thompson, Peter and Macklin, Robert, *The Man Who Died Twice: The life and Adventures of Morrison of Peking*, Allen & Unwin, Sydney, 2004

The History of The Times: 1884–1912, vol 3, The Office of The Times, London, 1947

Tunnicliffe, Wayne (ed), *John Russell: Australia's French Impressionist*, Art Gallery of NSW, Thames and Hudson, Sydney, 2018

Unsworth, Walt, *Everest*, Allen Lane, London, 1981

Wainwright, Robert, *Maverick Mountaineer: George Ingle Finch, the Wild Colonial Boy Who Took on the British Alpine Establishment*, ABC Books, 2015

West, Francis, *Hubert Murray: The Australian Pro-Consul*, Oxford University Press, Melbourne, 1968

West, Francis, *Gilbert Murray: A Life*, Croom Helm, London, 1984

Wilkins, Sir George Hubert, *Undiscovered Australia: Being an Account of an Expedition to Tropical Australia to Collect Specimens of the Rarer Native Fauna for the British Museum, 1923–1925*, Putnam, New York, 1929

Wilkins, Sir George Hubert, *Flying the Arctic*, Putnam, New York, 1928

Wilson, Duncan, *Gilbert Murray OM 1866–1957*, Clarendon Press, Oxford, 1987

Young, Geoffrey Winthrop, *Mountaincraft*, Methuen, London, 1949

INDEX

Academy Award, 63
Accident Investigation Branch of the Air Ministry, 35
Ackland, Michael, 136, 139, 143
Adventures of War with Cross and Crescent, 101
Age, The, 71, 72, 73, 74, 75
Alcock, Captain John, 30
Alexander, Samuel, 219
Allegro de Concert Op.3, 260
Alpine Club of London, 43, 50, 56, 57, 58, 59, 61, 66
American Geographical Society, 115
Amundsen, Roald, 110, 111, 117, 118, 123
Andrews, Malcolm, 99
Anquetin, Louis, 186
Antarctica, 108, 116, 117, 118, 119, 120, 122
Archer, Jeffrey, 67
Arctic Circle, 102-104, 110-115, 119, 122
Argus, The, 73, 74, 75, 78
Art Gallery of New South Wales, 185, 194, 195
Art in Australia, 195
Art of John Peter Russell, The, 176
Art Society of New South Wales, 177
Asquith, Arthur, 268, 270, 271
Asquith, Herbert Henry, 212, 263, 265, 266
Atalier Cormon, 178, 179, 180, 182, 188
Atlantic, The, 27, 28, 29
Australia and the Olympics, 247

Australia Felix, 135, 137, 145
Australian Broadcasting Commission, 170, 273
Australian crawl stroke, 225
Australian Flying Corps, 104
Australian in China, being the narrative of a quiet journey across China to Burma, An, 78
Australian Imperial Force (AIF), 104
Australian Labor Party, 156, 157
Australian Literary Society, 138
Australian Motorist Magazine, 22
Australian Sporting Hall of Fame, 247
Australian Tariff: An Economic Inquiry, The, 162
Australian Victories in France in 1918, 106
Australasian Boxing Championship, 229

Bacchae, Euripides, 207
Bach, Johann Sebastian, 129
Baker, George, 224
Baker, Reginald Leslie (Snowy), 223-249
Balchen, Bernt, 117
Balkan War, 100, 101
Balkan League, 101
Balkans, The, 46, 47
Ballarat Hospital, 77, 78, 126
Balliol College, Oxford, 209, 253, 254, 256, 264, 268
Barrie, Sir James, 208
Bartok, Bela, 214

Barton, Sir Edmund, 205
Battle of the Somme, 270, 271
BBC, 219
Beach, Bill, 255
Bean, C E W, 104, 105, 106, 107
Beaurepaire, Sir Frank, 232
Beddington, Frank, 255
Beethoven, Ludwig van, 261
Bell, Vanessa, 159
Belle Ile, Brittany, 181, 182, 184-189
Belloc, Hilaire, 153
Bennett, Floyd, 111
Bennett, Scott, 255
Bennett, Suzanne, 116
Berenson, Bernard, 264
Beresford, Bruce, 140
Bergson, Henri, 214
Bernard, Emile, 186
Besant, Annie, 41, 62
Bifertenstock, The, 44
Bigglesworth, Squadron Leader James, 24
Bisham Grange, 263
Bjornstjern, Bjornson, 132
Blackmore, Lou, 25
Bleriot, Louis, 123
Bloomsbury Group, 149, 153, 159, 167
Boats and Boat Racing, 255
Boer War, 206, 207
Bonacossa, Count Aldo, 44
Bonham-Carter, Maurice, 264, 265, 266
Boodles, 263
Borrow, George, 155
Borwick, Leonard, 272
Boxer Rebellion, 86, 87, 153
Boyd, Martin, 219
Braddon, Russel, 219

Bradman, Sir Donald, 246
Brahms, Johannes, 259
Bramson, Alan, 26
Brideshead Revisited, 203
Brigden, Professor James, 162, 165
British Aerospace, 36
British Conservative Party, 220
British Empire Michelin Cup, 19
British Foreign Office, 85, 87
British Labour Party, 22
British Legation, Peking, 86
British Liberal Party, 211, 220
British Museum, 108, 109
British Women's Temperance Association, 203
Brooke, Rupert, 51, 268, 269
Brooklands Motor Racing Track, 19, 32
Brown, Lieutenant Arthur, 30
Brown, Joseph, 193
Brown, Roy, 24
Browne, W Denis, 268, 270, 272
Bruce, Brigadier-General Charles, 53, 56
Bruce, Geoffrey, 54, 56
Bruce, Stanley Melbourne, 161
Buckley, Vincent, 143
Burke, Joe, 258
Burnell, Richard, 256
Burns Philp & Co, 252
Burns, Tommy, 235
Burton, Eilean, 158, 167
Butterworth, George, 272
Byrd, Commander Richard, 110, 111, 114, 115, 116, 117, 123
Byrd, Senator Harry, 123

Campbell, Jock, 46, 47, 65
Camsell, Charles, 152, 166

INDEX

Carey, Peter, 145
Carlyon Sahib, 205
Casals, Pablo, 260
Castle Howard, 203
Cavill, Dick, 225
Century of National Humiliation, 82
Cesbron, Achille, 184, 186
Cezanne, Paul, 177, 184, 195
Chaplin, Charlie, 242
Chester, Henry, 74
Chief Judicial Officer, British New Guinea, 207
Chiene, Professor John, 76
Chirole, Sir Valentine, 80, 81
Chopin, Frederic, 262, 267
Christie, Julie, 63
Churchill, Sir Winston, 214, 267, 268
Cixi, Dowager Empress, 84, 86
Claridges, 263
Clark, Axel, 141, 143
Clarke, Sir George, 94
Clarke, Patricia, 158, 167, 168
Classical Concert Society, 260
Cleary, Mike, 248
Cleaver, Hilton, 258
Coleman, William, 152, 167
Colonial Sugar Refinery, 226, 252
Columbia University, 210
Columbus, Christopher, 122
Committee for Intellectual Cooperation, 214
Commonwealth Grants Commission, 161, 164
Conder, Charles, 194
Conrad, Joseph, 153
Cook, Frederick, 110
Coombs, H C, 165

Cooper, Gary, 245
Cope, John Lachlan, 107, 108
Copland, Sir Douglas, 152, 154, 164, 165, 167, 168, 171
Cornish, Selwyn, 152
Corot, Camille, 177
Courbet, Gustave, 178
Crimean War, 80
Crocker, Sir Walter, 218, 219
Crown Street Public School, 226
Curie, Madame, 214
Cycle of Lyrics Op.4, 260

Daily Chronicle, London, 100
Daily Mail, 20, 21
D'Aranyi, Jelly, 260, 272
Darcy, Les, 239-241, 249
Darwin, Charles, 262
David, Hugh, 272
Davis, Wade, 39, 56
Debussy, Claude, 259
Degas, Edgar, 181
De Little, Mr, 16
Detroit Aviation Society, 110
Diamond Sculls, 251, 256
Dick, Mary Ann, 252
Disney, Walt, 245
Dixon, Sir Owen, 219
Dixon, Robert, 144
Dobell, William, 171
Dostoevsky, Fyodor, 130
Douglas, J W H T (Johnny), 233, 234
Downing, Professor Richard, 168-170
Drake-Brockman, Henrietta, 133
Drones Club, 262
Du Cane, Sir Charles, 148

Earl of Carlisle, 203
Earp, Professor F R, 154, 155
Edinburgh University, 76, 77
Eielson, Ben, 112-115
Eilean Burton: a feminist between the wars, 158
Einstein, Albert, 44, 214
Electra, Euripides, 207
Elegy for Strings in Memoriam Rupert Brooke, 269
Eliot, William, 143
Ellsworth, Lincoln, 110, 111, 117, 118, 120
Emperor of Japan, 88, 94
Empire Builders, The, 245
End of Childhood, The, 139
Enemy Within, The, 242
Engesser, Ernst, 259, 260
England Amateur Boxing Association Championship, 230
Ervine, Sandy, 60
Eton College, 252, 253
Euripides, 205, 207, 208, 209
Everest Committee, 50, 57, 58
Everest, Mount, 39, 49, 50, 52-61, 123
Everest, Sir George, 49

Fairbanks, Douglas, 245
Familiar Faces, The, 171
Farrer, Percy, 50, 52, 60
Federal Institute of Technology, Zurich, 44
Fellow of the Royal Society, 64, 67
Fighter's Paradise, 245
Finch, Agnes (Bubbles, ne Johnson), 48, 53, 59, 64, 67
Finch, Antoine Konstant, 43
Finch, Betty, 62
Finch, Charles Edward, 40, 41, 42, 43, 48, 62

Finch, Charles Wray, 40
Finch, Dorothy, 41, 42, 62
Finch, Edward, 62
Finch, Frederick George Peter Ingle, 46, 47, 61, 62, 63, 65, 67
Finch, George, 39-67
Finch, Laura Isobel (ne Black), 40-43, 47, 61, 62
Finch, Max, 41, 43, 44, 50, 59
First World War, 23, 45, 46, 90, 104-107, 157-159, 190, 211, 212, 240, 251, 266-272
Fisher, Andrew, 157
Fisher, Betty, 46, 47, 65
Fisher, Irving, 160
Fitzgerald, Sir Thomas, 76
Flack, Edwin, 231
Florey, Howard, (later Lord Florey), 219
Flying the Arctic, 115
Foreign Policy of Sir Edward Grey, The, 212
Forster, E M, 155, 167, 168, 169
Fortunes of Richard Mahony, The, 125, 127, 134, 135, 137-139, 141, 143-145
Four Stages of Greek Religion, 210
Franklin, Miles, 133, 134, 143
Freyberg, Bernard, 268, 271
Frogs, The, Aristophanes, 207

Galbally, Ann, 176, 178, 186, 189, 195
Gallipoli, 46, 107, 268-270
Game of Jiu-Jitsu, The, 154
Garnett, David (Bunny), 153, 154, 159, 165, 171
Garson, Greer, 139
Gassman, Vittorio, 140
Gaugin, Paul, 182, 184, 185, 186
Gaumont Pictures, 99, 100, 102

INDEX

Geelong College, 70
General Paralysis of the Insane, 127, 144
General Theory of Employment, Interest and Money, The, 163
Getting of Wisdom, The, 125. 128, 134, 140, 143, 145
Giblin, Lyndhurst Falkiner, 147-171, 258
Giblin: the Scholar and the Man, 152, 154
Giblin, William Robert, 148
Giblin's Platoon, 152
Gilbert, W.S., 199
Gilman, Peter and Leni, 53
Gilmore, Dame Mary, 133
Gladstone, W E, 201
Glasgow University, 203, 204, 206
Gobi or Shamo, 203
Godley, Hugh, 266
Golden Echo, The, 154
Goldman, Dr Ralph, 121
Gordon, Harry, 247
Grainger, Martin, 151, 152
Grainger, Percy, 260
Grant, Bernard, 101
Green, Dorothy, 140, 143, 145
Grant, Duncan, 159
Greer, Germaine, 133, 145
Grey, Sir Edward, 211, 212
Grierson, John, 99
Growden, Greg, 228, 245, 246, 247
Guangxu Emporer, 84, 87
Guillaumin, Armand, 181, 186

H G Hawker Engineering Company Ltd, 33
Hagger, Alf, 152
Haldane, Lord, 266
Hamilton, Sir Ian, 264, 270
Han Suyin, 91

Hardwick, Harold, 239, 248
Hardy, Frank, 238
Harford-Lloyd, Charles, 253, 265
Harris, Max, 193
Harvard University, 208
Hasluck, Sir Paul, 166
Hawker Aircraft Ltd, 36
Hawker, Bert, 26
Hawker de Havilland, 36
Hawker Harrier, 15, 36
Hawker, Harry George, 15-38
Hawker Hurricane, 15-36
Hawker, Muriel (ne Peaty), 26, 29, 30, 32
Hawker Pacific, 36
Hawker Pacific Aerospace, 36
Hawker Siddeley, 15, 36
Hearst, William Randolph, 116
Heinemann, 131, 137, 138
Henley, Francis, 264, 266, 267
Henley Royal Regatta, 255, 256, 258, 259
Henley Royal Regatta: A Celebration of 150 years, 256
Henry VIII, 209
Hepburn, Audrey, 63
Hillary, Sir Edmund, 66, 123
Hinckler, Bert, 37
Hinks, Arthur, 50, 51, 52, 53, 59, 60
Hippolytus, Euripides, 207
History of Ancient Greek Literature, A, 205
History of Rowing, 258
History of the Times, 80
Hitler, Adolph, 215
Hoch'sche Konservatorium, 259, 260
Holden, William, 91
Hollick-Kenyon, Herbert, 119
Home Rule for Ireland, 201, 211, 220

Howard, John, 219

Howard, Leslie, 245

Howard, Rosalind, Countess of Carlisle, 203, 204

Hudson Bay Company, 151

Hughes, Billy, 107, 157

Hughes, Robert, 145, 195

Hunt, Colonel John, (later Lord Hunt), 64, 66

Hurley, Frank, 104-106

Hutchins School, 148

Ibsen, Henrik, 130, 131

Imperial College, London, 45, 64

Indian National Chemical Laboratory, 65

Inner Temple, London, 202

Into the Silence: The Great War, Mallory and the Ascent of Everest, 39

It is not Dawn Till You Awake, 254

Jackaroo from Coolabong, The, 242, 245

Jacobson, Jens Peter, 131, 145

Jaivin, Linda, 88

James, Clive, 145

James, Henry, 155

Jenness, Stuart, 102

Jiu-Jitsu, 154

John Russell: Australia's French Impressionist, 189, 193, 194

Johns, Captain W E, 24

Johnson, Jack, 235

Johnston, George, 219

Jones, Jennifer, 91

Joplin, Mary, 78

Jowett, Benjamin, 209

Juan Shikai, 89, 90, 94

Jungfrau, The, 44

Kahn, R F, 163

Kanaka labour, 72

Kauper, Harry, 72, 73

Kearns, Jack, 239

Kearny, Ethel Rose, 236

Kellas, Alexander, 50, 52

Kelly, Frederick Septimus, 251-273

Kelly, Mary (Maisie), 252, 253

Kelly, Thomas Herbert, 252, 253

Kelly, Thomas Hussey, 252, 253

Kelly, William Henry, 252, 253

Keynes, John Maynard, 150, 159, 163, 165

King George V, 15, 29, 30, 35, 97, 115

King Victor Emmanuel of Italy, 97

Kings College, Cambridge, 149, 150, 165, 167, 268

Kings School, Parramatta, 40

Kingsford-Smith, Charles, 37, 114, 123

Kipling, Rudyard, 94, 155

Kitchener, Lord, 264, 266

Klondike gold rush, 150, 151

Knorr, Iwan, 259, 260

Kramer, Dame Leonie, 143

Kurz, Marcel, 50

Lane, Freddie, 225, 226

Landy, John, 246, 247

Larkin, Ted, 157

Last Race, The, 245

Latham, Christopher, 262, 272

Lawson, Henry, 143

League of Nations, 213-215, 220, 221

League of Nations Union, 213, 214, 215

Leander Club, 256, 258, 259

Legislative Council of New South Wales, 199

INDEX

Legros, Alphonse, 177
Leipzig Conservatorium, 129, 130
Lemmone, John, 261
Levanesky, Sigismund, 119
Liberal Woman's Association, 203
Lindbergh, Charles, 32, 114, 123
Lindrum, Walter, 246
Lindsay, Joan, 134
Lister, Charles, 268, 270
Liszt, Franz, 259
Livingstone, Dr David, 70
Lloyd George, David, 35, 212
London Daily News, 133, 138
London, Jack, 235
London Symphony Orchestra, 261
London University, 149, 176
Longstaff, Sir John, 188
Loren, Sophia, 63
Lost Impressionist, The, 176, 189
Love is a Many Splendoured Thing, 91
Lowes-Dickinson, Goldsworthy, 149, 167
Lucas, E V, 155
Lure of the Bush, The, 242
Lyndhurst, Lord, 148
Lyons, Joseph, 156, 161

MacDonald, Sir Claude, 86
Macfarlane Burnet, Sir Frank, 219
MacInnes, Colin, 219
Mackeller, Dorothea, 264
Mackenzie, Stuart, 256
Mackenzie-Grieve, Lt Commander Kenneth, 27, 29, 30, 32
Magdalen College, Oxford, 201, 253
Magdalene College, Cambridge, 93
Magellan, Ferdinand, 122

Mahler, Gustav, 129
Major Barbara, G B Shaw, 208
Making of a Mountaineer, The, 63, 67
Making of an Explorer: George Hubert Wilkins, The, 102
Mallory, George, 39, 50, 51-57, 59-61, 67, 264
Man from Kangaroo, The, 242, 245
Mandle, W F, 248
Manet, Edouard, 178
Mann, Thomas, 214
Manor, The, Mosman NSW, 62
Martinsart Cemetery, 271
Marshall, Alfred, 149
Mary, The, 29, 30, 32
Masefield, John, 134, 214
Matisse, Henri, 173, 188, 189, 193
Matterhorn, The, 44
Mattiocco, Anna Maria Antoinetta, 179-184, 187-189
Maughan, W Somerset, 264
Maurice Guest, 132, 133, 139, 142, 145
May, Gladys, 48, 49, 59
May, Robert (later Lord May), 219
Maynard, Jeff, 99, 100
McDonald, John, 195
McIntosh, Hugh D, 234-239, 244, 249
Mc Kenna, Reginald, 264
McLaren, Bruce, 36, 37
McLaren Racing Ltd, 37
McLeod, Karen, 133, 143, 144
Medea, Euripides, 208
Melba, Dame Nellie, 95, 197, 261
Melbourne University, 71, 147, 162, 163, 171
Melville, Sir Leslie, 165, 171
Mendelssohn, Felix, 129

Merchant Taylors School, London, 201
Meredith, George, 155
Merril, Caroline de Witt, 190-192
Michelin Tyre Company, 19
Mill, John Stuart, 201
Millet, Jean Francois, 178
Ministry of Home Security (UK), 65
Morrison, Alexander, 70
Morrison, George, 70
Morrison, George Ernest, 69-95, 153
Morrison, Ian, 91
Morrison Library, 88, 90, 92
Monash, General Sir John, 106
Monet, Claude, 173, 177, 181, 184, 188, 189, 195
Mont Blanc, 44
Monte Rosa, 44
Moorabbin (Harry Hawker) Airport, 37
Moorehead, Alan, 145
Most Immoral Woman, A, 88
Mountain Craft, 51
Mozart, Wolfgang Amadeus, 273
Murray, Lady Agnes (ne Edwards), 199, 201
Murray, Gilbert, 197-221, 264
Murray, Hubert, 197, 198, 200, 201, 202, 205, 206, 216, 217, 218
Murray, Lady Mary (ne Howard), 203-205, 206, 216, 218, 220
Murray, Terence, 198
Murray, Sir Terence Aubrey Murray, 198-199
Munro-Ferguson, Sir Ronald, 92
My Brilliant Career, 134
Myself When Young, 128, 139

Naifeh, Stephen, 180
Nasht, Simon, 99

Nehru, Jawaharlal, 65
New College, Oxford, 203, 208
New South Wales Amateur Boxing Championship, 227, 228, 229
New South Wales Irish Rifles, 206
New South Wales Swimming Association, 230
Nichol, Charlotte Ann, 174
Niels Lyhne, 131, 133
Niemeyer, Sir Otto, 164
Nieuport Goshawk, 34
Nobile, Umberto, 110, 111
Noble, Monty, 226
Nolan, Sir Sidney, 219
Norgay, Tenzing, 66, 123
North Pole, 110-114
Northcliffe, Lord, 20, 26, 30
Novak, Kim, 63

Oedipus Rex, Sophocles, 209, 264
Olivier, Sir Laurence, 63
Olympic Games of 1896, 231
Olympic Games of 1900, 225
Olympic Games of 1904, 231
Olympic Games of 1908, 231, 232, 233, 258
Olympic Games of 1932, 245
Olympic Games of 1936, 256
Opium Wars, 81, 82, 93
Order of Merit, 219
Ottoman Empire, 101
Owen, Wilfred, 272
Oxford Cambridge Boat Race, 254
Oxford University, 51, 201, 202, 203, 209, 214, 218, 220
Oxford Volunteer Training Corps, 212
Oxygen, 53, 56, 58, 60, 61, 66, 67

Palmer, Nettie, 143

INDEX

Papua New Guinea, 72, 74, 198, 207, 216-218
Papua of Today, 217
Papua or British New Guinea, 217
Paterson, Banjo, 15, 29
Pearl, Cyril, 74
Pearsall-Smith, Logan, 264
Peary, Robert, 110
Peck, Gregory, 139
Pepys, Samuel, 92
Permanent Trustee Company, 176
Phar Lap, 239
Piano Concerto no 4 in G , Op.58, 261
Picnic at Hanging Rock, 134
Pissarro, Camille, 177, 181, 184, 189
Pratt, Catherine, 143
Presbyterian Ladies College (PLC), 128, 134
Prince Alphonso de Bourbon, 265
Prince Leopold of Battenburg, 265
Prince Maurice of Battenburg, 265
Principles of Economics, 149
Powell, Enoch, 204
Power Without Glory, 238
Problem of Foreign Policy, The, 215
Pritchard, Katherine Susanna, 133, 143
Purchasing Power of Money, The, 160
Purdie, Edna, 143
Puyi, the Xuantong Emporer, 87

Qing Dynasty, 84-86, 89

Radic, Therese, 262, 267
Raeburn, Harold, 50
Ransome, Arthur, 168
Rats of Tobruk, The, 63
Ravel, Maurice, 259

Raynham, Fred, 19, 28, 29
Referee, The, 244, 246
Regents Park House, 135, 139
Regius Professor of Greek, Oxford University, 208, 209
Reid, Forrest, 169
Remarkable Friendship: Vincent Van Gogh and John Peter Russell, A, 186
Renoir, Pierre Auguste, 181
Research and Experiments Department (UK), 65
Rhapsody, 140
Ribblesdale, Lord, 268
Richardson, Ada Lillian Lindesay (Lil), 126, 128, 135, 137
Richardson, Ethel Florence Lindesay (Henry Handel) 125-145
Richardson, Mary (ne Bailey), 126, 127, 129-131
Richardson, Victor, 248
Richardson, Walter Lindesay, 126, 127, 135, 141, 144
Rio Tinto Company, 77
Rise of the Greek Epic, The, 208
Riviera Country Club, 245, 246
Roberts, Tom, 176, 177, 194
Robertson, Elizabeth Jane, 224
Robertson, George, 130-132, 135, 136, 138, 139
Robin, Jennie, 90, 91
Robey and Co, Lincoln, 175
Rodin, Auguste, 173, 182, 184, 188, 193, 194
Rogers, Will, 245
Rolls Royce, 16, 27
Roncoroni, Olga, 139, 142, 143
Roosevelt, Theodore, 88
Rosenberg, Isaac, 272

Ross, Winston, 120
Royal Aero Club, 20, 27
Royal Arsenal, The, 45
Royal Field Artillery, 45
Royal Geographical Society, 50, 57
Royal Meteorological Society, 107
Royal Naval Division, 267-271
Royal NSW Lancers, 228
Rugby Union, 150, 227
Russell, Bertrand, 211, 212, 264
Russell, John, 174-176
Russell, John Peter, 173-195, 273
Russell, Peter, 174, 175
Russell, Scott, 66, 67
Russian Revolution, 48
Russo-Japanese War, 85, 87, 93

Salon des Refuses, 177
Salter, Elizabeth, 176, 189
Savoy Grill, 263
Schumann, Clara, 259
Schumann, Robert, 129, 259
Scrambling Among the Alps, 43
Scriabin, Alexander, 259
Scotch College, 70, 128
Scott, Robert Falcon, 61
Searle, Henry, 255
Second World War, 65, 120, 215
Serenade for flute, harp, horn and strings, 261
Shackleton, Sir Ernest, 108
Shadow of Lightning Ridge, The, 242
Shaw, George Bernard, 208, 211, 216
Shaw-Stewart, Patrick, 264, 268, 271
Sherman, Harold, 119
Sisley, Alfred, 181, 184
Sitwell, Edith, 264

Slade School of Art, 176
Sleeping Acre, 245
Smith, Keith, 37, 108
Smith, Louisa, 98
Smith, Ross, 37, 108
Smuts, Field Marshal, 213
Snowy Baker Films, 242
Snowy Baker Story, The, 228
Snowy Baker's Embrocation, 237
Snowy Baker's Magazine, 237
Snowy Baker's Unfailing Liniment, 244
Society for Psychical Research, 137, 216
Society of Australian Writers in Britain, 219
Somme Lament, The, 273
Sopwith Aviation Company, 18-21, 23, 24, 26, 27, 33
Sopwith Camel, 24, 25
Sopwith Pup, 24, 25
Sopwith, Sir Thomas, 18, 19, 25, 26, 34
Sopwith Strutter, 23, 24
Sopwith Tabloid, 21, 22
Sopwith-Kauper gun interrupter gear, 25
South Australian School of Mines, 98
South Pole, 116, 117, 119
Spencer, Herbert, 201
Spiritualism, 126, 216
Spofforth, Frederick, 70
Sporting Novels, 246
Spurling, Hilary, 188
Stadiums Limited, 238, 239, 241
Stalin, Joseph, 97, 119
Stanley, Henry Morton, 70, 71
St John's College, Oxford, 201
State Library of New South Wales, 210
Stefansson, Vilhjalmur, 102, 103, 110
Stein, Gertrude, 264

INDEX

Stevenson, Robert Louis, 155
Streeton, Sir Arthur, 194
Strutt, Colonel, 53, 56, 60
Sutherland, Dame Joan, 219
Stead, Christina, 133, 145
Strachey, Lytton, 51
Sun Yat Sen, 89, 94
Sunburnt Country, A, 219
Suttor, Sir Francis, 228, 236
Sword of Valour, The, 245
Sydney Grammar School, 200
Sydney Smelting Company, 252
Sydney Symphony Orchestra, 253, 261
Sydney University, 204
Syphilis, 144

Tartakover, Theo, 230, 231
Taylor, Elizabeth, 63, 140, 246
Theme, Variation and Fugue for Two Pianos Op.5, 260
Theosophical Society, 41, 42, 62
Thomas, Lowell, 99
Thoughts Through Space, 119
Times, The, 67, 70, 73, 79-81, 85, 87, 88, 89, 91, 92, 133
Tolstoy, Leon, 130
Tooth & Co, 251
Toulouse-Lautrec, Henri, 178
Toynbee, Arnold, 220
Tracey, Spencer, 245
Trans-Siberian Railway, 85
Treaty of Nanjing, 81
Treaty of Tianjin, 82
Trojan Women, Euripides, 207
True Adventure Thrills, 100
Trumper, Victor, 226, 246
Tunnicliffe, Wayne, 189, 194

Ultima Thule, 135, 137, 138
Undiscovered Australia: being an account of an Expedition, 109, 115
Unfinished Autobiography, An, 200, 219
Union Club, 263, 265, 266
United Australia Party, 161
University of Melbourne, 126
US Army, Quartermaster General Corps, 121
US Navy, Office of Scientific Research, 121
Unseen Anzac, The, 99
Unsworth, Walt, 57, 59
Urantia, 119
Valentino, Rudolph, 246
Van Gogh, Theo, 180, 185, 186
Van Gogh, Vincent, 179-186, 190, 193, 195
Van Raalte, Mrs, 265
Vasco de Gama, 122
Vaughan-Williams, Ralph, 272
Versailles Treaty, 91
Vickers, Billy, 265
Violin Sonata in G Major (Gallipoli Sonata), 270
Von Richthofen, Manfred, 24

Wagner, Richard, 141, 259
Wainwright, Robert, 48, 51, 56, 57
Wallabies Rugby Team, 227, 232
Wallace, Sir Donald Mackenzie, 80
Walpole, Hugh, 134
Walter, Arthur, 92
Waugh, Evelyn, 203
Way Home, The, 135, 137
Webb, Beatrice, 94
Webb, Sydney, 94
Weiss, Ehrich (Houdini), 17
Wells, H G, 134, 211

West, Francis, 206
Westminster Abbey, 219
Wetterhorn, The, 44
White Panther, 245
White, Patrick, 143
White-Smith, Gregory, 180
Whymper, Edward, 43
Wickham, Alick, 225, 226
Wildenstein Art Gallery, 193
Wilkins, Sir George Hubert, 97-123
Wilkins, Harry, 97
Wilson, Sir Roland, 165, 171
Wilson, Woodrow, 215
Winchester College, 91
Wings of Ice, 100
Woolf, Virginia, 51
Wooster, Bertie, 262
Wren, John, 238
Yeats, W B, 268
Young Cosima, The, 139
Young, Geoffrey Winthrop, 51
Younghusband, Sir Francis, 49, 50

www.ingramcontent.com/pod-product-compliance
Lightning Source LLC
Chambersburg PA
CBHW070929150426
42814CB00032B/430/J